The Many Faces of Mary
a love story

Bob and Penny Lord

Journeys of Faith
31220 La Baya Drive # 110
Westlake Village, California 91362

Other Books by Bob and Penny Lord

This Is My Body, This Is My Blood,
Miracles of the Eucharist
We Came Back to Jesus
Saints and Other Powerful Women in the Church
Saints and Other Powerful Men in the Church

ISBN 0-926143-07-7

Preface

Sister Lucia explained to Fr. Eugene McGlynn, O.P., the Dominican priest and sculptor, that no matter how beautiful he made the statue, of the Immaculate Heart of Mary, it could never be as beautiful as Our Lady was when she appeared to the three children in the Cova da Iria. *(See Cover)*

Sister Lucia explains in her writings that, while the vision of the angel left the children physically weak and silent, the effect produced by Our Lady was very different. One praiseworthy explanation for the physical difficulty the children found as an effect of the angelic apparitions, while those of Mary brought such joy and even physical energy is this; the holy angels do not possess human nature. Mary does. Bob and Penny Lord, the authors of this book, describe Mary as *"Touchable"*.

Mary is greater by grace, than the greatest of the angels and saints in Heaven, collectively, next to Jesus Christ. St. Thomas Aquinas wrote that if anyone was to see even the lowliest of the holy angels, it would overwhelm us with the Holiness and Presence of God. Mary has more grace than all the angels and saints taken together. And yet, we have a greater familiarity with Mary than the angels whose Queen she is. *Mary is human.* She is a sister of our human race. Magnificent, the Immaculata is our very Mother in the order of Grace.

When the Church approves any apparition, such as Guadalupe, Lourdes, Fatima, as mentioned in this book, it is because the message is in harmony with the Gospels, with the teachings of the Church. It is as though God's Mother, a loving Mother concerned about the salvation of each one of her children, says, *"Here, let me show you. Don't you see what my Incarnate Son Jesus Christ said, and which the Evangelists carefully recorded in Sacred Scripture?"*

It has been my privilege during the Marian Year, (1987–1988) to welcome the most Rev. Alberto Cosme do Amaral, the official Bishop of Fatima-Leiria, to my parish in South Dakota for a national Marian Congress. That Bishop bears a special sense of urgency and reponsibility for the integrity of the Fatima message. It is well for us to discover if our devotion to apparitions of Mary are leading us to such marks of authenticity as found in the Fatima children.

There are three devotions, when based on solid Catholic doctrine, which will keep us authentic Catholic Christians. Devotion to Jesus Christ in the Holy Eucharist; devotion to God's Mother; and the devotion of loyalty to the Holy Father, the visible head of the church on earth.

Pope John Paul II, in his Sixth Encyclical, *Redemptoris Mater*, which he wrote in connection with the Marian Year, stated, **"The Piety of the Christian people has always very rightly sensed a profound link between devotion to the Blessed Virgin and worship of the Eucharist. Mary guides the faithful to the Eucharist.**

Pope John Paul II wrote further: **"In this context, the Marian Year is meant to promote a new and more careful reading of what the Council said about the Blessed Virgin Mary, Mother of God, in the mystery of Christ, and the Church. . . ."** *May such be the fruit of this book.*

May the Marian Year, the second only in the almost 2,000 year history of the Roman Catholic Church, lay to rest, once and for all, what Vatican Council II said of Mary, when for some years, many Catholics were confused into believing that this Ecumenical Council had downgraded devotion to the Mother of God. In Reality, as Pope Paul VI said, on the occasion of the promulgation of the *Dogmatic Constitution on the Church* (Lumen Gentium), its 8th Chapter on Mary spoke the most gloriously and extensively on Mary of any of the Church's previous 20 Ecumenical Councils.

I pray this book will lead readers to search more deeply into the official teachings of the Church, so as to discover more deeply the true face of Catholicism.

FATHER ROBERT J. FOX
YOUTH FOR FATIMA APOSTOLATE
EDITOR, MESSENGER OF OUR LADY

Dedication

Our Lady has so many friends. Just mention that you want to do something for Mary, and people come from the least likely places to help.

We would like to dedicate this book, first, to

Our Pope, John Paul II

who has such a love story with Our Dear Lady. He, more than any one person in our generation, has opened the doors and windows to allow Mary back into our lives. He has given us the freedom to openly proclaim our love for her. One of the most dynamic personalities in the world today, he goes to Mary as a child to his Mother.

Our Children

We would like to specially dedicate this book to our three children and our grandson—Our *Daughter*, Sr. Clare of the Consolation Sisters of St. Francis, who mothers the unloved and unlovable, and taught us to love; Our *Son* Richard who, we know is in the arms of Mother Mary, in Heaven, bringing petitions of ours to Our Lord Jesus; our *Adopted Daughter*, Luz Elena Sandoval. The Lord has given us Luz Elena to share in the Ministry. Sadly for Luz Elena, she shares the blood, sweat and tears, as well as the laughter. Then there is our *Grandson*, Rob Ziminsky, a loving Grandson, an affirming son, a faithful member of the Body of Christ, a brother to all he meets, listening, helping, available. He, by always being "there" for us, whether on Pilgrimage or at home, helped us to gather this material and these pictures. Our Children gave us a knowledge of Jesus and Mary, in our never-ending love for them, and their unconditional love for us.

John and Annabel Joyce

Annabel is our mentor, and our inspiration, our Mary on Earth. At times when things looked their darkest, when everyone told us to wait on this book, not to spend the time or money on it, Annabel and John lifted us up, pushed us, and encouraged us, spiritually, and financially. They have always seen the need for this book to be published, and did everything in their power to get it done.

Thank You, Gentle Lady

We would like to give particular thanks to one donor from Baton Rouge, Louisiana, who wishes to remain anonymous. She asks that her deceased parents and husband be remembered. You won't know who they are. But they know; Our Dear Lord Jesus and His Mother Mary know.

We Thank You for Giving Us Confidence

To the tens of thousands of people who have bought our first book, THIS IS MY BODY, THIS IS MY BLOOD, Miracles of the Eucharist. You've told us by the orders and letters that have poured into our office, that we're reaching you. You've told us that the Lord is speaking through us. You've asked us to write more books. Thanks to you, we have the confidence to present this book on Mary, our most special Lady.

We Thank You for Making It Happen

When we were near completion of this manuscript, we re-alized we didn't have the money to publish the book. We knew how important this book is, how much Our Lord, and Our Lady want you to read the many ways she loves you. We sent out an appeal for donations to help finance the publishing of the book, or for people to order in advance as alternate means of bringing the Ministry the money it needed for the publication of the book. Both donations and advance orders poured in. The Lord, through your generosity, has sent the money.

God Bless You, Mother Angelica

THE STAFF OF ETERNAL WORD TELEVISION NETWORK, AND THE SISTERS OF THE MONASTERY OF THE ANGELS IN BIRMINGHAM, ALABAMA—These holy people were the first to see the Lord working in our book, **THIS IS MY BODY, THIS IS MY BLOOD, MIRACLES OF THE EUCHARIST**. They brought us to Birmingham, and interviewed us on Mother Angelica's program. The public response was so great Mother brought us back again to make a television series, based on the book. EWTN has been a great help in spreading the word of our book and our Ministry throughout the country. Special thanks to our producer there, Lori Andrews, and all the true Christians at EWTN.

OUR BROTHERS AND SISTERS WHO DO THE WILL OF THE FATHER

Jesus used the words *Brothers and Sisters and Mother*, to refer to those who "do the will of the Father". We would like to specially name some of these brothers and sisters, and sometimes mother, whom you never meet, or hear of, but make up the discipleship of Jesus, Mary and Joseph, **JOURNEYS OF FAITH**. These are the people who work in the Ministry Office. They are the unsung heroes of our Apostalate. All the letters of acclaim are addressed to Penny and myself. We get to go on television shows, and share about our work, talk in Churches, in Halls, get to meet you and get loved and hugged by you. But without these people, who never get letters addressed to them, and never go on television, nothing would ever happen. Ours is a team effort, and the

Lord and Our Sweet Mary have sent us a special team. We would like to mention them by name here. They are **LUZ ELENA SAN-DOVAL, ROB ZIMINSKY, JOHN AND ANNABEL JOYCE, JOANNE SULKOSKE, AND HELMI KALCHSCHMID** Then there are our Long Distance Disciples, **TED & BEVERLY ANN MILLER, Orlando, Florida—JIM AND PATTI CUNNINGHAM, Gadsden, Alabama**, and **TERRY BARBER, West Covina, California**.

There are so many more of you out there that are responsible for this book. We sometimes believe that Heaven is allowing us to meet all the beautiful people my Mary has put in our path. We thank her for you. We thank you for answering her call to support us and our work. We know we'll meet you again, if not here on Earth, surely in the Kingdom. God bless you.

BOB AND PENNY LORD

Table of Contents

Vision of St. John Bosco of the Church, represented by
the ship, being attacked by enemies of the faith.
A great pope is raised up by God to lead the Church to
victory and a lasting peace through devotion to Jesus in
the Holy Eucharist and to the Blessed Mother.

Mary's Back, and She's Stronger Than Ever

"SUDDENLY THE POPE FALLS, SERIOUSLY WOUNDED. HE IS INSTANTLY HELPED UP, BUT, STRUCK A SECOND TIME, DIES. A SHOUT OF VICTORY RISES FROM THE ENEMY, AND WILD REJOICING SWEEPS THEIR SHIPS!"

The above is part of a dream experienced by St. John Bosco on May 30, 1862. He saw a large ship, with the Pope at the helm. Also, in his words,

"In the midst of this endless sea, two solid columns, a short distance apart, soar high into the sky. On the one side, a statue of Our Lady, the Blessed Virgin, stands high above the sea. At her feet is a large inscription, which reads 'AUXILIUM CHRIS-TIANORUM', (Help of Christians). On the other side, and much higher, is a Giant Host, at the base of which is written 'SALUS CREDENTIUM' (Salvation of Believers). The two columns stand tall and strong, warding off the thrashing of raging winds."

St. John Bosco describes smaller ships surrounding the large ship and the columns. Many of them attack the flagship, while others defend it. No sooner is the Pope killed than he is replaced by another pope. The battle continues. The new Pope tries to steer his ship between the two columns, but is having an extremely

difficult time of it because of the constant pummeling by the furious hurricane. Finally, he succeeds in bringing his ship between
the columns. He ties it up at each column. The wind cries out a
bloodcurdling shriek, heard round the world, and dies. The
enemy ships scatter in great fear, their battle lost, while the de-
fending ships sing out praises to Our Lord Jesus, as they, too, tie
up at the posts. A peaceful calm blankets the sea.

We chose to open our book on Mary with this vision, or
dream of St. John Bosco, because we believe there is a strong
connection between that dream and the work the Lord has commanded us to do. There was then, and is now, a great battle being
waged between the powers of good and evil for control of the
world, and destruction of two of the strongest powers we have in
the Church today, The Eucharist, and Our Mother Mary.

In 1985, we had absolutely no idea of writing a book on
THE MIRACLES OF THE EUCHARIST, although we had gathered more than enough material over a ten year period. We had
used our research to teach the Pilgrims we brought to the shrines
in our Pilgrimage Ministry. But the Lord was strong in His demand. In October of 1986, **THIS IS MY BODY, THIS IS MY
BLOOD, Miracles of the Eucharist** was published. But that was
just the beginning.

There was a great misunderstanding of the documents of
Vatican II regarding Our Lady's role in the Church, during and
immediately after the Council convened. Because of this, devotion to Mary went into a tailspin. Her best friends, the angels and
saints, were also affected. It was a complete sweep. It was as if
the whole world had gone crazy. This was not at all what Pope
John XXIII had in mind when he attempted to *open the windows
of the Church to let the Spirit flow*. The day before convening
Vatican Council II, he went in pilgrimage to the shrine of Our
Lady at Loreto, in Italy, celebrated Mass in the Holy House of
Nazareth, and prayed for Mary's protection of the upcoming
Council.

Long after the Council ended, the actual documents of Vatican Council II found their way to the rank and file of the Church. In reading them, it was very obvious that none of what actually happened was meant to happen by the Council. Actually, the praise of Our Sweet Mother Mary and the saints was a great tribute to the Council and its Documents. But it took years before anyone knew what they were actually saying. In 1954, Pope Pius XII declared a Marian Year. In 1962, Vatican Council II opened. In 1964, just ten years after the declaration of Mary's special Marian year, Vatican Council II declared a teaching, explaining Mary's place in the Church. In the same year, Pope Paul VI declared Mary **MOTHER OF THE CHURCH**.

But the damage had been done. Devotion to Mary stopped; novenas to Mary stopped; the Rosary stopped; magazines devoted to Mary ceased publication. But Mary made a statement in 1917 at Fatima, which was not meant just for Russia.
IN THE END, MY IMMACULATE HEART WILL TRIUMPH
And triumph it will.

SHE IS DAUGHTER OF THE FATHER—obedient to Him
MOTHER OF THE SON—leading us to Him
SPOUSE OF THE HOLY SPIRIT—moving men's hearts.

We Have Good News, and We Have Bad News
The Good News is that Our Lady has been through this before, and survived very well. This is not the first time that Mary has been attacked in the history of the Church. From the very beginning, she has been the target of jealousy and abuse. Every time strong devotion to Mary has taken place, it has always been followed by violent hostilities. Usually, these assaults begin with the heresies denying the Real Presence of Jesus in the Eucharist. They are almost always followed by onslaughts against Mary. We call this the Good News because we and she have always come out of it, *eventually*. The Bad News is that the *eventually* involves a great deal of struggle and persecution, both on Mary and her

believers. We have been in such times of persecution since Vatican Council II.

We're told that since the last approved apparition by Our Lady at Banneux, Belgium, in 1933, there have been 130 claimed visits from Mary prior to the reported apparitions in Medjugorje, Yugoslavia in 1981, which we will talk about in this book. **SINCE MEDJUGORJE,** we hear about the Lady from Heaven coming to places like Africa, and Cairo, and Ireland, to name a few. It will be some time before anyone properly analyzes what is happening in our time. While we're not attempting to comment on the authenticity of any of these claimed apparitions, we know one thing for sure. Mary's Back, and She's Stronger Than Ever.

Two weeks after we had sent the manuscript of our book on the **MIRACLES OF THE EUCHARIST** to the editor and typesetter, we left to bring a group of pilgrims to the Holy Land, Medjugorje, and the shrines of Our Lady in Europe. We had not considered a follow up book. *Remember, we knew absolutely nothing about publishing, or selling a book.* We were praying to the Lord to show us how to get the book on the Miracles of the Eucharist distributed.

During this Pilgrimage, Mary came to us in a very special way, with a mandate. She showed us on many occasions, the painting of that vision of Don Bosco's in 1862. She spoke softly, gently to our hearts. She invaded our sleeping and our waking hours. We knew, within two weeks of our departure for her shrines, that *this book had to be written.* But it had to be a very special book, for a special Lady, at a crucial period in the history of the world.

When we began formulating a book on Mary, we needed a word from her, a direction. Should it be another book on the apparitions of Our Lady from our personal research? Should it be our own experiences with Mary at different times in our lives? Should it be our experiences at the shrines of Mary throughout the world? Should it be about our feelings for Mary, our love for her, how it came about, how it's manifested itself over the years? Should it be about her love for us, and how she's protected and guided us all our lives, how she's stood by us when we rejected her? We needed guidance.

Who is Mary? Why is there such controversy surrounding this Lady, the most loving, the most beautiful woman in the history of the world? Why does she always visit us from Heaven? What does she say to us that has so much meaning for us? Why do we listen to her? Why do we *not listen* to her? Why is she under so much attack? Why does she keep coming back, when people are so cruel to her? Mary means so many things to so many people. What did she want us to say about her? We had to find out.

Our Journey began. We had visited many of the shrines of Mary over the years. We observed the effect Our Lady had on other pilgrims who visited the same shrines. We tried to write down our own feelings while we were at these holy places, but it was near impossible. While we focus on Jesus and Mary on Pilgrimages, at shrines like Lourdes and Fatima, we are so filled with emotions that it takes time to sort it all out. Oftentimes, we have to go off by ourselves to a quiet place to gather our thoughts. We had written background on all these shrines for our Good Newsletter, and for Pilgrims going on one of our Journeys of Faith to Mary's shrines. But we had never put it all together.

We developed a hunger for Mary. We searched out and made pilgrimages to lesser known shrines, such as Our Lady of the Victories in Paris, Pontmain, Banneux, Beauraing, and others that we had heard of. We looked for a theme, an overall message, which would apply to all the apparitions. We thought that each apparition was given for a particular person, or group of people, for a specific time in the history of a given part of the world.

The only thread of an overall message we could determine is that of Cana, her last recorded words in the Gospel, **Do Whatever He Tells You**. She's been more specific over the years. She calls for prayer, fasting, penance, reconciliation, and a return to the Sacraments. Other than that, the message of each apparition seems to be *unique* in itself. She never makes reference to her previous apparitions.

At Loreto, Italy, inside the Holy House of Nazareth, I told Penny I could feel a great closeness to Mary. I directed my attention to her statue above the main altar. I focused on her eyes.

I emptied my mind of everything but the vision before me. Only she was clear. Everything on the outer edges of my vision was blurred. I was at the brink of direct communication with her. I could feel her trying to reach me. She was speaking. I could almost hear her in my heart. But I lost it. The room became crowded with pilgrims; my concentration was broken. It was so frustrating. I knew she was trying to get through to me. The feeling was there! It actually became stronger, burning inside of me. But the words, breaking it down into human language had not yet come. I couldn't explain to myself or anyone else what had happened.

My mind traveled back to that warm summer day in 1983, when my Penny, or now I wonder if it wasn't Mary through Penny, coined the phrase, **THE MANY FACES OF MARY**. The late afternoon sun cast its shadows from the buildings onto the pavement of the sleepy, narrow Corso Boccalino, which leads to the Holy House of Nazareth in Loreto. The shops lining either side of the streets were still closed for their traditional Italian 3½ hour lunch period. It was warm. It was late July. The previous two week excruciating heat wave was but a preview of what August would bring.

As we walked down the street towards the famous shrine to Mary, we praised and thanked her for the relief from the heat the shadows afforded us. It was a lazy day, partly because of the heat, and partly because of the conversation with our luncheon guest. He was a young Italian manufacturer of religious articles, Paolo Georgetti. He was eager to know why people prayed to Mary under so many different names. He used the pretext that he was interested in manufacturing plaques of Our Lady, but we could tell from his conversation that he had been seriously flirting with the Jehovah's Witnesses.

My wife Penny, who has a great love for Mary, rattled off with great enthusiasm the various titles of Our Lady to which she judged people had the greatest devotion. "Let's see, there is Our Lady of Lourdes, Our Lady of Loreto, Our Lady of Fatima. Then you definitely need Our Lady of Pompeii, Our Lady of Perpetual Help . . ."

Young Paolo started to laugh. "But senora, how many ladies are there?" The sound of his laughter ricocheted off the buildings, assaulting the peaceful silence of the afternoon. It was like a shriek against our ears. We felt as if he had blasphemed.

Penny looked at him, her expression a combination of hurt, anger and defensiveness. "How many people are you? To your wife, you are Paolo, husband and lover. To your children, you are daddy, pillar of strength, provider. To your father, you are Paolo, son, successor to his business, learning your trade from him. To your mother, you are the baby she held inside her womb for nine months, and watched with pride as you grew up. To your contemporaries, you are Paolo, the friend. To your employees, you are Signor Georgetti, the *patrone*. Same Paolo, but different people, addressing different needs.

It's the same with Our Lady, only multiplied ten thousand fold. *Mary has many faces.* Each title of Mary answers a special need in those who reach out to her. And she answers the needs as a loving mother, an understanding friend, a trusting confidante, whatever you need. She's available. Don't ever underestimate the Many Faces of Mary". *There it was!!*

We went to Lourdes. Everyone who has spent any time at that mystical shrine has their own special place, their own special relationship with Mary. Our particular place is the Basilica of the Rosary. There is a mosaic of Mary inside the dome. She looks absolutely breathtaking. She wears her crown as Queen of Heaven and Earth. She's dressed in a white gown with a blue sash, and a cloak of ermine. Her arms and hands are outstretched. The expression on her face is very individual, very personal. It says different things to different people at different times. Each time we go to Lourdes, she says something new. Even if we visit the church a few times during one trip, she gives us a variety of messages. She has a smile on her face, and an expression in her eyes that is so young, so happy, so full of hope. Her eyes follow us all over the church. No matter where we walk, if we turn to look at Mary, she's watching us. The message we received this last time was *You're getting close. Don't stop searching. Keep your attention on me. You'll get the message soon.*

I came back to California after two pilgrimages to the shrines of Mary. Penny had to remain in Europe, waiting to bring the next group of pilgrims to the shrines. After each pilgrimage, I seemed to be on the verge of a breakthrough. But it still had not happened. I returned on September 6. Mary's birthday is September 8, and mine is September 9. I received the message from Mary in our Parish Church.

I attended Mass in our parish on September 8. I had completely forgotten it was the Birthday of Mary. Our Parish priest had been in the Room of the Apparitions in Medjugorje with me in July, but I hadn't seen him since we had returned from that Pilgrimage. On this day, he gave a homily in honor of Mary on her birthday. He said many things, but the one that stood out to me, **THE MESSAGE** that Our Lady was trying to give me, came through. I'm paraphrasing what he said, but the essence is as follows:

"In preparing this homily, I went through the Litany of Mary. It gives the various titles of Mary, some of which are **STAR OF THE SEA, GATE OF HEAVEN, MYSTICAL ROSE.** I thought to myself, she's not a star, or a gate, or a rose. These are the words of poets, and while they're very poetic, very inspired, and they attempt to place Our dear Lady in her proper position in Heaven, way above us, they don't tell us anything about who she really was, and is. She's a woman, a very special woman, a very strong woman, an obedient daughter, a loving wife, an unselfish mother, a friend, a confidante, and all love. It's good to put Mary on a throne, because she is our queen. But if we put her out of reach, we've made a mistake, because she is above all, **TOUCHABLE**."

Mary is Touchable! I had to travel 9,000 miles, and 60 days searching, struggling, praying for a word, only to come back to my parish in California. The speaker was not famous. He was not Fr. John Powell, or Fr. Ken Roberts or Fr. Richard Rohr. He was a simple parish priest, much like St. Jean Vianney, the Cure of Ars. The church was not a great shrine. It was our little parish church Our Lady used to give me my word. And the word I received is **Touchable**."

In all her apparitons, Mary reaches out to us, to help us. She becomes vulnerable; she allows herself to be touched. Battle lines are drawn. Attacks from the fallen angels are a guarantee. They hate her more than any human being the Lord has put on this earth. Good people are made to do bad things. Unbridled anger, pure hatred spews out of their mouths in denunciation of her. But then good things happen. *"In the end, my Immaculate Heart will triumph"*. Mass conversions come about. There are Healings of body and soul, reconciliation, return to her Son Jesus in the Eucharist. All of this happens because she is willing to be **Touchable**.

Our goal in this book is to make Mary touchable for you, as she is to us, as she was to the people she chose to visit on earth. We will try, with the inspiration of the Holy Spirit, to make her for you what she is for us. She is our friend. She can be your friend, too. We want to share with you the freedom to call on her the way you would your very best friend. When you reach out to her for help, or solace, have the confidence that she will take your hand, listen to you, console you, and lead you to her Son, Jesus. If she can reach you through our writing, she will have accomplished *her* goal, which is our mission.

We come back to the vision of St. John Bosco in 1862. What was Mary called in that dream? **HELP OF CHRISTIANS.** Our Lady wants to touch you. She wants you to touch her. She has used us to bring you closer to her, to give you the freedom to allow her to get closer to you. She has been waiting for you. Go to her now. She is your mother. Remember how you loved your mother as a child, and how she loved you. Happiness is just around the corner. Reach out and touch her.

Mary, My First Love

This book is sub-titled **"A LOVE STORY"**. It is truly that.
I'm reminded of the Scripture Passage at the end of Sirach 51:13

When I was young and innocent, I sought her
She came to me in her beauty,
and until the end I will cultivate her.
As the blossoms yielded to ripening grapes,
the heart's joy,
My feet keep to the level path because from earliest
youth I was familiar with her. . . .
I became resolutely devoted to her . . .
the good I persistently strove for.

I burned with desire for her,
never turning back.
I became preoccupied with her,
never weary of extolling her.

For her I purified even the soles of my feet
in cleanness I attained her.
At first acquaintance with her,
I gained understanding, such that I
will never forsake her.

My whole being was stirred as I learned
about her;
therefore I have made her my
prize possession.

Submit your neck to her yoke, that your mind
may accept her teaching.
For she is close to those who seek her,
and one who is in earnest finds her.

My relationship with Mary is a very personal one. She is my first love. I can talk to Mary. I can count on her. I have been in love with her for as long as I can remember. It's been an on again, off again romance with us, not on her part, but on mine. She's constant. She has always "been". When I've broken away from her, wrapped myself up in the glamour of the world, she stood by. When I thought I had outgrown her, didn't need her anymore, she waited. I always came back. She was always there.

Our bond is unique. I've never heard anyone speak of their feelings for her in the same way that I do. But I wonder if the truth is that others *do* feel as I do towards her, but just don't know how to say it. Or possibly they are afraid to say the words "I love you. I have always loved you." I've spoken to many people who have a special devotion to Mary. I've looked at their eyes as they speak of her, and what she means to them.

They say with their mouths, things like "I have a strong devotion to Mary", and "I always pray to Mary", or "She has never let me down". But their eyes betray their words. There's a cloudiness in their expressions, a wetness in their eyes that tells of a much deeper emotion than their lips proclaim. I wonder if they wouldn't rather blurt out, "I deeply love Mary. I always have. I put her on a pedestal, not the way you would a holy person, or a saint, but like that perfect woman whom you've found, and will love forever". I want to shout it from the rooftops. **"I LOVE HER!! I'M IN LOVE WITH MARY!!"** So, instead, I write a book.

Mary has guided me and protected me all my life, from the time my mother carried me in her womb. My mother, a good Irish Catholic girl, used to tell everyone that she had a dream while she was pregnant with me. In that dream, she found herself walking through a haze, towards a great light off in the distance. She was drawn to it. Though she had no sensation of walking, she got closer and closer to the source of the light. She could make out the figure of a woman holding a child. The haze lifted. She recognized Mary standing in front of her, holding what she assumed to be the Christ Child. The child was beautiful and radiant, but not as brilliant as Our Lady. My mother recalled that she thought this was unusual. Her belief was that Jesus would outshine everyone. The splendor of His Presence would overcome even the aura of His Mother.

She awoke from her dream puzzled as to why Our Lady would appear to her, holding the Baby Jesus, and why the aura surrounding Mary was greater than that of the child. She assumed the vision was a sign from Heaven that my birth would be a successful and healthy one. My mother went on to complete her pregnancy, and I was born a robust and healthy handful. Her attention was diverted to welcoming and taking care of the new member of the family. She forgot about the dream.

In her story of this dream, mother recounted that something uncanny happened as I grew into my third month. She had the strange feeling that she knew me, as though from another time, another place. I looked so familiar to her. She racked her brain for days, trying to unravel the mystery. Then one night she had the same dream again. Only this time, she understood why the child had not outshone Mary. The child in the dream, the same child Mary had held months before, was not the baby Jesus. It was me.

Mary said to my mother **"He is mine. Take care of him"**.

My mother kept faithful to the charge she had been given as well as she could for as long as she could. She was the victim of an alcoholic husband, my father. She suffered greatly, trying to salvage her marriage, and at the same time, take care of two young boys. The Great Depression ended. The war years came. There was plenty of money around for defense workers. But while other people amassed fortunes during the war, or at least little nest eggs for the future, my father spent all his money on liquor and friends. Neither my mother, my brother nor I ever saw "Happy Days are Here Again". Babies, we found ourselves going to every bar on the waterfront in Brooklyn, near the defense plants and shipyards, on payday, trying frantically to find my father to get a little money before it was all gone.

By the time the war was over, my mother was a beaten woman, without any self worth. Her youth and innocence had been stolen from her. The one chance my parents had at making something out of their lives, had been wasted. It was now behind them. The balloon of the big war money had burst. My father went back to the meager existence of struggling to make ends meet. My mother finally gave in to my father; she, too, became an alcoholic. They lived out their lives in misery and disappointment.

I don't mean to speak harshly of my parents. They were good people. I loved them very much. I'm sure they are both very happy and at peace with Jesus and Mary in the Kingdom. They were just victims. We know about victims. We see our children, victims, falling dead every day from the satan of drugs. We've lost almost a whole generation. In my parents' time, it was the satan of alcohol. They were victims of the Roaring 20's, the Flapper Days. Alcoholism was the socially acceptable behavior. They were completely overwhelmed by the culture of the anti-Christ prevalent in *their* day. When the great chastisement of the Depression overtook them, they were already addicts.

My mother was not able to fulfill the mandate Mary had given her. Mary, my lady, had to take over personally. She had plans for me from the very beginning. When I was very young, I felt the compelling desire to spend my life wrapped in the warm, protective cloak of Mary in the Church. I remember once, at age

11 or 12, wanting to go to Mass every morning during Advent at a local cloistered Monastery in the Bronx. The masses were celebrated at 6:45 A.M. That meant I had to wake myself at 6 A.M. because my father, who was the first to rise, didn't get up until 6:45 A.M.

In those days, we didn't use expressions like "Filled with the Holy Spirit". *I just had a thought.* Everybody else had a thought too. They thought I was crazy. I couldn't explain why I wanted to do it. I just did. It was very cold when I left the house at 6:20 to go to the Monastery. I'll never forget the gusts of cold winter air hitting my face, penetrating through my winter coat to my clothes, to my skin, as I opened the front door of my house each morning. At the beginning, right after Thanksgiving, it was cold. By the time Christmas eve approached, it was bitter. There were days of freezing rain, and days of gentle snowfall. But all the mornings gave me great peace, walking in the pre-dawn hours, just Jesus, Mary and me. I believe that year, 1946 or 1947, was the most beautiful Christmas I have ever experienced. I never felt so fulfilled at Mass. I can still recall the fragrance of burning candles and incense. From that time, churches have always had a special aroma for me. The voices of the nuns chanting their morning prayers still echo in the recesses of my mind.

Until I began to write this book, I never realized how much an 11 year old has a need for tranquility, for belonging. I was so at home in that Monastery. I didn't want to go back out to the cold world. I was in my mother's womb, warm and protected. My mother was Mary.

I thought I had a vocation to the priesthood. I never fantasized being a priest, wearing priestly clothes or doing priestly things. I envisioned myself in the Presence. I was not sure what Presence. Mary was there. The colorful saints, whose lives I had read, or had been read to me, were there. Jesus was very much there. That little monastery on Baretto Street in the Bronx was there. It was the hub. I believe that more than a vocation to the priesthood, I had an overpowering desire for relationship with people I was deeply in love with. I had never met them personally or physically. But they were all there, around me, speaking to me, touching me, loving me. And at the head was Mary, the indescribably beautiful Mary.

There is an expression used by the young people today, **"Get into the Real World"**. The confusion lies in determining what is the Real World and what is Fantasy. At age 14, I thought the real world was the world of girls, drinking and partying. That had been the world of my father. That world was calling me. My biological system had gone through the trauma of puberty, and with it my value system. Physical and emotional discoveries overpowered me. In addition, I broke out in pimples all over my face. As I grew into my teen age years, the distorted glamour of evil pulled me away from my true love. Eventually, it drew me away completely. The images I thought to be real, I learned in later years were fantasy, unreal. The only reality was the love I had embraced as a child, then walked away from completely as a young man.

There's a wise saying, *"The 35 year old man has to live with the decisions made by the 18 year old"*. Our whole lives are determined by the mistakes we make as young people. That should have been my fate. But my Lady didn't let it happen. She had too much work for me to do. She was willing to wait for me until I finally grew up.

Every now and then, Mary showed herself very strongly in strange ways, in strange places. For example, I worked at Radio City Music Hall as an usher during my high school days. I had become romantically involved with the girls in the Corps de Ballet, and the Rockettes. They were all older than I; but as long as I was willing to adopt their way of life, they accepted me. Although I was going to a Catholic High School, I had all but forgotten about Mary and the Saints. They didn't fit into my new life style. At about that time, somehow, a book came my way. It was called **THE SONG OF BERNADETTE**. It dealt with the apparitions of Mary to Bernadette Soubirous at Lourdes in the year 1858. Here I was, completely lost in this beautiful book on Mary and Bernadette. I was a contradiction, sitting in the Employee's

Cafeteria of Radio City Music Hall with all my new found show business friends, older girls and guys whose values had nothing at all to do with Mary or anything Marian. I still have that book from 1952. The cover is gone, as are the first 7 or 8 pages. But it is a very special book to me.

The pull from Mary was strong, very strong, but not strong enough. For a few months, I was renewed in my love for her and Our Lord Jesus, but then I began to backslide. Soon the transition was complete. I was back to my old ways. I had left her behind. Every now and then, she came back into my consciousness. But I conveniently pushed her out of my mind. Even during my time in the service, I was stationed in France, not 200 miles away from Lourdes, but I never went to visit her at her shrine. Paris was 600 miles away, yet I went *there* every chance I had. But when I was in Paris, I never visited the Chapel of the Miraculous Medal, or the Church of Our Lady of the Victories.

SEPTEMBER 23, 1957. Dates are very important. Jesus used numbers as symbols during His Ministry. In the history of the Church, many important events occurred on September 23. Padre Pio died on September 23, 1968. The first Eucharistic Congress in Abruzzi was held on September 23, 1921. I met Ernest Hemingway in the Yankee Stadium and got him to autograph one of his books on September 23, 1957. But the most important thing about September 23 is it is the day my Penny was born. And September 23, 1957 was the day Mary chose to place Penny in my path.

We refer at this time to St. Paul's letter to the Romans, Chapter 8, Verses 28–30. *We know that God makes all things work together for the good of those who love him, who have been called according to his decree. Those whom He foreknew He predestined to share the image of His Son, that the Son might be the first- born of many brothers. Those He predestined, He likewise called; those He called He also justified; and those He justified, He in turn glorified.*

I believe very strongly that God has planned out the lives of every soul He has created. While we have to say **"Yes"** in the same way that Mary said "Yes" in order for God to work in our lives, I believe that He has orchestrated a beautiful life for all of us, if we just get out of the way. I believe that God has had a plan for me since before I was born. I believe that Penny and I were chosen for each other from the beginning of time to be husband and wife. I believe that Mary came to me in the form of Penny, to be the instrument to bring me back to the Lord, and to give myself to Him through Mary in full time Ministry. These are things I believe. I know for a fact that Penny was given to me for my salvation.

In the early days of our marriage, Penny and I spent most of our time struggling to survive, much like any average married couple. Our Lord Jesus had to take last place, and with it, my Mary. But they waited. They knew what work we had to do, and they allowed us all the normal desires that young married couples have, a good job, beautiful children, a house, cars, money.

We worked hard. We have always been achievers. It was almost as if we had a check list. First we achieved the children, then the house, the cars, and finally the money. When we had achieved everything we wanted, we lost our 19 year old son, our precious boy, to an overdose of drugs. He was a victim of that world. Instead of blaming ourselves for allowing a society to exist that could destroy our children, while we were busy *achieving*, we blamed God. Doesn't everybody?

Still, Jesus and Mary waited. They gave us four years to mourn, to turn off God, Church, and each other. Then, on January 1, 1975, The Feast of the **Solemnity of Mary**, the first day of the Holy Year, they hit us over the head with a two by four. We will never forget it. It was a typical New Year's Day. We had stayed at home. Our daughter Cheryl, (now Sister Clare) had come over for dinner with our grandson, Rob, and a Jewish friend. The conversation centered around important matters, the Football games that day. We had dinner. After it was over, and everyone had left, I took the table cloth out to the patio to shake it out. Again, **I HAD A THOUGHT**.

We hadn't been to Mass on Sunday for four years. My *thought* was, *I'd like to go to Mass every day from now on.* First I called the local church, where we had never attended Mass, to find out what the schedule was. Then I went into the family room where Penny was watching television. I said, "Honey, how would you like to go to Mass every day from now on?"

Her reaction was normal. She was completely shocked. But she had a *thought.* "For many years he went to Mass on Sunday for me. I owe it to him, for whatever reason he has, to support him in this." The first day we entered the church, I had a feeling that I can't describe, except to say I had come home. The warmth I had felt as a child in the Monastery in the Bronx at daily Mass had returned. Penny said my eyes gleamed with love for Our Dear Lord in the Eucharist, and everything that the Church represented. She was afraid for a time that I was going to divorce her to become a priest.

That was the beginning. We have never missed the gift of the Eucharist one day from that time to this. We've given ourselves up to full time ministry. We don't earn the kind of money we were used to. We don't have the freedom to go anywhere, or do anything we want anymore. But the places we are not free to visit, we don't want to visit; and the things we cannot have, we don't want. We have come home. **LORD, IT IS GOOD FOR US TO BE HERE.**

The Tilma of Juan Diego—Our Lady of Guadalupe
Mexico City

Guadalupe, 1531: Our Lady Saves America

Fly with us up into the Heavens to envision God's view, an overall picture of the country of Mexico. The date can be anywhere from December 6 to December 9th of any year, based on the distance between the little village in question, and the famous Hill of Tepeyac in Mexico City, where the Mother of God, Mary Most Holy, radically changed the course of history just 39 years after Christopher Columbus set foot on the new world.

From our vantage point in the sky, we see little arteries and veins, made up of people. Groups of pilgrims awaken early in the morning. They gather together in the village square, laden down with sleeping bags, food and provisions for a week or more, and a great banner depicting Juan Diego's tilma, and the magnificent image of Our Lady. They begin their walking pilgrimage, for as few as 50 miles, and as many as 200 miles, praying, singing, dancing, in praise of Our Dear Lady, and the gift of power she has been given by her Son Jesus.

As they arrive at Mexico City, they present an overwhelming contrast, these poor farmers and shepherds from unknown villages deep in the heartland of the country, with the skyscrapers and fashionably dressed inhabitants of the big city. But strangely

enough, they're not out of place at all. They parade gaily down
the main avenue of Mexico City, waving to the people in the cars
and trucks, who wave back at them. Traffic is snarled for miles;
however no one appears to be concerned. All roads lead to the
outskirts of the city, to Tepeyac Hill. And all pilgrims follow those
roads to the great Basilica of the Virgin of Guadalupe.

It is said that in the normal course of events, 15,000 pilgrims
a day visit the shrine to Mary at Guadalupe. This however, is not
the normal time. This is the octave of the Feast. The numbers are
more into the millions. Most of the pilgrims make their headquarters in and around the Basilica. The high point for all is a long
visit to the miraculous tilma (poncho) of Juan Diego, which hangs
high above the main altar, on which is imprinted the Heavenly
image of Mary. Pilgrims spend hours at this shrine. They bring
roses, carloads of roses, because roses were the medium used by
Jesus and the heavenly angels to paint the portrait of His Mother
Mary on the tilma.

During any hour of the night on any day from the 10th to the
15th of December, a passerby can see hundreds of thousands of
pilgrims sleeping in the great plaza, surrounded by the old, sink-
ing Basilica on one side, and the new, modern Basilica at a right
angle to it. The pilgrims don't go to sleep very early. They dance
and sing through the night. But at some point in the wee hours,
they realize that the next day will be another celebration. They
finally allow themselves to fall into the sleep of the innocent, in
the knowledge and security that they are being protected by the
greatest powers in the world.

In order to get the proper perspective on this shrine, we
brought a Pilgrimage of Peace to Guadalupe in December of
1986, to see and experience first hand the shrine and the Feast of
Our Lady of Guadalupe, which falls on the 12th of December.
One of our priests put it best at his homily during Mass at the
Shrine.

**"IF YOU HAVEN'T SEEN IT FOR YOURSELF; IF YOU
HAVEN'T HAD THE PRIVILEGE OF BEING HERE ON THE**

FEAST DAY, YOU CAN NEVER IMAGINE IN YOUR WILDEST DREAMS THE TRIBUTE PAID TO OUR LADY HERE IN MEXICO."

Over the past 11 years, we have been present at, or brought pilgrimages to every major shrine in the world. We have walked the Way of the Cross at the Via Dolorosa in Jerusalem on Good Friday, and fought the crowds at the Tomb of Jesus. We have been to the Shrine of St. Anthony in Padua on the 13th of June, where pilgrims from all over Europe come to venerate the saint. We have been to Fatima on the 13th of October, in memoriam of the Great Miracle of the Sun, when over a million pilgrims take part in the ceremonies. We have been to Lourdes at the height of the Pilgrim season, where up to 250,000 pilgrims march in the Candlelight Procession. We have been at audiences with the Pope in Rome at Eastertime, when close to 100,000 pilgrims jammed St. Peter's Square. We attended a Mass at St. John Lateran's in Rome in 1979, celebrated by Pope John Paul II, with a procession of the Blessed Sacrament following, where the secular newspapers complained of traffic jams caused by crowds of over 200,000 walking with Our Lord Jesus and Pope John Paul II.

WE HAVE NEVER—NOT EVER—SEEN ANYTHING LIKE THE VENERATION AND PRAISE GIVEN TO OUR LORD JESUS THROUGH HIS MOTHER MARY AT GUADALUPE.

The closest estimate we could get was that on the day of the Feast, December 12, approximately *3 to 4 Million Pilgrims* attended the services. The official festivities actually begin on midnight of the evening of the 11th, when a special service takes place. It is called a **MANANITAS. The word, a Mexican coloquial expression, means a short musical composition to celebrate a famous person or event.** In this instance, however, it is anything but short. The most famous singers from every Hispanic country in the world, but mostly from Mexico, Central and South America, pay tribute to Mary by singing sweet praises to Jesus and the Lady who honored and saved them at Tepeyac Hill.

From the break of dawn on the 12th, there are Masses and

special services inside the Basilica. Outside the Basilica, in the great plaza, on the streets, all over the city of Mexico, festivities begin, spreading into the suburbs of the city, creating arteries of celebration in every hamlet and village in the country. And it goes on for days. Actually, the festivities begin with the *Feast of the Immaculate Conception on December 8*, which carries them through to *The Feast of Our Lady of Guadalupe on December 12*. It continues on through the 16th, when the *Christmas Posadas* begin. (Posada is a re-creation of Joseph and Mary being turned away from the inns) So for all intents and purposes, the festivities begin on December 8, and don't end until New Year's Day.

Back to the Feast Day of Our Lady of Guadalupe; the main Mass and the Blessing of the Roses takes place at 11 am. It is celebrated by the Bishop of Mexico City, with the Cardinal and Papal Nuncio in attendance. We were fortunate enough to have a reserved space in the balcony for our group. While we waited for the Mass to begin, (we arrived at 9:15 am) we were able to look down from the balcony into the great plaza. There were great multitudes of groups of pilgrims, dancing in native costumes. There were Indian dancers of many tribes, as indicated by the color and type of costumes they wore. There were Spanish dancers, wearing costumes from various periods from Mexican history.

They reminded us of the Little Drummer Boy story. He had nothing to bring to Jesus for Christmas except his ability to play the drums. So he gave Jesus all that he had. These dear people, so extremely poor that we in the United States, can not possibly conceive the level of their poverty, danced their hearts out in honor of the Lady from Heaven. They had nothing else to give, but Jesus and Mary were so pleased with the gifts they *did* give.

Their values were so outrageous by our standards. They cared not about leaving their homes unattended, because there was nothing in the homes worth stealing. They weren't concerned about their jobs. Most of them did not have jobs. But those who had them knew that if they were gone when they returned, the Lord would provide somehow.

It's said that with the exception of Christmas and Easter, the Feast Day of Our Lady of Guadalupe is the most celebrated Feast Day in existence, and that the shrine of Guadalupe is second only to St. Peter's Basilica in Rome as the most visited shrine in the World. Somewhere in the area of 15,000,000 pilgrims visit Guadalupe each year. *Pope John Paul II said that 95% of the Mexican people are Catholic, but 98% are Guadalupeans.*

Why? What's It All About?

In the early morning hours of **December 9, 1531**, the frost was still on the ground. All living things, such as flowers and grass, and leaves on the trees, had died for the winter, waiting for the warmth of Spring to breathe life back into them. Juan Diego was a simple Indian. He had been converted just recently to the Catholic Faith. He and his wife were baptized in the Church of Santiago, built out of the rubble of the destruction of the Aztec temple of Huitzilpochtli. Juan had risen from bed before dawn on this Saturday morning to attend Mass in honor of Our Lady of the Immaculate Conception. After Mass, he was to take lessons at the Indian school, run by the Franciscans, for those newly converted to the faith.

As he passed Tepeyac hill, a blanket of warmth and peace overtook him. He could hear the sound of sweet angelic voices singing above him, coming from the top of the hill. He had never heard anything like it before. He listened intently. They stopped. Then their voices echoed from a great distance. They began again. He was overcome by the angelic melody. After a short while there was silence again. Then one single voice rang out to him like a bell.

"Little Juan, Juan Dieguito".

This should have been unusual to Juan, because the voice was so young and sweet that it had to come from someone much younger than his 57 years, and yet she spoke to him as if he were her child. That didn't concern him, however. He darted up the hill as quickly as his legs could carry him. The sight he beheld filled his heart with such joy, he thought it would burst. But the dazzling beauty of what he saw before him made him freeze on the spot. He couldn't catch his breath.

There before him was the most beautiful lady he had ever seen. She was young; she was regal. She did not look *of this world*. He had never imagined anything that even closely resembled the vision before his eyes. He had no idea who she might be, but he didn't care. He wanted to be swallowed up by the elegance of the lady. Everything around her sparkled like the finest diamonds. Gold reflected from her garments. She wore the most exquisite gown he had ever seen. Even the rocks and bushes glistened from the reflection of her. She spoke to him.

"Juanito, the smallest of my children, where are you going?"

"My Lady and my child, I must go to your church in Tlatiloco, to continue the study of the divine mysteries taught us by our priests, who are missionaries of Our Lord."

The eyes, those piercing eyes, looked deep into his soul.

"Be it known and understood by you, the smallest of my children, that I am the ever Virgin Mary, Mother of the True God from whom all life has come; of the Creator, close to whom is everything, the Lord of Heaven and Earth.

I ardently desire a temple built for me here, where I can show and offer all my love, compassion, help and protection, for I am your Merciful Mother, wishing to hear and help you, and all those others who, loving me, invoke and place their confidence in me; therein to hear your complaints and remedy all your sorrows, hardships, and suffering.

And in order to carry out what my mercy seeks, you must go to the bishop's palace in Mexico and tell him that I sent you to make it clear how very much I desire that he build a temple for me here on this place. You shall tell him exactly all you have seen and marvelled at, and what you have heard.

Be assured that I shall be very grateful and reward you, for I shall make you happy and you shall greatly merit my compensation for the work and trouble that the mission I entrust you with will cause you. Now you have heard my command, my son, the smallest of all. Go now and give it your best effort."

Juan Diego did not know how to behave in front of this heavenly creature. He bowed as low as he could, and said,

"My Lady, I am going now to carry out your command. For the present, your humble servant takes leave of you."

He attempted to back down the hill, so as not to turn his back on the radiant lady. But he found himself slipping, and so he bowed again, turned his back and left. He kept turning around as he went down the hill. She was so beautiful, he didn't want to take his eyes off her. He couldn't get enough of her. She remained there until he was too low to see her anymore. He immediately set out for the Bishop's palace in Mexico City to tell him what Our Lady had commanded.

We find it unusual to think that anyone can just run off into town and visit the bishop. In our time, it's highly unlikely that if we just popped into the bishop's office, we could be received. However, at that time, Friar don Juan de Zumarraga, who had just been appointed bishop, was a Franciscan friar. It's possible that he even knew Juan Diego, because Juan had converted some 5 years before this time. There weren't that many Catholics among the Indians.

Whether it was that, or the aura that shone on the face of Juan Diego when he announced himself at the bishop's palace, he was given an audience with Bishop Zumarraga. Juan bowed low and knelt before this emissary of the Lord Jesus. He was very nervous. He did not have the gift of dialog, or so he thought. He had to speak slowly to be understood, because he spoke in Indian, and a dialect at that. The Bishop was Spanish, but he had an interpreter. Still, communication was not that easy.

Juan watched the bishop's eyes as he related the story of his visit from the Lady from Heaven. They were expressionless. He looked from the interpreter to the Bishop. Perhaps the interpreter was telling him the wrong thing. Why was the bishop not jumping up and down with joy? Juan could feel perspiration breaking out all over his body. It wasn't working. The Bishop didn't believe him. At the end of the story, the bishop said to him,

"You shall come again, my son, and I will hear what you have to say at greater leisure. I will look into the matter carefully from the very first, and give much thought and consideration to the good will and desire with which you have come."

The newly appointed bishop had no idea what a prediction he was making in the words he spoke to Juan Diego. Juan would definitely come again, and they would talk again, but the dear bishop was not expecting it to be as soon as it turned out to be. He was dealing with a matter of great importance, but he didn't know it; Juan Diego didn't know it. Only one person knew it; the Lady who shakes and moves. And she had a grave reason for moving and shaking.

Juan was completely crushed as he left his audience with the bishop. He dreaded the look of sadness he anticipated he would see on the face of the beautiful lady when he made his report to her. He went back to Tepeyac Hill, where she was waiting for him, and gave her an account of his unsuccessful interview with the bishop.

"Dear Lady and Child, I understood perfectly by the way he responded that he did not believe me. He may have thought I made up the story about your coming to me, and asking to have a temple built here, and that you didn't really ask for it. I seriously implore you, my Lady and Daughter, to give so great a message to an *important* person, someone well respected, in high esteem, that they will believe.

I am but a little man, a thin rope, a stepstool, a ladder, one of the least important of all people. You, my Child, smallest of my daughters, my Lady, send me where I am completely out of place, and have no standing. Forgive me if I cause you grief and make you angry with me, my Lady and Mistress."

The Lady remained calm, but her voice was very definite. She looked at Juan Diego's eyes, deep down into his soul.

"You listen to me, smallest of all my beloved children, and

understand what I am about to say. I have many messengers and servants. I could send any one of them to do my bidding, and they would be accepted without question.

But it is extremely necessary that *you* solicit my cause and help me. It's of the utmost importance that it be through *your* intercession that my wish be carried out. My little son, I urge and firmly order you to go *again* to the bishop tomorrow. Tell him again in my name, and be *sure* that he understands my position, that he begin work on the temple I ask for.

Be sure to impress upon him that it is I, the Ever Virgin Mary, Mother of God, who send you."

Juan was a simple man, but he could see a look of determination on that beautiful face, and hear the persistence in her voice. The die was cast. There was no way out for him.

"My Lady and my Child, please believe me, I don't want to cause you worry or concern. I will go gladly as you command. I will do as you command. I won't complain about the journey. But you must know that it's very possible that I won't be heard, and if I am heard, won't be believed. I just think that if the mission is as important as you say, you should get someone who is more capable than I of getting the desired results."

He looked at her to see if his last statement made any impression on her. She just stared at him. He quickly continued,

"But I will go to Mass before meeting with the bishop. I will pray all the way into the city. Then, towards sunset tomorrow evening, I will come back to you again, and give you a report of the bishop's response."

On the following morning, *Sunday, December 10*, Juan rose before dawn again. He headed for Tlatiloco (Mexico City) for Mass and instruction. From the time he had left the Lady the day before, his mind was completely taken with her. He couldn't get her out of his consciousness. She was so pretty; he couldn't believe how exquisite she was. She had to be Our Lady. No one that ravishing, with such a sweet voice, could come from anywhere but Heaven. He also thought of her determination. Without losing a bit of her delicacy, she was very firm in her demands. She in-spired him, not out of fear if he failed, but out of such great love for her that he would suffer anything, even death, to please her. Little did he know that her focus was life, and not death. Her mission was to *save* lives.

Juan prayed all the way into the city. He prayed to the Lord Jesus, to the Virgin Mary, the little lady at Tepeyac Hill, to his deceased wife, Maria Lucia, to all the angels and the saints. This assignment was so important. He didn't know why. But the Lady said it was important, and he didn't want to disappoint her, so it was important.

He could not get his mission out of his mind during the Mass at ten o' clock. He fought the distraction throughout the Mass. As per the Lady's instructions, he set out immediately for the bish-op's palace as the Mass let out. His heart pounded. His hands shook. He repeated in his mind, over and over again, the message he was to bring the bishop. He tried to think of ways to convince the bishop that he was not lying, and was not crazy.

This time, entrance into the bishop's palace was much more difficult than it had been the day before. The servants had been warned that he was a radical, or a lunatic; and in either event, should not be allowed in. Juan Diego, more concerned about dis-appointing the Lady than being disliked by the servants, de-manded to see the bishop. After much arguing and difficulties, he finally got in.

As he knelt down before the bishop, whose expression was not as kind today as it had been yesterday, Juan Diego wished for the whole thing to be over. He knew the only way, however, was to convince the bishop. He repeated his story, tears streaming down his cheek.

A change came over the bishop, as Juan spoke to him. His attitude of annoyance changed to one of genuine concern. The Holy Spirit instructed him. While Juan Diego had been receiving instructions, he had never been taught very much about the Mother of God except to adore her in keeping with her station as

Queen of Heaven and Earth. Remember, nothing like this had ever happened. Apparitions from Mary were very few in Church History prior to this time. The Indian converts had never heard of any of them. Where would this man, this simple, uneducated Indian, get these notions? They had to come from somewhere. If Our Lady were truly trying to speak to him through Juan Diego, there must be a good reason. The bishop decided to take it seriously.

He asked Juan Diego many questions. Where had he seen her? What did she look like? What exactly did she say? Juan repeated everything as it had happened. The bishop seemed particularly interested in Juan Diego's plea for Our Lady to get someone of importance to bring the message to the bishop, and her firm reply that it had to come from Juan.

At the end of the interview, the bishop told Juan that he could not accept his story on his word alone, and could not possibly act on it unless there were some sort of sign from Heaven. Juan didn't think this an unreasonable request. After all, if she really wanted the temple built as she had said, she should be willing to cooperate with the bishop. He asked the bishop,

"Senor, just what kind of a sign do you ask for. I will go and request it from the Lady of Heaven who sent me."

We're not sure if the bishop requested a particular sign, but it was agreed that Juan Diego would ask the Lady for a sign, which he would bring back with him. When Juan left the bishop's palace, the bishop had some of his trusted servants follow him, to see what he did. According to their report, when they got to the bridge at Tepeyacac, Juan disappeared. This angered the servants, whom we believe to be Indians, like Juan Diego. They went back to the bishop with a story that Juan had deceived them, or had made up the tale about seeing the Lady. They even recommended that if he returned, he should be punished severely, so that he wouldn't make up stories and tell lies again. The bishop took this as a sign that he should not believe Juan Diego, and dismissed the incident from his mind. *Or at least he tried to.*

Juan returned to Tepeyac Hill, where Our Lady waited for him. He explained in great detail the entire interview with the bishop. He emphasized the need for some sign from Heaven that it was truly *she* who was speaking through Juan. The Lady agreed, and told Juan to return the following morning, *Monday, December 11*, and she would give him a sign to bring back to the bishop, which he would have to accept. She told Juan to go home and rest, that she would see him the following morning. Juan was elated as he left Tepeyac Hill, both because he had pleased the beautiful lady, and *also* because this affair would soon be finished.

The next part of the story is so unbelievable, it has to be true. Juan Diego *forgot* to keep his appointment with Our Lady. We have to attribute this to his simple nature. What might have contributed to his distraction was that when he arrived home that Sunday night, he found his uncle, Juan Bernardino, sick to the point of death. Juan Diego went immediately in search of a doctor, who was able to give the uncle some relief from his excruciating pain, but diagnosed him as terminal. He would die in a short time. Juan spent the next day caring for his uncle. You would think that somewhere in the back of his mind there would be a gnawing about some really important thing he forgot to do. But there's no indication that he thought about Our Lady or his meeting, or the bishop at all.

During the night of Monday, December 11, the uncle's condition grew worse. He asked Juan to go and get him a priest. He wanted to confess his sins, and receive the Last Sacraments of the Church. Early on *Tuesday, December 12*, Juan got up and headed for Tlatilolco to bring a priest back to his uncle. The first inkling we have that Juan remembered the meeting with Mary came when he approached Tepeyac Hill. He had to pass there to get to the city. He realized that if he went the same way he had the previous two days, she would be waiting for him. We're not sure if Juan was afraid of being chastized for not having kept his appointment to bring the sign to the bishop, or as he told the Lady, he didn't have time to take care of her request this day, because of his uncle.

Juan decided to avoid confrontation. He went around the other side of Tepeyac Hill, in order to *avoid* meeting the Lady. But as he passed near the place where they had met, he saw her walking down towards him. She asked him,

"What is the matter, my little son? Where are you going?"

Juan's reaction reminds us of the little boy who got caught with his hand in the cookie jar. He acted as if nothing had happened.

He bowed down before her, and spoke. "My Child," he began, "my littlest Daughter, Lady. I hope you are well and happy. Did you sleep well? Are you in good humor and health this morning, my Lady and little Daughter?"

Juan went on to tell her about his uncle, how he was sick to the point of death, that Juan had to get a doctor for him and nurse him the whole day, and now he was on his way to her house (the Church) in Tlaltiolco to get a priest for him. He continued,

"But even so, I'll return here right away, tomorrow, to take your message to the bishop. I promise not to deceive you. First thing tomorrow, I'll be here."

The Lady stopped Juan Diego with her sparkling smile, before he could say another word. She spoke to him gently but firmly.

"Listen to me and understand me well, my son, smallest of all. You have nothing to be worried about. Have no anxiety about your uncle. He will not die now. Is this not your Mother here next to you? Are you not here in the shelter of my loving shadow? Are you not safe here within my loving bosom? What else is there to worry about?

At this very moment, your uncle is being cured. He will be well."

Juan Diego breathed a sigh of relief. He believed what the Lady was telling him. With this burden lifted from his heart, he was able to concentrate fully on what Our Lady wanted from him. He begged her to send him to the bishop with the message immediately.

She asked him to climb up the hill to the place where they had met previously.

"There you will see many flowers; gather them carefully and place them together in your tilma; then bring them down and show them to me."

Juan Diego mumbled under his breath as he climbed the hill. *Simple he might be, but not stupid.* Flowers never grew up in that place, much less at this time of the year. There was frost covering the ground. How could anything grow up there now? But he was wise enough not to question the beautiful Lady, so he followed her instructions. His eyes grew wide as he reached the appointed place. In an area where previously there had only been thistles, thorny plants, cactus and mesquite, he saw the most beautiful Castillian roses of assorted varieties and colors. They were out of season for the most fertile ground, much less for this barren soil.

He gathered them carefully, and placed them in his tilma (poncho), being sure not to crush any of them. Then he retraced his steps to the other side of the hill, where she was waiting for him. The world's greatest decorator took the flowers from him, and rearranged them in his tilma. How must Juan Diego have felt having this exquisite child/woman standing so close to him, actually touching him? There was a fragrance about her, so much richer than that of the beautiful roses. It filled his nostrils. He became heady from it. After she had arranged the flowers to her satisfaction, she instructed him to close his tilma, so that they could not be seen.

"My little son, these various roses are the sign and proof that you must take to the bishop. Tell him in my name that they will make him understand my wish, and he must carry it out. You are my ambassador. You are most worthy of my confidence. Now, most important, do not unfold your outer garment or reveal the contents to *ANYONE* until you are in the bishop's presence. Tell him everything I've said to you. You can do it, Juan. I will be with you."

Juan held the flowers close to his chest, being careful not to bruise them, as he walked towards the city and the bishop's palace. He repeated the Lady's message over and over as he neared his destination. He wanted to be sure he didn't forget one word she had said, even her slightest inflection. He was confident now. He had the sign. The bishop had to realize that nowhere in the country could he find roses like these at this time of the year. There was no place they could have come from, other than Heaven. He would believe that Our Lady was speaking to him, and everything would be fine.

What he didn't take into consideration was that there would be two forces working at the bishop's palace that day. Our Lady would be there, but the evil one would also be in attendance. Satan had been in control of Mexico for the last ten years. He had good reason for not wanting this sign to come to the attention of the bishop. He *knew* what would happen. So he put all his forces to work around the residence of the bishop. When Juan arrived at the palace, the guard refused to let him pass. The servants who had lost him the other day, came out and began berating him. He just stood there, his head drooping, not knowing what to do. A long time passed.

The servants realized that Juan was carrying something inside his tilma. Their curiosity got the best of them. They asked what he had there. He did not answer them. They crowded around him, demanding to see what he had inside the cloak. He knew what his instructions were, but he also knew that this crowd would not be satisfied until they saw something. So he opened his tilma slightly to show the roses inside. They marvelled at what they saw. They knew how impossible it was to have Castillian roses at this time of the year. They wanted them. They began to grab at the roses. But as they grabbed a rose, it disappeared, and turned into a painting on the tilma. This shocked the servants.

They ran to the bishop to tell him what was happening, that Juan Diego was here with the sign from the Lady. The bishop, believing that this was important, allowed Juan into his office. The Indian knelt as before, and repeated the entire story over again.

He told him about the Castillian roses on the hill, and how Our Lady had arranged them, admonishing Juan that no one should see them before the bishop. Juan ended his report with the words **"RECEIVE THEM"**. With that, he opened his tilma, whereupon all the roses cascaded to the floor.

Juan looked for an expression of surprise and joy from the bishop as the roses came into his sight. Juan's eyes followed the roses to the floor, and then looked up at the bishop. He was surprised to see that the bishop was not looking at the precious roses at all. Neither was the interpreter, who was standing next to the bishop. They were both staring intently at Juan Diego's chest.

He watched incredulously as their expressions changed from surprise to fearsome awe, to exalted reverence. Both men fell to their knees; tears of joy streamed down their cheeks. Juan looked at the tilma, to see what the reason was for their bliss. Before their eyes, the three men saw the image we call Our Lady of Guadalupe take form. It was not there as the roses first fell out of the tilma. It was only beginning. In a short period of time, the entire image was complete, the only true picture we have of the Blessed Virgin, designed by the Master Designer, and painted with joy by the Angels. In this glorious moment in time, the destiny of Mexico was altered. Our Lady had come to the Americas, to change the course of history.

Throughout the account of the Apparition, we hear Our Lady speak of the importance of having the bishop build the temple. She insisted that Juan Diego had to be the one to bring the message to the Church of Mexico. Why, we ask ourselves? It was so difficult. Had she used a more prominent person, as Juan had suggested, wouldn't it have been easier? Wouldn't she eliminate the risk of not being accepted?

Why Mexico?—Why 1531?—Why Juan Diego?

When we began research on the Miraculous Apparition at Mexico City in 1531, we thought that the reason Our Lady chose the New World was because she had been rejected and treated so badly at the hands of the European powers during the Sixteenth Century. The rumblings of the Protestant Reformation were spreading throughout Europe. Heresies were surfacing daily. The great hate campaign being waged by heretics and agnostics was first against Our Lord Jesus in the Eucharist, and secondly, His Mother Mary, who had treated them with nothing but love. It seemed very reasonable that she shake the dust from her heels, and turn her attention to the New World. All this may be true, but there was more, much more.

The Spanish Conquistadores and their great leader, Cortez, have been romanticized in books and films for centuries. Their exploits have been fantasized as glamorous escapades of daring adventurers, depicted by Errol Flynn and Tyrone Power. Sadly, the truth of it is that this was one of the darkest periods of humanity, on a par with the atrocities of Adolph Hitler and Joseph Stalin, filled with wholesale massacre, and the final destruction of a great civilization, the Aztecs. The worst part of it is that it was all done in the name of Jesus.

One particular example of the Spanish mistreatment of the Indians almost lost Cortez his great victory in Mexico. Pedro de Alvarado was one of Cortez' most trusted and valiant captains. While Cortez was in another part of the kingdom, he left Alvarado in charge of their headquarters in Tenochtitlan. The Indians had been given permission to hold a religious ceremony. A promise was given that there would be no human sacrifice, a ritual among the Aztecs which was considered by the Spanish as *inhuman*. The Aztecs came unarmed.

Several hundred young Indian nobles gathered for the ceremony. They were dressed in religious loin cloths, and wore jewels appropriate for their station. The entire proceeding was overseen by armed Spanish guards, who watched from the entrances of the temple.

For absolutely no reason, towards the end of the dance, the Spanish guards pulled out their swords, and proceeded in unison to attack the young Indians. They killed every one of them brutally, mutilating their bodies completely. Then they waded through the pools of blood and ripped the jewelry off the mangled corpses. It was possibly the most barbaric act they could have performed.

When Cortez returned, he sensed the hostility in the air. His captain, Alvarado, tried to come up with a lame excuse as to why his soldiers committed this lunatic act. The attitude of the Indians towards the Spaniards changed drastically. The troops of Cortez were almost destroyed in that city because of this incident.

On the other side of the coin, during the battle that immediately followed between the Spanish troops and the Aztecs, 72 Spaniards were taken captive, and rushed to the temple for Aztec sacrifice. They were made to dance naked around a statue of a god, with plumes on their heads, and fans in their hands. Then their bodies were bent over a pointed rock. Their chests were cut open, and the hearts ripped out of the living bodies. The pulsating hearts were offered to the gods, while the bodies were thrown down the steps of the temple to be ripped apart and eaten by the Indians. Spanish troops could see this atrocity being performed from a distance. In terms of warfare, we would say that this is a cruel way to torture and kill your enemies. But in the eyes of the Aztecs, they were not executing prisoners of war as much as performing a religious ceremony. This was the same form of human sacrifice to which they subjected as many as 20,000 of their own people each year.

There are no good guys in the world when it comes to colonization and conquest. The history of the world is streaked with the red blood of innocent victims of imperial powers. No one is free from guilt. We will not make any judgments about Spain or the Aztec empire. Let it suffice to say that in the period between the Conquest of Mexico by Cortez in 1521, and Our Lady's appearance to Juan Diego in 1531, there was a mammoth struggle between opposing cultures and philosophies. The rulers who took over after Cortez' decisive victory, became despots. They didn't understand the brilliant culture of the people whose lives they controlled, so they treated them as slaves and *worse*, animals.

The Spaniards sent over a group of Franciscans to convert the Indians to Christianity. There was a common ground between our faith belief and the teachings of an Aztec god, Quetzelcoatl. Their tradition says he was a great prophet who appeared at Chouala in 700 A.D., and taught the people a civilized religion along the lines of Catholicism. The Indians who converted to Christianity were able to live in peace and harmony with their rulers, but there were too few, and time was running out.

The situation had come to a head just about the time when Our Lady chose to appear to Juan Diego on Tepeyac Hill. The Indians were at the point of organizing a revolution, to massacre every European in their land. History tells us that it was almost the eve of the revolution when Our Lady came. It's been determined that at the time of Our Lady's appearance, the Aztecs were capable of killing every European in Mexico. There was a great need for God to bring these two peoples together. He chose His Mother as the perfect instrument, as He had done fifteen hundred years before, at the Annunciation in Nazareth.

It was important for Our Lady to come to the Indians. They had to embrace Christianity, and the Spaniards had to accept the Indians as human beings, rather than strange, mystical animals. The apparition at Tepeyac Hill was the catalyst that brought them together. In the course of 7 years, **8,000,000** Indians converted to the Catholic Faith. Nothing like that has ever happened in the history of our Church. What had been wholesale massacre became wholesale conversion. The Holy Spirit filled the land on a much greater scale than in Jerusalem on the day of Pentecost. Reconciliation between the Spaniards and the Indians came about. Peace came to Mexico.

The Miraculous Tilma of Juan Diego

As for the miraculous tilma of Juan Diego, critics and enemies of Our Lord Jesus and His Mother Mary have spent the last 450 years trying to disprove that this was a work of Heaven. The cloth on which Our Lady chose to have her image imprinted is Cactus cloth, which has a life span of no more than 20 years if it is *not painted on.* If it is painted on, it lasts about 6 years. This cactus cloth, which was used by Juan Diego for many years prior to Our Lady's visit from Heaven, has never decomposed, more than 450 years later.

At one time, authorities in the art field tried to simulate the circumstances of how the tilma might have been painted by human hands. Investigations began as early as the middle of the sixteenth century, using whatever tools were available to the artistic and scientific communities of the day. It has continued till today, with the latest scientific and computerized equipment available.

Jody Brant Smith (a Non-Catholic) wrote a book a few years ago, called **THE IMAGE OF GUADALUPE—MYTH OR MIRACLE**, in which he and a colleague, Dr. Callahan, (a Catholic) performed extensive experiments on the Image of Our Lady, such as infra-red photography, ultra violet photography, and computer-enhanced black and white photography. They were trying to determine if a sketch had been made underneath the painting, which would have proven that the painting was done by human hands. They were also trying to determine what kind of colors and pigments were used in the painting.

Prior to issuing the findings, the author **(remember, a non-Catholic)** made the following statement:

Some may find it ironic that in our skeptical age the tools of science have been used not to disprove but in some degree to authenticate miracles of the past. Our discovery of the absence of undersketching in the image of Guadalupe and our inability to account for the remarkable state of preservation of the unsized cactus cloth as well as the unfading brightness of the paints or dyes used in the original parts of the painting put Dr. Callahan and myself firmly in the ranks of those who believe the Image was created supernaturally.

With all the information they were able to gather from the use of the sophisticated equipment at their disposal, they were not able to determine with certainty what pigments or dyes were used to make the portrait. They were easily able to rule out thousands of possibilities, but were not able to make definite conclusions as to *what was used.*

Two other areas they were not able to explain with any certainty was why the paints had not hardened and cracked in the period of 450 years, and why there has been no fading. We must remember here that until the middle of the 18th Century, there was nothing to protect the tilma from the people touching it, or from the lights and smoke from incense and candles.

There are more aspects of the Image of Our Lady that *cannot* be explained than can be explained. For instance, there is the brilliance of the colors. Up close, the colors are not as bright as they are at a distance. The clarity, the sharpness of the design is greater the farther away one goes from the painting. The colors of Our Lady's face change as one goes farther back. In tests done on the tilma, it was determined that it had never been treated. In order to paint on canvas, it has to be treated before the paints are put on. Also, when paint is applied to canvas, it clogs up the holes, making it impossible to see through the canvas. Juan Diego's tilma can be seen through. The colors can be seen from the front, but not from the back. On a normal canvas, the pigments of the paints seep through to the back, but not so on the tilma. On the back is what looks like a large green leaf, covering the image of Our Lady. It can't be seen from the front. By the same token, none of the colors can be seen from the back.

The Image takes on a different size. When we attended Mass at the Great Basilica on the Feast Day in 1986, a man came out on the altar holding a banner of Our Lady of Guadalupe. The man was average height, about 5 foot 9 inches. To the left and above him was the painting of Our Lady, relatively close to the man. The image on his banner was probably 4 foot in height. The Image of Our Lady up on the Altar is only 6½ foot high, and yet it looked at least three times larger than the image on the banner.

The Portrait Within the Eye

It does appear that with each technological or scientific advance made by man, the miracles of the past are verified. The

Twentieth Century brought with it new advances in the field of Photography. Photos by the billions have been taken of the Image of Our Lady of Guadalupe.

In 1929, one Alfonso Marcue Gonzalez was examining close up photographic negatives of the Portrait. It's much easier to see the image in a negative than in a positive. He clearly saw the figure of a man in the eyes of the Madonna. In 1951, Carlos Salinas, using more sophisticated techniques, affirmed the theory, and was able to identify the man as **JUAN DIEGO**. In the 30 years from the 1950's to the present, gigantic strides have been made in the field of photography, as we've noted above. It has now been determined that there is not only the image of Juan Diego in the eye of the Lady, but three other people, who have been identified as the Bishop, Juan Zumarraga, the interpreter, and another un-identified person, whom they believe to be a woman.

Assuming on the *wildest of possibilities*, that a human hand had been able to paint the portrait of Mary on the rough cactus cloth without an undersketch, *and* assuming that he was able to fit into the eye the image of the four people, *all of this without any brushstrokes, by the way*, the brilliant Lady from Heaven throws another curve at her doubters. The images in the eye are distorted, according to the curve of her eye.

There has to be some place in time when the doubters and critics of the authenticity of the Portrait of Mary have to finally give up. There are just too many unexplainable phenomena here. For 450 years, people have been trying to disprove this Miracle from Heaven. The more they try to discredit it, the greater the evidence materializes in favor of its authenticity.

We went to Guadalupe, not to verify the legitimacy of the Image, but to live the experience, as pilgrims, to bring you the true pulse of the work Mary has done and continues to do in Mex-ico. We never really expected to come back blabbering idiots, but that's what she did to us. We cannot pass anyone we know, or speak on the phone, without raving about our **GUADALUPE EN-COUNTER**. We insist to everyone we come in contact with, that next year they will join us as we pay homage to my Magnificent Friend, Mary, in one of the most outstanding ongoing miracles we have ever beheld.

Would you believe we almost did not go on this Pilgrimage to our Lady of Guadalupe? We had read many books on the apparition. We had more photographs than we could possibly use. Why did we have to go? But as December 9 approached, we found ourselves like Lucia at Fatima, and Mirjana at Medjugorje. We were drawn to the shrine by a power we didn't understand, and were helpless to control. She wanted us there, and she would have her way. So, we packed our bags, and did as we were told. What fools we were to think that she wouldn't use the same persuasive powers on us that she has used throughout the centuries, from Juan Diego in Mexico, to Bernadette Soubirous, in Lourdes, to Marija Pavlovic of Medjugorje. We went, we saw, we felt, and we are hopelessly in love with Our Lady of Guadalupe, Our Lady of the Americas. Why not?

The Bishop speaks to the Lady—Altar of Basilica of Guadalupe
December 12, 1986—Mexico City

Paris, 1830: Mary and Her Miraculous Medal

Paris is called the *City of Lights*. It is also called *Sin City*. It is one of the most sophisticated cities in the world. Among the more fashionable districts or Arrondissements, as they are called, is the Rive Gauche, or Left Bank. It has long been a haven for artists, attempting to capture on canvas the magnificence of the Cathedral dedicated to the most elegant lady in Paris, or the world for that matter, Notre Dame de Paris, Our Lady, my Mary. Boulevard St. Germain boasts avant-garde boutiques, cafes and restaurants. At the intersection of Boulevard St. Germain and Boulevard Raspail is a giant department store with many annexes. It is called Bon Marche, or Good Deal.

Sandwiched in between two of the annexes of this mammoth store on a side street, is a small courtyard, at the end of which is a chapel. From the street, all that can be seen is the address, 140 Rue du Bac, and a little plaque, hardly noticeable to the bustling shoppers trying to avoid the cars that race down the street at breakneck speed. The plaque shows both sides of the Miraculous Medal. The little sign underneath reads *"La Chapelle de Medaille Miracleuse"*. It's not difficult to recognize those who know where they are, as opposed to those who do not. The worshipers wear an expression of awe on their faces as they enter these hallowed grounds.

The contrast from outside to inside is incredible. Outside is a jungle of humanity, embracing the world and all its trappings. Hawkers set up their tables in front of the store, promoting "Sale" items, merchandise without which the average housewife cannot possibly live. But as you walk through the portals of this court-yard, you experience something that *no one can live without*. A peace and serenity blankets you. On the left wall as you walk down towards the chapel, reliefs of the life of St. Catherine La-boure and the miraculous gift given to her are shown. But you find yourself magnetically drawn to the end of the courtyard, be-cause you know that's where it all began, 150 years ago.

The area around Boulevard St. Germain looked much differ-ent in 1830, when Zoe Catherine Laboure entered the mother house of the Sisters of Charity. While it was still a part of the Left Bank, it was not as built up as it is today. Paris was in an uproar at the time. She had just come through one of the most devastating times in the history of France, the French Revolution. During this plague on humanity, the Church was one of the main targets for persecution. Churches were desecrated; sacrileges committed on their altars; in particular, Notre Dame of Paris. Priests and nuns were tortured, and exiled from the country at best, or killed at worst. The Revolution fell, as it had to, because it was so satanic. But the attitude of the government towards the Church remained.

It was followed by the reign of Napoleon Bonaparte. While he reopened the Churches, he also attacked the Church. He battled with Rome, was excommunicated, and put the Pope under arrest. After his reign ended in 1815, havoc broke out again in Paris; the Church had to go underground again, hiding out in the monasteries. By the year 1830, a new revolution was in the mak-ing. The Bourbon king, Charles X, made a frantic attempt to re-store the power of the country to the throne as it had been before the Revolution. The people were not having any of it.

We know Our Dear Lady was upset about how her priests

and nuns, as well as the laity were being treated. She had always been so loving to her children. It was she whom Jesus allowed to intercede on our behalf. We drove Him beyond reconciliation, and yet, because of her, He allowed His arms to be held back. It did not seem that mankind was going to get any better. It was time for tribulation. But the Mother, the loving Mother, asked *again* for one more chance to reason with her children, and *again*, the gift was given by the Son to the Mother. She searched the earth for a suitable soul, an innocent, pure vessel, who would be worthy and willing to be filled. Mary has never been known to back down from a battle, so why not begin her strategy for the salvation of France in the steaming streets of the city which had been her greatest supporter, but had become her greatest enemy? Paris was no match for Mary.

In order to begin in the city, we have to first go out to the country to find our suffering servant. Our Lady's plan takes us to a little farming community in Burgundy, Fain-les-Moutiers, where a young girl, Zoe Catherine Laboure, had been touched by the Lord. She wanted to enter the religious life from early childhood, but, being an obedient daughter, had to wait until she could get her father's permission, which was not quick in coming. Mary had to influence Catherine's situation greatly to finally bring her into the Mother House of the Sisters of Charity on the Rue du Bac as a Novitiate.

Catherine had a dream when she was barely 19 years old, that she was in her Parish Church at Fain-Les-Moutiers. An old priest, whom she had never seen before, was celebrating Mass. After it was over, he beckoned Catherine to come to him. She panicked, although she didn't know why. She ran from the Church and the old priest.

Next she found herself in a room beside the bed of a sick person. The old priest was standing next to her. He said to her

"My child, it is good to care for the sick. You run away from me now, but one day you will be glad to come to me. God has His designs on you! Do not forget it."

She never forgot the dream, but continued to work at home for her father until she was 22. She asked to join the Sisters of Charity. His reply was an emphatic "No!" However, Our Lady was working her plan. *A thought came to the father.*

He had a son in Paris, who owned a restaurant. He thought that by sending Catherine to the big city, with all its lure of worldliness, she would soon forget her ridiculous notions about becoming a nun. However, unwittingly, he was playing into the hands of Mary. When the young girl came to Paris, she found that her struggles were as bad as, or worse than they had been in her little village. Paris can be heaven or hell. The determining factor for Catherine was the life she was exposed to. She suffered for a year under this torture. Perhaps our Lady wanted her to understand the difference between the fantasy of the world, and the reality of her dream to be a nun. When Mary felt that Catherine had had enough, she removed her from Paris, temporarily.

An aunt, Madam Hubert Laboure, who worked as the principal of a young ladies' finishing school at Chatillon, suggested that Catherine come there. Catherine was willing to do anything to get out of Paris, so she went. But she found very quickly that the luxurious surroundings of the school were not at all in keeping with her background or desires. So our Lady had shown her another side of life, that of the gentility. Had she not been exposed to this lifestyle at an early age, she may have desired it in later years. Catherine realized that this was not for her either. *She had been touched.* Her heart yearned to be close to Jesus in the Sisters of Charity convent.

THE PLOT THICKENS. There just *happened to be* a convent of the Sisters of Charity in Chatillon. Catherine made a visit there. As she was ushered into the parlor, she froze. There on the wall was a painting of a priest. *It was the priest in her dream.* He seemed to be looking at her. When she asked who the priest was, she was told it was St. Vincent de Paul, *The Founder of the Sisters of Charity.* Catherine knew she was *home.* This was where the Lord wanted her to be.

We believe that stubborness, when used for God's purposes, can move mountains and men's hearts. In this instance, Our Lady was able to work with the stubborness which father had passed on to daughter. As Catherine's father was adamant about her not entering the convent, Catherine was as unbending that she would. With the help of Our Lady through the aunt, his sister, Catherine's father grudgingly gave his consent. At the beginning of 1830, Zoe Catherine Laboure entered the convent of the Sisters of Charity at Chatillon-sur-Seine.

We mentioned that Paris can be heaven or hell. When Catherine returned on April 21 of that year, it became heaven for her. She did not go back to the restaurant, or the worldly life of the Paris she had left. She entered the convent of the Sisters of Charity at 140 Rue du Bac, an address which would become famous very shortly, thanks to Our Lady and the cooperation and assistance of this young postulant.

Catherine was made to feel at home almost immediately after she arrived at Rue du Bac. Three days after she got there, the body of St. Vincent De Paul, which had been hidden during the French Revolution, was returned to Paris, in solemn procession, and installed a block away at Rue De Sevres. She felt so close to this man who had personally called her to be a part of his ministry. Other than that, her time was spent in serious pursuit of her vocation.

The summer of 1830 was unusually hot. There had been some relief around Bastille Day, July 14. A great storm fell on that day, which managed to reduce the festivities to local drunkenness in the bars. It also brought with it a certain amount of coolness for a few days. But by the 18th, the heat was mounting again, with no sign of relief in sight. With the heat came a fearful unrest among the people.

July 18, 1830 saw great activity at the Motherhouse of the Sisters of Charity on the Rue du Bac. The next day was the feast day of St. Vincent de Paul, the father in faith of their community. Preparations had been made for weeks for the festivities to be held

on July 19. Catherine had worked hard during the day with the
other sisters, to insure that the chapel and the convent would be
spotlessly clean for the feast.

On the night of July 18, Zoe Catherine Laboure was in a
deep well deserved sleep. She heard her name called. She awoke
to the sound of a young child.

*"Come to the Chapel. The Blessed Virgin is waiting
for you."*

Catherine's first response, half out of shock, and half out of
drowsiness was,

"But how can I go across the dormitory? I will be heard."

"Be calm." the child replied. *"It's half-past eleven. Everyone is asleep. Come. I am waiting for you."*

As she rushed to get dressed, and catch up with the child,
she became aware that he was an Angel, most likely her Guardian
Angel. Had he said **THE BLESSED VIRGIN** was waiting for her?
She thought that was what he had said. Or was she still asleep?
She was sure she was dreaming as she floated down the hall towards the chapel. All the lights were brightly lit. She couldn't
believe that none of the other nuns had awakened.

She entered the chapel. It was all aglow, candles burning
throughout the little church. She looked around the room. She
was alone, except for the child. He led her to the foot of the altar,
where she knelt. She prayed. She waited. All that had happened
was registering in her brain. Was she really waiting for the
Blessed Virgin? The little boy, Angel, had said that. Or had he?
She looked towards him. His concentration was on the tabernacle
containing the Blessed Sacrament. She prayed more.

She heard a rustling sound, like someone walking in a silk
dress. She turned in the direction of the sound. The Angel said,

"Here is the Blessed Virgin" .

Catherine's heart pounded furiously. From out of nowhere,
the most beautiful lady she had ever seen, appeared before her.
Catherine caught her breath. She knew without asking, that this
was the Mother of God. Catherine thought to herself, *this is how*

Mary would look. But she's so young, so exuberant. The Lady sat in the director's chair, reserved for the priest during Mass. A wave of emotion swept over Catherine. She had to be close to Our Lady. She fell to her knees at the foot of the altar, and embraced the knees of the exquisite visitor from heaven.

Mary sat with Catherine for what seemed like an eternity. She instructed her in the proper behavior of a nun. She also gave her private secrets, many of which were revealed towards the end of Catherine's life, and others which have never been made known. Some of the things we do know are as follows in Catherine's own words. Our Lady said to her,

"Our dear Lord loves you very much. He wishes to give you a mission. It will be the cause of much suffering to you, but you will overcome it, knowing that what you do is for the glory of God. You will be contradicted, but you will have the grace to bear it. Don't be afraid. You will see certain things. You must report them. You will be given the words through prayer.

The times are evil. Misfortunes will fall upon France. The king will be overthrown. The entire world will be overcome by evils of all kinds, but. . . .

But come to the foot of this altar. Here, great graces will be poured upon all those who ask for them with confidence and fervor. They will be bestowed upon the great and the small."

This was the most unusual and intimate apparition of Our Lady's that we have ever researched. She allowed this child to sit at her knees, and put her hands in the lap that had held the baby Jesus. Mary poured her heart out to this young girl. While talking about some of the outrages which were in store for France and the Church, Mary held back tears, but finally broke down and cried.

We are allowed to witness the humanity of Mary, the compassion, the love and concern she has for us. There's a helplessness about her that wrenches us at the deepest part of our soul. This sympathetic mother, so good, so loving, cries at our viciousness towards each other. We have to wonder how she can still love

The chair Our Lady sat in during apparition to Catherine Laboure July 18, 1830

Our Dear Lord loves you very much. He wishes to give you a mission.
Incorrupt body of St. Catherine Laboure
Chapel of Miraculous Medal, Paris

us in our wickedness. Why do we always mistreat this all loving human being, who concerns herself with our welfare so much?

Why does she torture herself for us? She has never done anything wrong. She has never committed a sin. She watched her Son suffer and die a cruel and inhuman death for our sins. Hasn't she had enough? Why should she have to continue to suffer for us?

The primary message that first night to Catherine was that she would have to endure much suffering, but Mary would be with her. The young postulant could have confidence that she would be successful in her mission, even when all seemed hopeless, if she followed the instructions of her heavenly Mother.

As quickly as the Lady had come, she faded away. Catherine was alone in the chapel, except for the young child. He accompanied her back to her dormitory. When she returned to her bed, the child faded away also, just as Our Lady had.

Catherine didn't sleep that night. She was too excited. She couldn't believe what had just happened to her. Her mind raced through the events of the evening. She heard the clock strike two. She had been with Mary for almost two hours. She repeated in her heart all the things the Lady had told her. A Mission! She was being honored with a special mission! But what was it? Mary didn't tell her. Catherine was not concerned; she knew that when the time was right, Our Lady would let her know exactly what she wanted.

Some of Mary's predictions to Catherine began to occur within a week of the apparition. Riots broke out in the city. Dead bodies littered the streets. King Charles had tried to rescind all the rights given the people by the Constitutional Government approved by his predecessor, King Louis XVIII. The entire middle class rose up against him. During the "Glorious Three Days" of the Revolution, Paris was a bloodbath. The king was deposed, and fled the country. The revolutionary forces refocused their attacks on the Church. It was a repeat of the revolution of 1793. Priests and religious were slaughtered.

However, Our Lady kept her promise to protect the spiritual children of St. Vincent de Paul. No harm came to St. Catherine or the sisters of the Rue du Bac. A new king took the throne, King Louis Philippe. He was a figurehead, which was what the people wanted. He had virtually no power. France went back about the business of running their country, not well, but their way. Paris quieted down, and Catherine continued with her novitiate.

Our Lady appeared to Catherine again on Saturday, November 27, 1830. There was none of the intimacy, none of the special closeness they shared in July. Mary did not even look at Catherine during this apparition, nor did she speak to her directly. Catherine received the message through inner locution. Our Lady had a definite purpose for this visit. She went directly to the heart of the matter.

Catherine was in the chapel for evening meditation. All the sisters of the community were there also. It was quiet time. A reading had been given, and the sisters were now meditating about how this insight affected their lives. Catherine's reflections were interrupted by a familiar sound. It was the rustling of the silk dress of her Heavenly friend. Catherine thought her heart would burst. She immediately opened her eyes and looked in the direction of the sound. To the right of the altar stood Our Lady, more resplendent than Catherine could remember. When she wrote of the apparition years later, she recalled in detail how Our Lady was dressed. The vision was indelibly etched on her soul. Mary stood on a globe, and held a golden ball at arm's length, as if she were offering it up to God, her eyes directed towards heaven.

In an instant, brilliant lights radiated from her hands downward. Catherine could see that the lights came from rings Mary wore, three on each finger. They were of various sizes. Catherine noticed that rays did not shine forth from each ring. Mary explained the reason as she spoke to Catherine's heart. The Lady said,

"The ball which you see represents the whole world, especially France, and each person in particular. These rays symbol-

But come to the foot of this altar. Here, great graces will be poured out upon all who ask for them.

Altar where Our Lady gave us the miraculous medal
Chapel of Miraculous Medal, Paris

ize the graces I shed upon those who ask for them. The gems from which rays do not fall are the graces for which souls forget to ask."

Catherine was in a state of ecstasy, completely swallowed up in the joy of the vision. The golden ball vanished from Our Lady's hands. Her arms went down, hands pointing outward, in an attitude of welcoming. The rays focused themselves down to the globe on which the Lady stood. An oval frame formed around Mary, with the following words written on it:

O Marie concue sans peche priez pour nous
qui avons recours a vous

Oh Mary conceived without sin,
Pray for us who have recourse to you

The voice of Mary spoke to the heart of the young postulant again.

"Have a Medal struck after this model. All who wear it will receive great graces; they should wear it around the neck. Graces will abound for persons who wear it with confidence."

The image turned. Our Lady disappeared, to be replaced by a large **M**. A bar went through the M, from which extended a cross in the middle. Underneath the M were two hearts, one surrounded by thorns, symbolizing the Sacred Heart of Jesus, and one pierced by a knife, with droplets of blood dripping from it, symbolizing the Immaculate Heart of Mary. Twelve stars surrounded this image in the shape of an oval.

Slowly the image faded, and disappeared.

This visit by Our Heavenly Mother set into motion a series of events which were felt immediately around the world, and to this day is a very strong part of our Marian devotion. Catherine had been sharing the apparitions with her confessor, Fr. Aladel, from the beginning. Mary gave him the difficult task of having her wishes fulfilled. The priest wasn't sure he believed what the young girl was telling him. In addition, these apparitions occurred while all hell was breaking loose in Paris. Although his community, the priests of St. Vincent de Paul had been spared from the attacks of the revolutionaries, his priorities were definitely not the possible ramblings of an over enthusiastic nun-to-be.

Our Lady cautioned Catherine to tell no one of her visions except her confessor. She took Mary literally on this. She would not cooperate with Fr. Aladel's request that she tell her story to a tribunal which was set up to determine whether a medal should be struck. The entire burden as to the truthfulness of Catherine's statements was on his shoulders. He didn't have the luxury of the tribunal hearing her story, and judging whether or not she was telling the truth. The priest had to do that, and then convince the tribunal of the authenticity of the apparitions.

Catherine had an urgency to have the medal struck. Mary had an urgency. Fr. Aladel did not share their urgency. Mary had not chosen to tell him directly, but through an intermediary. He did not have the brilliance of the beauty of Mary to spur him on, as did Catherine. There were times when he balked, and gave other things more importance. The vision of November 27 was repeated 5 different times, at 5 key periods, to motivate Catherine into jolting the priest into action.

When the apparitions repeated themselves, Catherine knew she had to confront the priest again. She trembled each time she entered the confessional to do battle with him. There were reports of loud knock-down drag out fights between Catherine and her confessor. At one point, she was so disheartened she asked Our Lady to get someone else to do the job, because the priest would not believe her.

Doesn't this sound similar to Juan Diego's plea at Guadalupe?

We thank Our Lord Jesus for the gift of His Mother's patience, that she doesn't just get disgusted, throw up her hands, and give up on us.

We believe that one conversation between Catherine and Our Lady, which was then repeated to Fr. Aladel, finally spurred him on to action.

Catherine said to Our Lady, in response to a complaint that nothing was happening,

"But my good Mother, you see that he (the priest) doesn't believe me"

Mary responded, "Never mind. He is my servant, and **HE WOULD FEAR TO DISPLEASE ME"**

This was most likely the single most important statement Our Lady could have made. She knew what the results would be. It ripped into the heart of the priest. He trembled at the thought of displeasing the Mother of God. He used as justification the fact that many of the predictions Our Lady had made to Catherine had come to pass, especially regarding the revolution in France, and the persecution of the religious orders. But we really think the fear of God, or in this instance, the Mother of God, was put into his heart.

The medal which was struck in 1832 was not originally called, nor was it meant to be a "Miraculous Medal". It was called the Medal of the Immaculate Conception. Our Lady had promised "abundant graces", and she kept her promise, more than anyone could have imagined in their wildest dreams. Reports by wearers of the new medal flooded the little convent of the Sisters of Charity on the Rue du Bac. Physical cures, conversions, miracles of every sort were reported.

The Archbishop of Paris, Archbishop de Quelen, who had authorized the medal to be struck, was one of the first to experience a miracle from Our Lady as a result of the use of her special medal. An excommunicated archbishop who had sided with Napoleon Bonaparte against the Vatican, had become very hardened against Mother Church. Archbishop de Quelen went to visit him on his deathbed. The dying archbishop would not relent in his anger against the church. But as Archbishop de Quelen was about to leave, his former colleague called him back into the room and asked for reconciliation. He was given the last rites of the Church, and died the next day, in peace.

The Conversion of Ratisbonne

The most famous as well as dramatic account of a miracle attributed to Our Lady's intercession through the Miraculous Medal is that of Alphonse Ratisbonne. He was an Austrian Jew, very well off in material possessions, a man of the world. He harbored a great hatred for Catholics, and all things pertaining to the Catholic Church. This was due in part to the conversion of his older brother, George, to Catholicism. To make matters worse, he also became a priest. Alphonse never forgave his older brother, but blamed the Church for bewitching the man.

In retrospect, it becomes so obvious that the bizarre incidents leading up to the dramatic instance of Ratisbonne's conversion could not possibly have been coincidence. A Master plan was launched to bring this angry man to the bosom of Mary, from which he would never leave. Prior to his upcoming marriage to a Jewish girl in Austria, Ratisbonne *thought it would be nice* to travel to Malta. Needless to say, he never arrived there. A succession of mishaps brought him to a city he vowed he would never visit, the center of Christianity, Rome. While in the ancient city, he did another thing which was completely out of character for him. He made the acquaintance of a newly converted Catholic, Baron Bussieres.

During a raging argument with Bussieres, in which Ratisbonne spewed his hate for the Catholic Church, Bussiere was able to get the Jew to wear the new medal to Mary from Paris, as a dare. He was even able to convince Alphonse to write down the words to the **MEMORARE**, and repeat the prayer. Ratisbonne accepted the challenge with outright mockery. He allowed the Baron's daughter to put the medal around his neck.

Our Lady then put a dying man, Comte de la Ferronays, in the path of Bussiere. They met at a dinner party in Rome. Baron

Bussiere discussed Ratisbonne with the Comte, who promised to pray the Memorare for him at the Church of St. Mary Major. The Comte de la Ferronays went to the Church, and prayed twenty Memorares for the conversion of the angry Jew. After having prayed, he returned home, and died the same day.

Ratisbonne wanted to leave Rome. He went to Baron Bussiere's home to thank him for his courtesy, which was his custom, and to return the medal to him. Bussiere, not wanting to lose Alphonse, asked him to accompany him to the Church of St. Andrea's, where Bussiere was to make funeral arrangements for Comte de la Ferronays. The fact that the Comte had prayed for Ratisbonne made him feel obligated to join his friend.

While Baron Bussiere made arrangements in the sacristy, Ratisbonne wandered about inside the church. He had a feeling he should leave. As he turned towards the front door, a huge black dog blocked his way. The animal was vicious, baring his fangs. Ratisbonne was frozen in his tracks. He couldn't move. Suddenly the dog disappeared. Directly in his path, at a side chapel, a brilliant light glowed. Ratisbonne looked up to see Mary standing there, above the altar, in the pose of the Miraculous Medal, which he still wore around his neck. He looked up at her. Her face was peaceful, but her eyes bore deep into his soul. He could not stand the brilliance of the light. He had to look away from her enchanting face, her captivating eyes. He looked at her hands, which, according to his own words, "expressed all the secrets of the Divine Pity". She never said a word, but he "understood all".

The vision lasted but a few minutes; the effects a lifetime. When his friend emerged from the sacristy, he found Ratisbonne on his knees, sobbing. He insisted on being baptized immediately. The story spread all over Rome. In a matter of months, Alphonse Ratisbonne was baptized, received First Holy Communion, and was Confirmed. He went on to become a priest, taking the name **Marie Alphonse Ratisbonne**. He joined his brother in Jerusalem to form the Daughters of Zion, whose ministry was to evangelize among the Jews. He tried to meet the Sister who had been given the vision of the Miraculous Medal, but without success. Catherine's gift was *hers*, and Ratisbonne's experience was *his* own to cherish for the rest of his life.

By 1836, millions of the medals had been distributed throughout the world. The unusual quality of the medal was that it was most effective in seemingly impossible situations. Cures of the hopelessly incurable, conversions of the worst enemies of the Church were noted, as well as miracles of every kind. The original title of the medal was forgotten, because everyone called it **THE MIRACULOUS MEDAL**. Eventually, the official name was changed to the "Miraculous Medal", and a feast day was instituted by the Vatican in its honor.

Catherine Laboure was transferred to a hospital for old people called Enghien, on the outskirts of Paris. She spent the next 45 years taking care of the sick, as St. Vincent de Paul had predicted in her dream, when she was 19 years old. She was completely inconspicuous, though many of her sister nuns suspected that it was she who had been given the gift of the vision of Mary. She cared for old sailors, whose foul language and abusive behavior towards her was almost more than she could bear.

Her life in the hospital was one of total submission to her vocation. She fought against her humanity to achieve as high a level of spirituality as possible. She suffered greatly. She experienced a spiritual dryness, which is common to all saints. (She could not feel the presence of the Lord in her life. During this time, she had to rely on Faith alone) St. Therese of Lisieux, the Little Flower, referred to it as "The Dark Night of the Soul". St. Teresa la Grande, of Avila, the great mystic and Doctor of the Church, lived through 20 years of Spiritual dryness. On her road to spiritual perfection, Catherine had to pay her dues, and she did.

She never gave her secret away. Finally, she was ordered by her confessor to write down everything that had happened. She wrote of the events in the chapel first in 1841; then wrote again in 1856 and a last time in 1876, the year of her death. It was in these writings that Catherine revealed that Our Lady had not wanted the figure on the front of the medal that we see today. She had wanted the image which showed her holding the globe in her extended hands, to be the front of the medal. This was not possible because of the difficulties the engravers would have in recreating the three dimensional aspect of the image.

Our Lady had asked for a statue to be made of the image she preferred, that which depicted her holding the world in her hands. It was not made. Catherine was furious on more than one occasion because of this. Towards the end of her life, she feared that Our Lady would be unhappy with her because she had not accomplished this. However, before she died, her mother superior had a statue built of the image which Our Lady had wanted for the medal. It stands in the Chapel of the Miraculous Medal today.

Catherine surrendered herself into the arms of Mary on December 31, 1876. Her mother superior wanted her to be interred in the chapel at Reuilly, but was not able to figure out how it could be done. Through the intercession of Mary, she was shown the way, and Catherine was buried in Reuilly, not in the chapel, but *beneath it*. On May 28, 1933, she was beatified in St. Peter's Basilica in Rome.

As part of the Canonization process, the body of the saint had to be identified. In a solemn procession, her coffin was removed from the vault under the chapel at Reuilly, and brought to the Mother house at Rue du Bac in Paris. In the presence of the Archbishop of Paris, civil officials, and various doctors, the coffin was opened.

We have to envision our Heavenly Family gathered also in this room, including choirs of angels, with Our beautiful Lady of the Miraculous Medal, St. Vincent de Paul, and St. Catherine in the foreground. As the lid was removed, the choir of angels broke out in hymns of praise to the power of God, for what the humans beheld was the body of St. Catherine, which had been in the ground for 57 years, *completely incorrupt*. Our Lady had given her a gift reserved for her most special people, including St. Bernadette of Lourdes, and we're told, Jacinta Martos of Fatima.

Today, more than 110 years later, that body is more beautiful than when she was alive. It's as if Our Lord Jesus honored Catherine by leaving us her body in this remarkable state. You have but to go to the Chapel of the Miraculous Medal, on Rue du Bac in Paris, sandwiched in between those two department stores on the notorious Left Bank. St. Catherine Laboure, canonized in 1947, is waiting for you, to prove what a beautiful contradiction Mary gives us.

This apparition has a great deal of meaning to us. It was the first instance in *modern times* when the Mother of God visited us. There had been no mention of an apparition by Our Lady since 1531, when Our Lady of Guadalupe came to Juan Diego in Mexico. There were many messages given the people of God. The most important truth given to us in Paris in 1830 was **THE IMMACULATE CONCEPTION.**

There was a great need for the doctrine of the Immaculate Conception of Mary to enter into the consciousness of the people. A radical heresy, Pantheism, had taken hold of most of Europe. *Pantheism claims that man is on a level with God, equal to Him. God is not a being, but is manifested in all the forces of the universe.* It began as a belief in 1705, when the term was coined by J. Toland in England. Originally, only the intelligentsia understood and accepted the heresy. But by the French Revolution, it had sifted down to the common man. They were led to believe, and accept, that because of the great strides being made by man, as a result of the Industrial Revolution, they didn't need God anymore.

Pantheism is a direct contradiction with the centuries old belief of Catholics regarding the Immaculate Conception of Mary. Our belief that only Jesus and Mary were born without sin clashed with the new heresy of man being equal with God, which had caused confusion and division. There was a need to make the truth clear to the faithful.

Mary began her crusade for renewal of devotion to her Immaculate Conception on the Rue du Bac in Paris. She continued pressing the point home until Pope Pius IX officially proclaimed the doctrine of the Immaculate Conception on December 8, 1854. In the event that there was still any doubts in the minds of the faithful, she appeared to St. Bernadette Soubirous at Lourdes in 1858, and made the statement **I AM THE IMMACULATE CONCEPTION**. In 1846, the Immaculate Conception was declared Patroness of the United States, and in 1913, the cornerstone was laid for the National Shrine of the Immaculate Conception in Washington, D.C.

Sweet Mary has always loved us. She comes to us in times of trouble. She ignores the hostilities against her, but fights like a tiger to protect her Son against attacks. France of the Middle Ages had a sincere love and devotion to Mary. Cathedrals in honor of her were built almost every year in the 12th Century. We believe that her first appartion to us in the modern world, in Paris, and her subsequent apparitions in France at La Sallette in 1846, Lourdes in 1858, and Pontmain in 1873, were strong attempts on her part to bring her beloved children of France, the eldest daughter of the Church, back to the fold.

The battle goes on, but she shows no signs of weakening. She's up to it. She's dug her heels into the earth, and promises not to give up on us, as long as there's still time, and even a handful of believers. We wonder, though, how many believers there are, and just how much time is left.

Panoramic view of the Shrine of Our Lady at La Salette, France

La Salette, 1846: Our Lady Who Wept

The visit of my Mary to earth on September 19, 1846 is usually referred to as **OUR LADY OF TEARS** or **OUR LADY WHO WEPT**. We sometimes believe that the only reason she is not weeping all the time is because she has the Beatific Vision of her Magnificent Son to comfort her. There's an expression, "You can't get hurt if you don't stick your chin out". She always sticks her chin out. She is always being hurt. If we study the history of the world, in particular the 16th through the 19th centuries, we become alarmingly aware that we've hurt Mary very deeply. However, very seldom do we ever hear her complain about the outrages committed against her. During her apparition to St. Catherine Laboure, she cried because of the chastisement that would come to France, and to the Religious Orders.

The irony of her visit to the two simple French children high above the tree line in La Salette, France, is that, again, the tears she shed were not for herself; *she cried for us*, her children. What an example she is, the suffering servant. What a heart she has. No wonder there is such devotion to her Immaculate Heart. It is so big; there's enough room in her heart for the whole world.

The excitement and devotion which flourished in the wake

of Mary's apparition to Catherine Laboure in Paris in 1830, and the phenomenal spread of the Miraculous Medal that followed in its path, brought many people back to the Church and Mary. But by and large, Satan was still in control. The situation had not changed that much, or the word had not spread far enough in the succeeding 16 years. 1846 found France as anti-Church as it had ever been, only more self centered and materialistic.

The mountain people had never paid too much attention to what went on in the big city. They had their own set of problems that had nothing to do with the national politics of the country, or the power plays and backstabbing in the parlors of Paris. While it's true that the national attitudes finally found their ways into the villages and hamlets, they really didn't need any encouragement for their attitude towards the Church. Their lack of faith was more because of apathy; the Church was just there, like an old shoe.

The French had indeed become cultural Catholics, that is, Catholics in name only. They were only involved with Church for Baptism, First Holy Communion, Weddings, and Funerals. Sunday was no longer a day of worship and glorification of God. It was a workday just like any other. The churches were empty. *First Holy Communion* was more often than not, *last Holy Communion*. Children were not taught prayers in the home. There was no example set by the parents. God was some far off figure who had nothing to do with their lives. If He truly existed, He was not concerned with *their* problems.

Their attitude towards God was a contradiction in terms when one considered where they lived. The majestic panorama of the mountain was such evidence of the splendor of God, His Perfect artistry, His Perfect Love. As far as the eye could see were beautiful mountains, one more elegant than the other, broken by streams of fresh water running down to the valleys. Little houses, nestled in the side of the mountains, were scattered throughout, adding patches of color to the scene. This could only be the work of a Supreme Being. No human architect or artist could ever have conceived such a plan. Sadly, though, many of the gifts of the

Lord are either unappreciated, or taken for granted. This beauty was wasted on the citizens of La Salette. Their attitude was "You can't feed your family landscapes."

Into this setting, we bring two children, Maximin Giraud, age 11, and Melanie Mathieu, age 15. They both came from the nearby town of Corps. As small as Corps was, 1300 inhabitants in 1846, the two had never met. But then, neither was part of the social circle.

Maximin was the product of a drunken father, and an uncaring stepmother, who had no time for him. Her main concern was taking care of the children *she* had borne her husband. The husband passed most of his time at the local cafe, spending the little money he earned on drink. Maximin was small for his age, but he was healthy. One night, a farmer from nearby La Salette met Giraud in a cafe, and talked him into letting Maximin tend his cows for a week. The boy had no experience in this field, but the farmer convinced his father that it was a simple task, which he would have no trouble handling. That's how Our Lady got Maximin to the mountain on September 19th of that year.

Melanie Mathieu, on the other hand, was an experienced cowherder at age 15. Hers was a large family from the other side of Corps. She was loved by her parents, but they were unable to take care of her. She was sent out into the streets to beg at an early age. When she was 8, she baby sat for money. They hired her out at age 10 as a farm helper. She never experienced a parent's warmth, a mother's touch, or love of any kind at the farms where she worked. She was not a person to her employers, with whom she lived; rather, she was treated as one of the farm animals. The farmers were only interested in what she could produce, not her physical or mental state. They didn't care whether she was happy or sad, sick or well. A scrawny girl, she was very plain, quiet, and sulky. But who could blame her? She had been virtually alone from age 10 to 15, when she met Maximin on the mountain of La Salette.

They had one thing in common, these two children from

different parts of the same town, whose upbringing had been completely different. They both had an overpowering desire to be loved by a mother. This was the most important form of nourishment they lacked. Little did they know that their Real Mother watched over them from the day of their birth, and all through their life, so that she could give them the gift of this moment in time.

The farms they worked at were near each other. Melanie and Maximin met on Thursday, September 17, when Maximin arrived from Corps. Melanie didn't like Maximin. He covered up his shyness and insecurity by acting brash and stupid. She thought him silly. Actually, the farmer who had talked Maximin's father into sending him up to La Salette didn't care for him either. After the first day, he was sorry he had asked for the boy. Maximin was lightheaded, flighty. He couldn't remember simple orders.

The following morning, Friday, September 18, the children went up the mountain together, but each went to a different slope with their respective cows. Maximin had brought a goat and his dog with him. It was an uneventful day. But being young, they planned on having a beautiful, adventurous time the following day, Saturday, September 19. That's the way with young people. Each day is a new day, a new adventure.

The morning passed. The children had brought the cows up, watered them, then ate their lunch together. They met with some other herders for a short time. The noon sun warmed them; their eyes became heavy. They both fell asleep in the pasture. Two hours later, Melanie woke with a start. She panicked. She looked around nervously. Where were the cows? They were nowhere to be seen. She awakened Maximin, and the two ran up and down the slopes, looking for their charges. When they found the cows quietly eating grass on the other side of a slope, they breathed a deep sigh of relief, and ran back towards the place where they had left their lunch, to gather up their knapsacks.

As they approached the edge of a ravine, Melanie stopped. A burst of bright light in the shape of the sun glistened in front of her. It was brighter than the sun, causing Melanie to shade her eyes from its brilliance. She looked away and closed her eyes. Then she returned her focus to the spot. It was still there. She was frightened. She called out to Maximin.

"Memin" that was his nickname, "come see the light shining down here."

Maximin could tell by the sound of her voice that something was wrong. He ran towards her.

"Where is it?" he shouted.

She could hardly speak. "There", she pointed weakly in the direction of the unusual light.

The globe grew larger and larger before their eyes. Melanie was mesmerized by the dazzling light. She dropped the stick which she used to keep the cows in line. Both children wanted to run, but their legs were like lead. They couldn't move. The globe opened. They were able to make out the figure of a woman inside. She was brighter than the sphere, if that was possible. She was seated, as if on a rock. Her face was covered by her hands. Her shoulders heaved. She was weeping. The two looked at each other, but did not move.

Maximin, not knowing what to say, blurted out to Melanie,

"Hold onto that staff of yours, and I will hold onto mine. If it does anything, I'll give it a good clout."

The lady raised her head. The two children gasped. There in front of them was the most beautiful face they had ever seen, or imagined. She was awesome. She was still crying, but even in tears, she was breathtaking. Her arms crossed her breasts. She looked up at the children, with so much love in her eyes that all fear left them. They melted in the warmth of her gaze. She opened her arms to them. Then she spoke.

"Come to me, my children. Do not be afraid. I am here to tell you something of the greatest importance."

Her voice lilted. It sounded like music. It was warm and loving, but firm. She commanded with a gentleness that relaxed them immediately. She spoke in French, which they did not understand that well. They spoke in the local patois. They realized, however, that she wanted them to come to her. Their hearts racing, they approached her. She met them halfway, gliding in their direction. The globe followed her, encompassing her in its splendor. She came so close to them that they were enveloped in the globe also. She had a sweet, fresh fragrance about her, a light scent of roses, but different from anything they had ever smelled. Her clothes sparkled as she moved towards them. She continued to cry as she spoke to them.

"If my people will not obey," she said, "I shall be compelled to loose my Son's arm. It is so heavy, so pressing that I can no longer restrain it.

How long have I suffered for you! If I would not have my Son abandon you, I must pray to Him constantly. But you pay no attention to it. No matter how well you pray in the future, no matter how well you act, you will never be able to make up to me what I have endured on your behalf.

I gave you six days for working. The seventh I have reserved for myself. But no one will give it to me. This is what causes the weight of my Son's arm to be so crushing. In addition, the cart drivers cannot swear without bringing in my Son's name. These are the two things which make His arm so heavy.

If the harvest is spoiled, it is your *own* fault. I warned you last year by means of the potatoes. You paid no attention. Quite the opposite. When you found out that the potatoes had decayed, you swore; you blamed my Son. They will continue to spoil, and by Christmas time this year there will be none left."

Maximin did not understand a word the lady said. Melanie struggled, and was able to pick out key words, but much of it was lost on her also. Mary was aware that the children were having a problem understanding French. She saw Melanie give a look to Maximin, who had a blank expression on his face.

"Ah, you do not understand French, my children. Well then, listen. I will put it in another way." Then she spoke in the local patois. She repeated what she had told them. Then she continued.

If my people will not obey I shall be compelled to loose my Son's arm it is so heavy, so pressing that I can no longer restrain it. Our Lady weeps for her children La Salette, France

Well, my children you will make this known to all my people. Our Lady of La Salette with Melanie and Maximin La Salette, France

"If you have grain, it will do no good to sow it, for what you sow the animals will eat, and whatever part of it springs up will crumble into dust when you thresh it.

A great famine is coming. But before that happens, the children under seven years old will be seized with trembling and die in the arms of their parents. The grownups will pay for their sins by hunger. The grapes will rot and the walnuts will turn bad."

Our Lady turned to Maximin and spoke to him privately. Melanie knew it was a secret for Maximin alone, because although she could see the lady's lips moving, and she was as close to the lady as Maximin, she couldn't hear a word. The lady then turned to Melanie, and imparted a secret to her also.

THEN SHE GAVE US THE SIGN OF HOPE

"IF THE PEOPLE ARE CONVERTED, THE ROCKS WILL BECOME PILES OF WHEAT AND IT WILL BE FOUND THAT THE POTATOES HAVE SOWN THEMSELVES."

She turned to the children. "Do you say your prayers well, my children?"

Maximin avoided her eyes, looking down to the ground. The two of them answered. "No Madam, hardly at all."

She looked so lovingly at them. "Ah, my children, it is very important to do so, at night and in the morning. When you don't have time, at least say an 'Our Father' and a 'Hail Mary', but when you can, say more."

Then she returned to the subject at hand.

"Only a few old women go to Mass on Sunday in the summer; everybody else works every Sunday all summer long. In the winter, when they don't know what to do with themselves, they go to Mass only to make fun of religion. During Lent, they go to the butcher shop like dogs". (This was a reference to the lack of fasting and abstinence during Lent)

She looked around her. She sighed a heavy sigh. She turned

her eyes in their direction, completely swallowing them up in the beauty of those eyes. She spoke to them in French.

"Well, my children, you will make this known to all my people."

She turned from them slowly. The meeting was coming to an end. She stepped across the stream, and then stopped. She never looked back at them. She repeated her previous command.

"Well, my children, you will make this known to all my people."

She continued to move up the slopes. The children followed her. She glided along the ground, without so much as bending a blade of grass. Then she was raised into the air. As she looked up to Heaven, the children noticed for the first time that she was not weeping. She looked off in the distance one last time. The globe which surrounded her glowed brighter than before. She began to fade. The light remained for a short time, and then *it* faded. She was gone.

This was the shortest apparition we will write about but one of the most significant. Mary established a pattern here that she would continue to use again in Fatima, and more recently in the as yet unconfirmed apparitions at Medjugorje, Yugoslavia. She begins with doomsday prophecy. In the instance of La Salette, Our Lady was making reference to the Great Potato Famine that plagued Ireland in 1845, and had reached disaster proportions by 1846. She also predicted further famine, plagues and suffering for France. These were all predictions of things to come, which did in fact occur. Close to a million people died as a result of a wheat shortage in Europe. The grapes of France were destroyed by a pestilence. Children did indeed die in their mother's arms.

But It Didn't Have to Happen

She gave us a way out in La Salette.

IF THEY ARE CONVERTED, THE STONES AND ROCKS WILL BE CHANGED INTO HEAPS OF WHEAT, AND POTA-TOES WILL SOW THEMSELVES.

Perhaps the chastisement would have been worse if many had not heeded her message, and returned to the Church.

In Fatima, she predicted the rise of the Soviet Union, and World War II.

BUT IN THE END, MY IMMACULATE HEART WILL TRIUMPH.

Perhaps the ravages of World War II would have been worse if we had not responded to her pleas.

In Medjugorje, the message is the same. Great times of tribulation are coming our way. But if we pray, fast, and return to the Church, if we reconcile with our neighbors, the chastisement will be lessened.

We were told in 1987 that Jesus is pleased with the way the world, **IN PARTICULAR THE WEST** is responding to Our Lady's warning at Medjugorje.

The Apparition by Mary to Maximin Giraud and Melanie Mathieu was approved by the Bishop of the area 5 years to the day after Our Lady came. On September 19, 1851, the letter authorizing devotion to Our Lady Of La Salette was proclaimed to the people.

In all instances where Mary shows her love by visiting us in an apparition, we can be sure that the devil is close by. La Salette was no different. From the very beginning, there were divided camps among the religious and the laity. Four of the priests who took part in the official investigation did not believe that an authentic apparition had taken place.

One of them resorted to the most unethical means, including writing anonymous stories discrediting the appearance by Mary. Another priest, who felt he had been slighted by the bishop, took out his anger on Our Lady of the Mountain. Even the assistant pastor to St. John Vianney, the Cure of Ars, twisted the saint's words to make it appear as if St. John Vianney did not believe in the apparition at La Salette, which was certainly not true.

All of these diabolical acts were finally discredited but they threw doubts into the minds of the people. All that's needed is the slightest suspicion to turn us away from the graces Our Lady is so anxious for us to accept.

Then there was the problem of the childrens' behavior. We have to remember that this was actually the beginning of Our Lady's apparitions to children on earth. Nobody knew who Mary had appeared to in Paris in 1830. They knew it was one of the nuns, though, and the natural association one makes with nuns is holiness. We also have to realize that St. Catherine was not subjected to the notoriety that came with being a visionary. She was able to live anonymously, without those particular pressures.

These children were in the public eye from the very first day. It was probably assumed that the children were saints, or should have been, if they had been chosen by the Mother of God. They were not saints. They were simple children, on whom this gift of love was bestowed. But with the gift came the responsibility of living up to it. Whether it was fair or not is not the issue. They just weren't able to handle it.

It was assumed that they would enter the religious life, which they tried to do. But neither was able to cope with it. They both lived in torture for the rest of their lives. Their conduct cast a shadow on the authenticity of the apparition, even after it had been approved by the Church. But the power of Mary was stronger than the power of evil. Her message was accepted and acted upon. La Salette became a great place of pilgrimage. It remains that way until today. One of the greatest gifts of La Salette is the amazing number of conversions that have taken place there. The Sacrament of Reconciliation is extremely strong. There are many stories of people who had been away from the Church for years, experiencing complete changes of heart at this holy place. This is exactly what she asked for.

We have to stop for a minute to share on the children. The series of apparitions in modern times by Mary began with the Miraculous Medal in 1830, and continued on through La Salette, Lourdes, Pontmain, Fatima, Beauraing, Banneux, and the most recent reported apparitions in Medjugorje, Yugoslavia. With the exception of Paris, in each of these instances, she chose to make her presence known to unsophisticated, unlearned children. Maximin and Melanie were the first in this series of visionaries. There were no guidelines as to how they should behave. There were no predecessors, on whose example they could fashion their lives.

We are all given free will. Jesus and Mary ask us to come to them freely, of our own volition. They do not want robots. The gift of surrender to the Sacred Heart and the Immaculate Heart has to be freely given. The fact that we have to fight our own human nature all our lives to be able to give this gift makes it an even greater sacrifice. While we have abundant graces to help us through the hard times, we have to say "YES", and accept them.

My Mary is an unconditional giver. She did not make stipulations with the children at La Salette. She came to them because she loved them. She asked them to plead with us to save ourselves from the wrath of Jesus. She told them to spread the message, which they did. We're sure that Mary grieved for these two children as she watched them walk through the rest of their lives in suffering. We have to believe that she did everything she could to bring them closer to the Lord. We also believe that Our Lady was waiting to welcome them into the Kingdom when they closed their eyes for the last time.

Without making a judgment about the children after the apparition, I find it hard to believe that anyone who had been given the gift of actually seeing this most perfect creature of God could ever turn away from her. Whether the vision had been for an instant, the blinking of an eye, or a short period of time, as was the apparition at La Salette, I think it would be imprinted on my heart for the rest of my life. I would never forget it. Everywhere I went, I would search for that vision, that face. I would like to believe that Melanie Mathieu and Maximin Giraud did the same.

La Salette is a difficult pilgrimage place in terms of bringing groups. It is high up on top of a mountain in the French Alps. The first time we went there, we wondered how high we would have to climb with our huge tour bus. At one point, my grandson, Rob, pointed to the top of the mountain. We could see a tour bus the size of ours. It looked like an ant. Rob said, "That's where we have to go". Everybody laughed. No one believed him. P.S. That was how high we had to go.

Possibly because of the difficulty in getting to the top, La Salette is a shrine that is not taken for granted. Tourists don't go up there. *Pilgrims do*. They boast about having made the journey up the great mountain. The attitude at the top is one of reverence and prayer. Mary's message of conversion is the keynote of this shrine. Chapels of Reconciliation are in great numbers. There is one church dedicated to the shrine. It is almost always filled with pilgrims, praying in petition and thanksgiving to Mary.

Mary speaks to us very clearly on top of this mountain, above the tree line. What the local people of 1846 failed to realize about the gift of this mountain, is that it is close enough to Heaven, and far away enough from the distractions of the world, that when Our Lord Jesus and His awesome Mother Mary speak to us here, we are able to hear them. Our great task is to listen to what they are saying to us, and **ACT ON IT**.

Our Lady at the Grotto of Massabiele
Lourdes, France

Mary looks to her Son in the church
Basilica of Our Lady of Lourdes, France

Lourdes, 1858: If I Should Ever Forget You. . . .

There is a quotation in Sacred Scripture regarding Jerusalem that reads: "JERUSALEM, JERUSALEM, IF I SHOULD EVER FORGET YOU . . ."

There are many holy places that this passage would apply to including Jerusalem. But for us, when we hear this passage, our minds race to that mystical place where honor is given to Our Lord Jesus through His Mother Mary, her shrine at Lourdes in France.

LOURDES, LOURDES, IF I SHOULD EVER FORGET YOU. . . .

Lourdes is such a tribute to, and affirmation of, the love and care, the concern, patience, and attention that is showered on us by our Heavenly Family. It is also a magnificent prayer of faith the world has been given in the the desire of Our Sweet Mary, *Bernadette's Aquero (Dear One)*, to take care of our physical and spiritual needs. The natural question we are asked after we have visited Lourdes is, **"DID YOU SEE ANY MIRACLES, ANY CURES IN LOURDES?"**

Praise you, Jesus, we have seen so many miracles, so many gifts from Son to Mother, and Mother to children. Lourdes is the

Wedding Feast of Cana, multiplied a thousand fold. We can just picture Jesus and Mary up in heaven. "Mother, it's not my problem", and Mary, just smiling, saying to us "Do whatever He tells you". Miracles abound in Lourdes.

We have **SEEN MIRACLES** in Lourdes. We have seen **CURES** in Lourdes. In order for us to witness to the physical cures the Lord has given us at Lourdes, we have a man in our little Parish church who was cured of terminal lung cancer in the baths in Lourdes.

There is also a doctor in our village, who was a very unhappy man. He found early in his career that he didn't like dealing with people. He gave up his general practice to become an anesthesiologist, so that he wouldn't be required to have personal contact with patients. He had a son who was a member of our Junior Legion of Mary. The father did everything to block the boy from coming to our meetings. Either he would not bring him to our home on the evenings of the meetings, or he would bring him late, and pick him up early. The doctor was very angry with the Church.

The children of the Legion grew up. Many of them moved away. Our Junior Legion of Mary was disbanded. But one day, some years later, the doctor's son called us on the telephone, and asked us to pray for his father, who had a brain tumor. He said to us "Jesus and Mary listen to your prayers." We told the boy we were on our way to Lourdes; we would pray at the shrine, and go into the baths for his father's cure.

At Lourdes, Penny went into the baths for this doctor. Normally, the women only sit down in the baths, while the men are completely submerged. Without Penny saying a word to the volunteers, they submerged her, so that the back of her head was in the water, the same place where the doctor had the tumor.

Our daughter, Sister Clare, called us the following day, to ask what we had done the previous day. She said the doctor had called, to say he had experienced a burning sensation in the back of his head, followed by a renewal of energy.

That was in 1981. The doctor still has the tumor, but it has been in remission since that day Penny went into the baths. He has made a pilgrimage of Thanksgiving to Lourdes, as well as to Knock. He has had a complete conversion. Today, he embraces the Church passionately. He said to us on one occasion, "I'm thankful for my cure. But if I should lose my new relationship with Jesus and Mary, I would rather die."

He is now the *unofficial* doctor for our local seminary. He begs for free medicine, lab work, and x-rays for the seminarians. The rector of the seminary told us recently that Dr. Bill has saved the seminary nearly a million dollars in medical expense over the last 6 years. So we can say with certainty that cures and miracles occur at Lourdes.

But physical healings are not the greatest miracle of Lourdes. What is the Miracle there? Is it solely in the fact that the Mother of God came here to visit a young, uneducated girl? Is the miracle the many cures that have taken place here? Is it the *Spring*, the miraculous waters that have poured out for the last 130 years, and show no signs of letting up?

Indeed, all these things are miracles, gifts from Our Lord Jesus through His Mother, His loving, giving Mother. But I believe that these were just the beginnings of a greater miracle, a catalyst of the real miracle, the ongoing miracle, the miracle of *Church*. The word *Catholic* stands out like a neon light in Lourdes. At any given time, tens of thousands of Catholics from hundreds of points on the earth can be found here, praising God, loving His beautiful Mother, and saying, **"YES, LORD, THANK YOU LORD, I BELIEVE. I TRUST YOU WITH MY LIFE".**

We're told that in France, the eldest daughter of the Church, less than 5% of the Catholic population go to Church and receive the Sacraments. We're not about to argue these statistics, but if they're true, all these people must be at Lourdes each time we visit there. We have seen *Faith* in Lourdes, that if, spread over the entire world, would be strong enough to give us peace forever.

What Is It All About? What Happened in Lourdes?

Why did Mary come? What was so important at this time in history, in this country? It's easy in retrospect to understand the need for divine intervention in 1858. The Church had gone through one of its worst periods possible in Europe. It had not quite recovered from the French Revolution. New governments, new revolutions attacked the Church and the people. In 1848, the Archbishop of Paris was murdered when yet another revolution took place in France. It then spread itself to Rome. The Pope's Prime Minister was murdered. The Papal Palace was attacked. Many were wounded or killed. It became violent to the point of driving Pope Pius IX out of the Vatican State. Belief and trust in the promise of Jesus waned badly. It seemed as if the Church was tolling its death knell. Louis Napoleon brought his French troops to the aid of the Church temporarily, and the Pope was able to return to Rome. But the calm was shortlived. The war clouds loomed over the horizon again. Satan poised his troops in preparation for the final destruction of the Church.

In 1854, in the midst of this, and in the face of massive opposition, one of Mary's staunchest supporters, Pope Pius IX proclaimed to the world what had been believed down through the centuries, but had never been made a *Dogma* of the Church. **THE IMMACULATE CONCEPTION** was declared fact, and all Catholics were required to believe this. There had been a popular heresy spreading throughout Europe at this time, Pantheism, which claimed that man was equal with God. By this proclamation, Our Lord Jesus through the Pope declared that with the exception of Jesus, *only* Mary was conceived without Original Sin. The rest of the human race are heirs of Adam and Eve, and all that goes with it.

This proclamation caused more problems than it meant to solve. Rumbling went on *inside* the Church, and *outside* in Protestant circles. It was outrageous, they said, to give this singular honor to a *woman*. Shades of Lucifer! He, the once favored angel of God, made this same statement when told that a woman would be Queen of Heaven and Earth, of all the Angels and the Saints. His pride couldn't take this. He and his band of angels revolted against God and Heaven. The cry of Mica-el, (Who is Like God?) reverberated the Heavens. With Michael the Archangel at the helm, the loyal angels of God cast Lucifer and his pack down into the black hole of hell. Lucifer has hated the name of Mary since that time. Under the influence of Satan, the enemies of the Church claimed Mary was from Adam as we all are; that she came into the world with the same stain of sin that everyone else was born with. "It was one thing for the peasants, the uninformed, to believe in this superstition", they ranted. "How could the Church make this farce into dogma?"

Our Lady of Patience, my Mary, who has never given up on us in 2,000 years, waited. One year went by. The situation was bad. Two years went by. Not much change took place in the attitudes of her children towards the new Dogma of the Immaculate Conception. The third year passed. But still she waited. And then she did the predictable. She found a remote town of no great importance, and within that speck on the earth, she chose a simple child of the poorest family in the region, and led her to a garbage dump. From that vantage point she was to send out a message to the world for all time, loud and clear, confirmation of Pope Pius' IX dogma, in the statement she made in the 16th Apparition on the Feast of the Annunciation,

QUE SOY ERA IMMACULADA CONCEPCIOU
I AM THE IMMACULATE CONCEPTION

She even spoke the words in a local patois, or dialect, rather than the language of the country, to a child who had no idea what the words meant.

But wait, we're getting ahead of ourselves. Whenever we talk of Lourdes, we get so excited that we go off in many directions. We have to go back to the beginning, to that cold winter day in February, 1858, when my Mary blessed this hamlet with her presence. In 1858, Lourdes was not on the map. It was a sleepy little village nestled in the Pyrenees mountains in the south of France. Lourdes is not known for its great weather. Even now the temperature is cooler, and the area more prone to rain than the rest of southern France. This particular winter of 1858 was bitter, especially for the Soubirous family. Their life had been difficult for many years.

The father, Francois Soubirous, was a "good old boy"; he had a great need for acceptance. In the early days of his marriage to Louise, they had a Mill, the Boly Mill, where St. Bernadette was born. They had a modest business, and their life was good. But when Francois went to the local cafe, he had to buy drinks for everyone. When people bought flour from their mill, any hard luck story would be good enough for Francois to extend credit to them. When they didn't pay their bills, he understood their sad story. But his creditors didn't understand *his* sad stories, and so, in short order, he lost his business and the mill.

By the year 1856, his family had been dishonored to the point of being forced to live in a one-room former prison in Lourdes, called The Cachot (the Cell, or Lock up). The reason it was no longer used as a prison was because it was considered below human living standards. Into this hovel, Francois and Louise Soubirous, and their four children moved. Le Cachot is approximately 15 by 20 feet. These are intolerable living conditions for 6 people. *(To explain violence in Ghetto situations, scientific experiments have been done on laboratory rats in cramped quarters. It is a scientific fact that when they are placed into these crowded conditions, they fight with and eventually kill each other.)* Yet the cousin of the Soubirous family, named Sajous, who lived above them, testified that he never once heard them quarrel.

To add to their disgrace, Francois was put in prison on suspicion of having stolen some flour from a local mill, where he had worked temporarily. The only evidence against him was that his living conditions were so bad he became the most logical suspect. It was *so* logical to the local police, that although Francois had never been accused of a crime before, they put him in jail. The Soubirous' lived below the poverty level. In those days, there was no welfare, but if there had been, they would have been prime candidates. When the father worked, he received wages slightly less than what was paid to hire out a horse. Louise did domestic work, but between the two of them, they could not bring in enough money to support their family. Yet, somehow they survived.

Into this background, we bring Bernadette Soubirous, an illiterate, extremely unhealthy little 14 year old girl. We sometimes think it's a shame that she was involved with the apparitions at Lourdes. She is such a pillar of strength, such a dynamic saint on her own, without the gift of the great privilege she was given. Or maybe it *was* because of the apparitions by Our Lady. However, it's important to point out that Mary has appeared to many people over the centuries, and very few of them have become saints. During the time of Bernadette, there were the two children from La Sallette, whose lives would never have been considered exemplary, in light of the fact that the Mother of God had come to them. The children of Pontmain, Beauraing or Banneux are not being considered for any special praises by the Church. But then there is Bernadette, special Bernadette.

Our Lady picks the people whom she graces with her presence very carefully. On the surface, most of the time, there doesn't seem to be any rhyme or reason for her choices. One of the feelings most frequently expressed regarding a visionary is **WHY HIM, WHY HER, WHY THEM?** While it's true in the case of Bernadette that we may never have heard of her without the apparitions, she would always have been a strong defender of the faith in her own simple way, would have led a holy life, and would have been a saint, even if she were never canonized.

Bernadette was always a good girl, a holy girl, a humble girl. For someone as famous as she became, she had no exaggerated impressions of her self worth. When asked how she felt about receiving such a special gift from Our Lady, she made the statement "What do you think of me? Don't I realize that the Blessed Virgin chose me because I was the most ignorant? If she had found anyone more ignorant than myself, she would have chosen her." In another instance, she said of herself, "The Blessed Virgin used me like a broom. What do you do with a broom when you have finished sweeping? You put it back in its place, behind the door."

February 11, 1858 started out as just another cold winter day in Lourdes. There had been snow in January. The remnants could be seen all over the town in the form of snow-capped mounds of dirt, white accents coloring the trees and buildings. After the snowfall, the weather turned colder, causing much of the snow to freeze over into ice. Earlier on this particular day in February, there had been a bitter cold rain. It had stopped, but a light drizzle remained. Cold winds whipped through the little village, searching for breaks in the armor of coats, scarves, mittens and boots. It was not a good day to be out.

The sharp winds penetrated the walls of the Cachot, causing a chill to run through Louise Soubirous. She looked to their meager supply of twigs and branches which were used for the fireplace. It was almost gone. This was not only their sole source of heat for the house; they also used the fireplace to cook their food. Most people had supplies of firewood piled high for this purpose, whereas the Soubirous' had to be content with wet twigs and branches which smoked up their little dwelling place. Louise was concerned that the smoke would bother Bernadette's delicate lungs, but she had no choice. The child would have to cough; they could not afford to buy the wood they needed.

Her husband, Francois, rested on the bed. He had worked for a few hours earlier in the day. It was the first work he had gotten in some time. He wasn't really tired, but he wanted everyone to know how hard he had labored for the family. He felt a spark of hope. Perhaps things were going to take a turn for the better. Louise understood her husband. She didn't want to take away from him this moment of accomplishment.

She turned to the girls, Bernadette, her oldest and sickest, and Toinette. She didn't want Bernadette to go for the wood. Bernadette, on the other hand, wanted to go out. She felt she was a drain on the family because of her illness. She was also suffering cabin fever, from being indoors so much. She was self conscious because she couldn't do all the things the other children could. She begged her mother to let her go with Toinette. Finally, Louise gave in. She was to ponder for many years to come if their lives would have changed so drastically had she not let Bernadette go that day. She had no way of knowing as she watched the two girls leave the house that the Bernadette who left would never return. She had been touched by the Lady from Heaven; and would never be the same.

We take you to a place high in the sky, so you can watch the drama of February 11, 1858 unfold, where heaven and earth meet, the divine touches the human, and the world is affected for all time. On earth, we see Bernadette and Toinette frolicking through the town, picking up a playmate, Jeanne Abadie. They don't even know where they are being directed. Their chore is to pick up firewood, wherever they can find it. At the other end of the spectrum, we see the clouds open, and a bright light appears from Paradise, moving slowly towards earth. The little girls wind their way through the town, then down the hill in the direction of the River Gave. From our vantage point, we can hear choirs of angels singing joyous hymns in anticipation of the miracle that is to take place. If we could see into God's dimension, we would be able to witness these angels surrounding and carrying the most magnificent creature the Lord has ever placed on the earth. Slowly, they descend from the Heavens, the drama building. We can feel our hearts pounding as the angels and the Queen get closer and closer to earth.

The children approach the River Gave. They see a cave on the other side. It's the Grotto of Massabiele, a garbage dump. But it's dry inside. They can see sticks and twigs on the ground. Bernadette hesitates crossing the river, for fear she will catch cold. Her mother will kill her if she finds out that Bernadette even entertained the idea of crossing. The girls chide her. She feels a flush of anger and resentment rise up in her cheeks. She takes off her stockings and begins to wade across the water. At the same time a streak of light flashes across the sky at meteoric speed. We don't know if the other children see it. But as Bernadette walks out of the water, she is thrown to her knees by an unknown force. Before her is a brilliance that is indescribable. It's dazzling, yet there is a softness, a warmth, a shimmering, but oh, so much more. She looks to an alcove at the right of the grotto. She is speechless. The choir of angels reaches its highest pitch as the eyes of Bernadette and the Lady meet. An electric beam rivets the gaze of the two together. Bernadette feels her heart swelling. She is afraid it will burst. She cannot breathe. She trembles; her fear turning into excitement, wonderment. She can't take her eyes off the Lady. It has begun. The Queen of Heaven comes to speak to her people. God puts aside the laws of nature, and creates **MIRACLE!**

What emotions went through Bernadette as her eyes met the gaze of Mary? Did she melt? Was she swallowed up in the warmth of the most exquisite Lady she had ever seen? Was she electrified? Being a simple girl of limited vocabulary, she was never able to, or chose not to divulge those deep feelings. But dear Lord, what must it have been like? I have been in the room of the Apparitions at Medjugorje during the time Our Lady visited the children. I saw nothing, yet the feelings, the presence of Mary was so strong that it ricocheted off the walls. It was all around us, nurturing, affirming, loving. But I could never adequately put my feelings into words. I don't think an earthly language exists that can fully express the heights of emotion, the impact of such an experience. There just are no words.

St. Thomas Aquinas, one of the most brilliant minds of our Church, after having had a vision of Heaven, stopped all his writing on the Summa Theologica, considering everything he had ever done "so much straw" when compared to what he had experienced. We'll never know exactly what Bernadette felt. But we can dream; we can ponder.

Bernadette did not want to tell anyone what had happened at the Grotto. She could not help but share it with her sister and Jean Abadie. But she did not want it to go beyond them. Children being what they are, however, the word spread like wildfire; the results of which were predictable. Jean Abadie spread the story around the town, while Toinette told her mother. Louise Soubirous beat both children. She ordered them not to go back to the grotto, or to spread any more lies. Secretly, she feared that Bernadette was hallucinating as a result of her illness.

Two days later, however, the girls managed to coerce their father into allowing them to return to the Grotto. This time they took 7 girls with them, and armed themselves with candles and holy water. Our Lady appeared to Bernadette again. She was the only one who could see Mary. The other girls just knelt in silence and awe. Satan must have possessed Jean Abadie that day. She climbed to the top of the mountain above the grotto, and rolled a large stone off the cliff, which landed near the grotto. All the girls ran for their lives. But Bernadette didn't notice what had happened. This was the first time that anyone was aware that she was in a different world. She was in a haven, which was to be her greatest source of strength in the coming days and years. It was called. . . . .

ECSTASY!! The expression is used in each of Bernadette's Apparitions. *"She went into ecstasy." "The ecstasy lasted 45 minutes."* We know that at these times, she was completely oblivious to everything around her. After this first ecstasy, during the second apparition, she had to be carried from the grotto to the home of Antoine Nicolau, the miller at the Savvy Mill. She was not aware of what was happening until she reached his house. In the course of other apparitions, she was under observation throughout the ecstasys. One time a woman lanced her shoulder with a large pin. Bernadette didn't react. During the same apparition, a candle she had been holding fell. The flames and burning wax touched her fingers for a few minutes. She was not aware of it. Nor did she have any scars from it. She was in **Ecstasy**.

This is what she held onto during the times of trial, which encompassed most of her life after that first meeting with the Lady. This is how she endured the attacks not only from her family and the secular world, but also from within the Church. To be sure, for her entire life, more people considered her a liar, or a lunatic, than a mystic. Many of those who did believe in the apparitions, were extremely jealous of Bernadette.

What happened during these special, private times? Can we even begin to fantasize what their time together was like? Where did they go? Did they soar to the heights of Heaven? Did they float gently back to earth? Did they talk? Did Mary fill this dear child with her exalted presence? Did Mary's eyes penetrate the soul of Bernadette as they had during that first brief encounter? Did she fill the future saint's heart with so much joy that she would be able to withstand the years ahead?

Bernadette was a guarded girl, and in later years, a cautious woman. She held onto those things that were hers alone. There was a boundary line that no one dare step over, a restricted place that was not to be shared. She was very strong and firm in this regard. She stood up against public officials, church officials, bishops, cardinals, anyone who tried to invade her special world. She had paid the price. She was willing to do whatever was necessary to accomplish the Lady's goal. She said "Yes" to Aquero, and Mary gave her the strength she needed to be a sign to the world for the rest of her life. The ever protective mother and friend made the time without her bearable.

She was to need this strength for the days ahead. People stopped her in the street to curse at her. One woman slapped her. The police chief called her into his office to interrogate her. He could not budge her, or make her change her story. Then the imperial prosecutor descended upon her. In the face of all these high ranking officials, Bernadette maintained a stubborn calmness, coupled with proper respect. The feeling she left both officials with was that she was sincere, but not at all frightened by their threats.

Bernadette's mother was firm in her refusal to allow her child to return to the grotto. But Louise Soubirous was never in a position to be firm about many things. She was so dependent on other people for her very livelihood, she couldn't take a chance on offending her employers.

Madame Milhet was one of these employers. She was somewhat bizarre. She was a combination of conservative Catholic and spiritualist, which did not put her in good standing with the Church. She was not in Lourdes when Bernadette first saw the Lady. When she returned, and heard the story, she thought the vision could be her dead 27 year old niece, whom she was sure was trying to contact her from the spirit world. Madame Milhet was a very strong woman. When she suggested something, it was to be taken as an order.

She came to the Cachot, bearing gifts of chicken and wine for the family. She began the conversation by offering Louise more work each week, which meant the family would no longer have to live on the edge of starvation. Having dangled this carrot before the eyes of Bernadette's mother, she then suggested a plan in which she and a friend would accompany Bernadette to the grotto, very early in the morning, so that there would be no one else around. Bernadette's poor mother had no choice but to give in. Madame Milhet also recommended they bring pen and paper, so that Bernadette could ask the Lady to write dwn who she was and what she wanted. She was sure the Lady wouldn't mind.

Just to show you the way Mary works when she wants something, at this moment, no one except Our Lady knew, that Bernadette was ready to throw herself at the feet of her mother, and beg to return to the Grotto; and the mother was ready to allow the child to return. Bernadette didn't know the mother's thoughts; the mother was not aware of what the child was thinking. The suggestion of Madame Milhet was Mary's way of bringing the whole affair together. Our Lady does use the strangest people to do her work.

Thus, it came to pass, by this uncanny set of circumstances, that Bernadette was allowed to return to the Grotto on Thursday, February 18th. This was an important day for Bernadette. Within a few minutes after having knelt, she went into ecstasy. Mary came to her. She asked the Lady to write down who she was, and what she wanted. The Lady smiled broadly, and spoke to Bernadette for the first time. "It's not necessary". She looked at Bernadette very lovingly. She spoke again. "Will you do me the honor of returning here every day for a fortnight (Two weeks)?"

Bernadette could feel her heart leap for joy. She promised gladly to return. The Lady's expression became somber. She looked at Bernadette almost sadly. She spoke very softly, "I cannot promise you happiness in this world, but in the next."

The young girl did not understand what Mary meant at that moment. She was so filled with happiness at the prospect of being with the beautiful Lady for two weeks, she couldn't think about anything beyond this time. She was to know the meaning of the Lady's words very shortly. They set the stage for Bernadette's life. But it was all right. It was enough, having this Heavenly vision before her. She made her **FIAT**. She said "Yes" to the Lady.

Thursday, February 25th was a very special day for Bernadette, the authenticity of the apparitions, and the future of Lourdes as a major Marian shrine, (although no one knew it at the time.) It rained relentlessly that morning. Bernadette walked down to the

Grotto of Massabiele from Le Cachot with her mother and her aunt Bernarde. Both ladies tried to protect the sickly girl from the weather, but the winds and rain lashed at their bodies, through their clothes. They felt the cold down to their bones.

When they arrived at the Grotto, to their amazement, there were over three hundred people gathered there, sitting in the rain, trying to protect themselves from the weather, their main focus to get and maintain good seats.

Bernadette had had a meeting with the blustery Cure Peyramale the day before. She conveyed Our Lady's wishes for a chapel to be built there, and for people to come in procession. This was just a small example of Bernadette's courage. Most adults would be frightened to ask the Cure the time of day; the reputation of his violent temper was well known throughout the town. But the Lady had told her to go to him, and she did. As the child repeated Mary's request, the priest about went through the ceiling. In a voice which could be heard all over Lourdes, he *commanded* the Lady to perform a miracle whereby the rose bush at the Grotto would bloom roses in February. Bernadette's mother was frightened that the Lady, if there really was one, might not perform the miracle demanded by the priest. She wasn't sure how her daughter would stand up under this pressure, and possible ridicule. Louise Soubirous was anxious about this particular day. For her, the test of the rosebush was a test of the Lady.

For Bernadette's part, she maintained an attitude of cool politeness towards the priest, showing the proper deference for his position, and his ranting; but she only bothered the Lady with his foolish requests because he had told her to, and she was obedient to his demands. We really don't believe she took him all that seriously. How could she be frightened of this priest when she basked in the light of the glorious Lady from Heaven?

At any rate, Bernadette repeated to Aquero the request by the Cure Peyramale for Our Lady to perform a miracle with the rosebush in the grotto, in which the roses would instantly burst into bloom, here in the middle of a very bad winter. But this was to be an important day in the history of the Apparitions, and Mary had neither time nor patience to listen to the blustering of the local parish priest. She ignored the request, and motioned Bernadette to come very close to her, to where the child could almost touch the feet of Our Lady. Bernadette was overcome with emotion, being so near to the Lady; she kissed the Rose Bush, causing little drops of blood to appear on her nose. Mary spoke to her in the local patois.

MARY—Go to the spring yonder and drink and wash yourself.

Bernadette jumped backwards, keeping her eyes on the Lady, wanting so to please her. She thought to herself. Spring? What Spring? She assumed Aquero meant the mill stream, and so she fell to her knees, and began to slide towards it. When she had almost reached the place, she turned back to be sure this was what Mary had meant. Our Lady shook her head. It was not the right place. The child thought, it must be the River Gave. She headed for the River, which was some distance away. Mary called out, **"Not to the Gave, please"**. Even the way she said it made Bernadette wince. Apparently the Lady was not pleased with the River Gave.

Bernadette was at a loss to know what the Lady meant. She twirled around uncertainly, then started back towards Mary. Our Lady repeated the message: **"Go to the spring yonder and drink and wash yourself"**. Then, in an effort to help the girl, she added **"Go eat the plants you will find yonder."** Bernadette looked around, wondering where she could find plants to eat. Over to the right in a corner was a small clump of grass sticking out of the rock. She ran over to it, and began to chew it. The grass tasted bitter, but she did not mind. So far, so good. She had taken care of the last part of the request. But where was there a spring to drink from? She looked around desperately, as if there were a time limit involved. She was afraid if she did not obey Mary's commands immediately, the Lady would realize how stupid she was, get disgusted and leave.

There was nothing there but some wet ground near the grass. Approaching a state of panic, she dropped to her knees, and began to dig in the dirt with her hands. She looked like a little squirrel, burrowing into the earth. Down a ways, she felt liquid, most likely from the last flood, she thought. But if this was what the

Lady wanted, she would give it to her. The obedient daughter dug deeper and deeper until there was a little puddle, just enough water to cup in her hands. She tried to get it out of the ground, but wound up picking up a combination of water and mud. She washed her hands and face, getting mud all over herself. Then she tried to cup enough water in her hands to drink. What she accomplished was swallowing a handful of mud. Almost immediately, her stomach rejected it; she began to gag. She couldn't get it out of her throat. Her mother and aunt ran to her with some water; the sorrowful figure vomited up the dirt, grass and water. The insensitive crowd began to laugh when she covered her face with mud. When she vomited, they became hysterical. Surely, she was mad.

Bernadette cried hard tears, partly because of the physical discomfort of the mud in her throat, partly because she was embarrassed, but *mostly* because she had failed the lady. Her mother was noticeably angry as she took the child away. Everybody else left the grotto, mumbling that the whole thing was lunacy, and Bernadette had gone crazy. The attention of the onlookers was so much on Bernadette that no one noticed a little puddle of water filling up the hole Bernadette had dug, which overflowed and began to trickle, forming a pool. This was the beginning of the **MIRACULOUS SPRING**, which has not stopped flowing from that time to this.

From this time forward, every time Mary appeared to Bernadette, she asked her to drink and wash in the spring. By this time, the child could cup her hands and get enough water to drink. The people assumed that this was a special ceremony just for Bernadette and the Lady. But as we can see 130 years later, and as the people at Lourdes came to realize shortly after the Apparitions, Our Lady was really talking to the people through this ritual she had Bernadette perform. She wanted all of us to *"Drink and wash ourselves in the spring"*.

On Thursday, March 4, the fortnight ended. For the last visit from Our Lady, close to ten thousand people crowded the Grotto, and the banks of the Gave River. Nothing spectacular happened. Our Lady repeated her request for the Chapel to be built there, and for people to come in procession. The local priest, Cure Peyramale, now secretly sided with Bernadette, but publicly repeated his commands for the Lady to tell him who she was, and to make the rosebush at the Grotto bloom. When Bernadette mentioned this to Our Lady, she just smiled at his commands. People had taken sides as to who believed Bernadette, who thought she was a liar, and who felt she was crazy.

As far as the world was concerned, the apparitions had ended. Bernadette had done her part. The Lady gave her many messages, and now it was over. But what had really happened? Why had she come? What was she trying to say?

Bernadette tried to go back to a normal life, but that was not to be. She was stopped everywhere she went. The local police and city government continued to question her. When she was forced to answer them, her attitude was very obviously reserved. Priests and bishops descended on her like locusts. Believers and curiosity seekers alike, continued to go to the Grotto. Bernadette, however, stayed away. She tried to concentrate on her school work, and on her religious education, which was so much more important to her now. She wanted desperately to receive Our Lord Jesus in Communion.

We have said throughout this narrative that Bernadette was a simple girl, almost illiterate, but never did we mean to give the impression that we thought she was stupid. Her behavior throughout the fortnight of the apparitions towards her questioners, police chiefs, mayors, priests and the like, give witness to the fact that she was bright. Her life *after* the apparitions affirms this.

We can't help but wonder then, what those next 3 weeks were like for her. We read in Franz Werfel's "The Song of Bernadette" that a period of peace and tranquility came over Bernadette. In the midst of all the questioning, the sightseers, the ambitious clergy, she maintained a *calmness*. She had something to look forward to. She knew that the Lady would come back again. She didn't know when, or how many times, but that was not important. She would be back; it was not over yet. Bernadette spent her time reminiscing about the two weeks that had passed, the times with Our Lady, and the anticipation of seeing her again. She didn't go back to the Grotto. When the time was right, Mary would let her know; then she would return.

THURSDAY, MARCH 25, The Feast of the Annunciation.
Bernadette wakes up like a shot, in the middle of the night. Her body is raised out of the bed to a sitting position. Her heart pounds so loudly she is sure it will explode. She knows; she can feel the call of the Lady, her "Aquero". The girl's entire body tingles with anticipation. She has to go to the Grotto. Before 5 in the morning, she can wait no longer. She tells her parents, bundles up as best she can, and leaves.

As she walks out of the "Cell", the Cachot, a blast of winter wind hits her full force. The powers of darkness are screeching, calling in all the evil spirits available, to make it difficult, even impossible, for this moment to happen, for the young girl to keep her rendezvous with the Lady. This has to be an important meeting; satan has pulled out all the stops. He lashes out at her with torrents of cold wind. As she walks the distance to the Grotto, a small crowd builds behind her. It's as if there's a radar screen, a network, something uncanny, that the people of Lourdes know her movements so early in the morning. They follow behind her. She is oblivious to everything but the direction in which she walks.

At the Grotto, there is already a small crowd of believers assembled. Word has gone quickly from door to door in the small village. Soon lights go on in the homes, and people file out, half dressed, rushing to the Grotto. Bernadette sees, as she arrives, that Our Lady is waiting for her. She runs to her special spot, where she kneels. Her aunt passes her a candle, which she takes unconsciously. The winds stop suddenly. She is blanketed by the warmth of the vision. Bernadette goes into a trance. This is the deepest ecstasy she will ever experience. As in previous apparitions, she gets up at times and walks deep within the grotto, talks very seriously with the Lady, and returns to her spot. This happens a few times.

Bernadette tells us that in this apparition, she asks the Lady to identify herself three times. The Lady smiles. The child pictures Cure Peyramale, shouting out his demand that the Lady tell Bernadette who she is. Bernadette tries a fourth time.

In Bernadette's own words,

"Aquero (the Lady) drew apart her clasped hands, and let

both her arms hang down. Then she put her hands together again at the level of her breast, lifted her eyes towards Heaven, and said

'I am the Immaculate Conception'"

The sky opened up. The clouds disappeared, and the Heavenly Hosts of Angels shone as they had on that Blessed Day in Bethlehem. Choirs of Angels sang in praise of the Glory of God. A beam of light shot down from Heaven to the alcove, surrounding the magnificent creation God had made. Cherubim and Seraphim floated down and positioned themselves around Mary. A soft breeze enveloped the child and the Lady. Bernadette could feel the tingly flush of warmth that emanated from Our Lady.

The cycle was complete. A miracle that had occurred before the beginning of time, the Immaculate Conception of Mary, passed down through the years as tradition, proclaimed on earth by Pope Pius IX in 1854, was confirmed by Heaven in 1858 in this little grotto nestled deep in the Pyrenees, in a hamlet of no consequence, to this chosen saint, who had no idea what the words of the Lady meant.

My Mary is so splendid. Her unpredictability is so predictable. She has such a great heart. She loves her priests so much. She had to give this priest, Pope Pius IX, the courage of his convictions. She stood behind him and fortified him. She loved this little girl so much, she created a bond between them so strong it would support Bernadette the rest of her life.

We're told in the annals of the history of the Apparitions of Mary to Bernadette at Lourdes, that Our Lady appeared two more times at the Grotto of Massabiele, on April 7, and again on the Feast of Our Lady of Mt. Carmel, July 16th. Knowing my Mary the way I do, I have to believe that she was always with Bernadette, both physically and spiritually. I can't accept that they were ever separated again. But as John the Baptist said before her, *Bernadette decreased while Our Lady and the shrine at Lourdes increased.*

The message went out to all the world, and has never stopped. A local stonemason, Louis Bouriette, had become blind in one eye, some years before the time of the apparitions. He had been present on the day when Mary asked Bernadette to wash her face and drink from the spring that didn't exist. Bouriette never shared with anyone else, but a *feeling* overcame him, that he should put the water from the spring on his eye. Secretly, he had his daughter go down to the Grotto, and take a pack of mud from the area where Bernadette had dug. He didn't tell the child why he wanted it. She went dutifully to the Grotto, and brought back a mud pack to her father. He hid himself not only in a barn, but in a far corner of the barn, to avoid being seen by anyone.

He put the wet mud on his eye, and prayed to Our Lady. When he took the pack away, the grey cloud that had always covered the eye was gone. He opened the door of the barn, and was thrown back inside by the shock of light that penetrated his senses. He fell to his knees, crying. He could see!

Bouriette went back to the Grotto to get more mud. His vision was still foggy, but he was no longer blind. When he arrived, he saw that the area was no longer a mud spot. Water trickled from the mud. It was a spring. He called Antoine Nicolau, who in turn called some of the local millers. They all agreed that the Lady had truly performed a miracle. She had told Bernadette to drink from the Spring, and here was a spring. They worked through the night by torchlight. They dug out a big hole where Bernadette had dug. They made a wall around it with rocks. Then they followed the vein of the spring, opening it up to allow the water to flow freely. By the time they finished, there was a basin the size of a Baptismal Font.

Our Lady had a plan from the outset, which was beginning to unfold, first with Bernadette attempting to drink from the spring that wasn't there; then the cure of Bouriette's blindness, and his discovery of the spring. The heavenly design continued when Antoine Nicolau had the *idea* of channeling the water into a basin. The stage was set. Mary had put all the pieces into place. Now for the finale.

There was a young child of two, the Bouhourots child. He had been convulsive from birth. The parents could not afford medical care, and so they had Louise Soubirous apply hot packs on the child, and shake him when the convulsions were at their worst. On this particular day, the child was having such extreme convulsions, they feared he was dying. And on this particular day, Louise Soubirous was nowhere to be found.

The mother was in a state of panic that only mothers can identify with. The other ladies of the neighborhood tried to convince her that the child's death would be the kindest healing for all concerned. The young husband agreed; they could have more children. But a mother is a mother. She is like a mother lion, when her young are endangered. The only mother who could sympathize with Mrs. Bouhourots was the greatest Mother, Mary. She had the child's mother recall Bernadette trying to drink water from the Spring. It became an obsession. The woman could not get it out of her consciousness. She didn't know why. She couldn't understand the significance. But it was there before her.

She stood, watching her son dying before her eyes. Finally, when she couldn't take it anymore, she wrapped the child in a blanket, and ran for all she was worth down to the grotto, closely followed by her friends who were sure she had lost her senses. The mother plunged the child into the freezing March water of the spring. By this time, he was emitting the death rattle. The mother cried out to Our Lady, *"Accept him, or give him back to me, O Virgin"*. She kept the child in the water for 15 minutes. She fought off the neighbors and friends who had gathered around the basin. They thought she was killing the boy. She could feel the presence of Mary beside her, crying with her. Then, when she felt he had been in the water long enough, she wrapped him in the blanket and brought him home. The convulsions had stopped. The child slept the whole next day. When he awoke, he sat up for the first time in his life and laughed. The Miracle of The Baths Had Begun.

For the first 50 years, the cures and miracles were attributed mainly to immersion into the miraculous baths. But Our Lady's plan was not yet finished. When organized pilgrimages began to go to Lourdes, a custom was initiated, called **THE PROCESSION OF THE BLESSING OF THE SICK**, in which a procession began from the Grotto of Massabiele, all the way around the grounds of Lourdes, down to the front of the Basilica of the Rosary. The sick were lined up in front of the Basilica. The very last person in the Procession was **JESUS**, in the Blessed Sacrament. As the celebrant faced the people from the front of the Basilica, and raised the King of the World in the monstrance, cries could be heard from various parts of the shrine. Litters pushed through the crowds, moving very quickly to the hospitals. Miracles had occurred! Those of us who have a great devotion to, and faith in the power of the Eucharist, call these, **MIRACLES OF THE EUCHARIST AT LOURDES**. Today, the people at Lourdes attribute half the cures to the Miraculous Baths, and half to the Miracle of the Eucharist in the Procession of the Sick.

There are special places in Lourdes for each pilgrim who goes there. Many spend most of their time at the Grotto, praying to Our Lady. Others go to the Blessed Sacrament Chapel, just below the Basilica of the Immaculate Conception. Our Lord Jesus is always there in the Blessed Sacrament, loving, blessing, helping, healing. Mary is alive and well and living in Lourdes. It is one of the major shrines in the world. It is a place of great hope, and great joy. There is a magic in Lourdes that has never left since my Lady visited here for the first time in 1858.

Bernadette left Lourdes in 1866 for the Convent of St. Gildard in Nevers, France, 600 miles to the north of Lourdes, and 300 miles south of Paris. The prediction of Mary to Bernadette on February 18, 1858, followed her all her life. *"I cannot promise you happiness in this world, but in the next."* Victor Hugo, a

French novelist and playwright of the 19th Century summed it up well. He said Our Lady asked Bernadette to **EAT BITTER HERBS AND DRINK MUDDY WATER.** This was to be the pattern of Bernadette's life. She bore it well not only during the time of the Apparitions, but also for the 13 years she spent in the Convent of St. Gildard in Nevers. During her life in the convent, she was tortured by one of the sisters.

Mother Marie Therese Vauzou was her Novice Mistress, and later her Mother Superior. During Bernadette's Canonization Process, it was determined that the superior took great pleasure in degrading the little saint in front of all the sisters. She is quoted to have told her superiors, as well as priests who visited the convent, and just about anybody who asked, what her feelings were towards Bernadette. Some of her statments were,

"OH, SHE WAS A LITTLE PEASANT GIRL. . . . IF THE HOLY VIRGIN WANTED TO APPEAR SOMEWHERE ON EARTH, WHY WOULD SHE CHOOSE A COMMON, ILLITERATE PEASANT INSTEAD OF SOME VIRTUOUS AND WELL INSTRUCTED NUN?"

"I DO NOT UNDERSTAND WHY THE HOLY VIRGIN SHOULD REVEAL HERSELF TO BERNADETTE. THERE ARE SO MANY OTHER SOULS MORE LOFTY AND MORE DELICATE. REALLY!"

Franz Werfel, the author of THE SONG OF BERNA-DETTE, speaks of a face to face encounter between the two, in which the older superior spews her hate and anger for the child. To paraphrase his words, Mother Vauzou says to Bernadette *"Who are you that the Blessed Virgin should appear to you? I've given up my whole life for the Church. Why didn't she come to me?"*

Bernadette's illness became worse during her years in Nevers. Many of her sister nuns suggested she go to the baths at Lourdes. Bernadette's reply was. . . . . *"I have made the sacrifice of never seeing Lourdes again. I have only one ambition, that of seeing the Blessed Virgin glorified and loved."*

Bernadette died in 1879. Mother Vauzou refused permission for the process of canonization to be initiated during her lifetime.

But Our Lady would have her way. As soon as the mother superior died, the cause for canonization was opened. Bernadette was officially made a member of the illustrious Communion of Saints in 1933, less than 60 years after her death. In addition, the body of Bernadette has never decomposed. When we bring our pilgrims to the Chapel of the Saint at the convent of St. Gildard in Nevers, they cannot believe that they are looking at the actual body of the little saint. After the initial shock, they agree that St. Bernadette is more beautiful today than the day she died.

There is a small book available at Nevers, written in many languages, called THE BODY OF SAINT BERNADETTE, by Fr. Andre Ravier. It is a compilation of documents in the Archives of the Convent of St. Gildard, of the Diocese and the City of Nevers. It authenticates that her body was never embalmed or preserved in any way, nor did it contain chemicals which could cause natural preservation.

The officials of the Church in Lourdes have tried to bring the body of Bernadette back to the land of her birth. But her promise not to go back, not to let anything detract from the glory of Our Lady there, has been kept all these years.

Mary is a good friend. She is faithful and loyal to those who love her. Bernadette gave up her life at Lourdes, for Mary, her Aquero. She was rewarded for that, or perhaps it is we who have been rewarded. When I kneel at the altar rail at Nevers, less than ten feet away from the beautiful shepherdess of Lourdes, I think she's sleeping. I feel a closeness, a kinship with St. Bernadette. She is truly the unsung heroine of Lourdes.

While at the Convent of St. Gildard, Bernadette was once asked by a young child "Sister, have you seen the Virgin Mary? Was she very beautiful?" Bernadette's answer was

"OH! SO BEAUTIFUL THAT WHEN ONE SEES HER ONCE, HE LONGS TO DIE TO SEE HER AGAIN!"

**Go and wash yourself in
the fountain**
The Healing Baths at
Lourdes

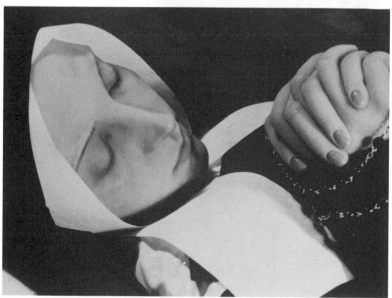

I cannot promise you happiness in this world, but the next
The Incorrupt Body of St. Bernadette—Nevers, France

St. Bernadette Soubirous at the time of the Apparitions
Lourdes, France

Candlelight Procession every night at Lourdes, France

Procession of Blessing of Sick Eucharistic Miracle at Lourdes, France

Mary Comes to Pontmain, France— 1871
My Son Allows Himself to Be Touched

Jesus loves His Mother so much. He gives her great power. But why not? Mary, the perfect Mother, never asks anything for herself, not even recognition. Everything is for her Son. She, on the other hand, loves *us* so much, she always comes to us, to help us, to guide us, to plead with us, to plead for us.

We have one complaint, however. She picks the most out of the way places to visit us. If it's not a high mountain place, like La Salette, where you take your life in your hands to get up there, it's a village in the middle of nowhere, where there are no decent roads as in the instance of Fatima, and no directions, as at Medjugorje, and for our purposes in this apparition, Pontmain, France.

Pontmain is not even a town, but a village. It's not on the map. No one in the United States talks about it, because no one knows where it is. Yet, it's a very special place, very out of the way, but so wonderfully out of the way that it remains untouched. It's very much like Loreto, Italy, in that it's not on the main circuit of pilgrimage shrines. There is no reason why we were able to

106

find this place, except that Our Lady had determined that she wanted us to go there, so that we could spread her message at Pontmain to the world.

The rest of the world may never have heard of this place, but to the people of the village, and the surrounding towns, Pontmain is the place where everything happens. The presence of Our Lady in this shrine is very strong, as in all the small shrines we have visited. (Beauraing, Banneux, Loreto) Everything centers around the Basilica of *Our Lady of Hope* in Pontmain. All the Weddings, Baptisms, First Holy Communions, Confirmations, everything is celebrated at this Church. The first time we were there, on a Saturday in May, 1977, there were three different First Holy Communion ceremonies, for three different groups, from three different schools in Brittany.

Pontmain is a small village on the borderline between the Normandy and Brittany sections of France. It is very small, situated between Fougeres and Mont St. Michel, which is on the Normandy Coast. The first time we visited Our Lady of Hope, in the summer, offshore breezes from the English Channel provided refreshing cool air to the area, as a relief from the summer heat. But when we returned in the winter, the soft, cool breezes had turned to cold, howling winds, bringing icy weather to the entire area, and through our insulated jackets. The local inhabitants choose to stay indoors by the fireplace, during these times, to protect themselves from being chilled to the bone by the gusty winds.

The winter of 1871 was such a time. January was an especially brutal time for man and beast. Those who could avoid it, did not venture out into the weather. But unfortunately, not everybody could stay at home.

France was still going through its period of chastisement. Those in high places in the government had not heeded the pleadings of Our Lady at the Rue du Bac in Paris, or La Salette, or more recently to the little shepherdess, Bernadette Soubirous in Lourdes. They were engaged in a war with the infamous Bismarck, and his mighty Prussian troops. The French had been so involved in killing their own, and attacking helpless nuns and priests, they didn't know how to handle a *real enemy*. Prussia was able to march through France with ease. Paris had been captured, and enemy troops were working their way through Le Mans towards the coast. Bismarck had known all the strengths and weaknesses of his adversaries. He anticipated their every move, and countered with a shrewder one. There was only one force he had not counted on. How could he? This one enemy was beyond his comprehension. He had no way of knowing her power; he didn't know her. He was taking on the **Mother of God**.

The little people, the common folk, flocked to their churches, to the shrines of the Rue du Bac, La Salette, and Lourdes. They prayed, fearful that it was too little too late, but hopeful, knowing that Our Lady was a merciful Mother, that their prayers would not fall on deaf ears. Rosaries, stations of the cross, confessions, fasting, communions, all were offered up to their Heavenly Mother in a desperate plea for help.

We can just picture in our mind's eye, millions of angels carrying all these prayers and offerings up from the earth and laying them at the feet of their Queen. They had to run out of room in Heaven for all the prayers and petitions offered up. At one point, Mary's beautiful eyes might have looked out over the land she had tried so hard to protect, that she had loved so much. We can imagine a sadness coming over her sparkling eyes. Perhaps a tear slipped down her velvety cheek, and descended to the earth; when it landed, an explosion of energy lit up the entire sky. It happened on January 11, 1871. Scientists called it an Aurora Borealis. The faithful called it **MARY TO THE RESCUE**.

On earth, the residents of Pontmain were trying to continue their lives as if all were well. Normally, these villagers wouldn't be affected by the goings on in the center of the country. After all, they were just farmers. But this war had hit everyone. Many of the young men of Pontmain had answered the call to duty. They were somewhere in the war zone, but no one knew where, or how they were. Stories of the massacres the French were suffering at

**But pray, my children
God will soon answer
your prayers**
Our Lady's Apparition
Pontmain, France

A beautiful Lady was suspended above Guidecoq's barn—
Pontmain, France

the hands of their enemies, found their way back to the town. Wagons, filled with wounded, moved along the main roads in disaster proportions. In addition, the Prussian troops had gotten to Laval, a town extremely close to Pontmain.

On the evening of January 17, the men of the Barbedette family were working in their barn. Dinner would be ready soon, but they wanted to get finished with their chores before going inside. It had begun to snow lightly, not like the other days. The winds had died down. The pure white powder fell gently, as if it had come directly from Heaven. Monsieur Barbedette, known as Bierot, his sons Eugene 12 years old, and Joseph, aged 10, were all working side by side. It was about 6 in the evening. Supper would be ready soon. They wanted to get their work done before they were called in to eat. In the recesses of their minds was concern over the third Barbedette son, Auguste, who was away fighting the war. The father felt that by working, he could take his mind off his fears; but it was not happening. Not an especially religious man, he found himself praying his rosary under his breath. A neighbor woman, Jean Detais, came by with rumors about the war situation, and possible news about the son Auguste.

Eugene could not get over how gently the snow had fallen outside. He couldn't hear a sound. There was not the slightest breeze blowing, much less the gailstorm winds that had buffeted the area earlier that day. He walked to the door of the barn. He didn't want to hear any bad news about Auguste. He thought that by walking away from it, by not listening to Jean Detais, he could prevent it from happening. The night cold air was refreshing. He looked outside. The snow had stopped. He remarked to himself how unusual it was that the sky was so full of stars, though there was no moon that night. He looked around him. He was immediately frozen to the spot.

Above neighbor Augustin Guidecog's house, about twenty five feet in the air, **A BEAUTIFUL LADY WAS SUSPENDED IN THE AIR**, her arms outstretched. She was looking at him, and smiling. He had never seen anything like her in his life. Her eyes gleamed like stars. Her teeth were pearl white. They sparkled as she smiled at him. To the 12 year old Eugene, she was a lady, but she appeared to be about 18 to 20 years old. She wore blue, but dark blue, darker than the sky. Her dress was long and loose; her sleeves flowed, and on her collar was a band of gold. There was a black veil on her head, topped by a gold cap which resembled a crown. A thin red band ran across the cap. She wore blue slippers tied with gold ribbons.

The neighbor woman noticed the boy standing in a daze at the door. He was staring up into the sky. She went over to him to see what was the matter. He asked her to look up in the sky and tell him what she saw.

"I see nothing." she answered.

Eugene looked at her incredulously. How could she *not* see a lady suspended in air. It was the most unusual sight he had ever seen, and she couldn't see it. He called his father and brother to look up at the sky. Bierot could not see anything, but young Joseph's expression turned to joy as he looked up above Guidecoq's barn.

"I see a beautiful lady". he exclaimed. He proceeded to describe the scene in detail, just as Eugene had seen it.

The father, Bierot, ordered the boys back into the barn to finish their work. He told Jean Detais, the neighbor, not to mention what they had said to anyone. She promised that she would not. The boys returned to the barn. Bierot took one last look before he closed the barn door. What could it be that they had seen? There was nothing unusual in the sky. The stars were brighter than he remembered seeing them before, but that was probably because the wind had blown all the clouds away.

The spark of a thought kept gnawing away at the back of his mind. He had been working with the boys all day. Their behavior had been normal. They hadn't acted silly. As a matter of fact, there had been a serious tone to the day. They were all worried about the well-being of Auguste. It would have been out of character for them to take a sudden turn to silliness, as he had first attributed their claim about a lady in the sky. Then, he thought, they didn't see the lady at the same time. First Eugene saw her, and then Joseph. They both described her in the same way. Bierot took one last look in the sky, shrugged his shoulder, and went back to work.

The boys could not get the beautiful lady out of their minds. Her gaze warmed them, as if she had covered them with her mantle. The eyes, those cobalt blue eyes that pierced them, the sparkling teeth, the delicate features of her face, formed an indelible impression on their mind. They worked quickly, which was not like them at all. When they had finished their work, they raced each other to the barn door. They pushed it open, and looked out. She was still there. She was still smiling at them. She was radiant.

Bierot called his wife; maybe she would see something. This was driving him crazy. Mrs. Barbedette came to the barn door. She looked up, but saw nothing. Her husband was somewhat relieved. However, as a precaution, just in case it was a vision from Heaven, they all knelt down to say five Pater Nosters and five Ave Marias. Then they went into the house for supper.

The boys wolfed their food down, so that they could run back outside to see if the Lady was still there. As soon as the last mouthful had been finished, they ran outside the door again. She was still there. The mother asked them to describe how tall she was.

"She's about the same size as Sister Vitaline."

This gave the mother an inspiration. She called the nun, asked her to look up into the sky, to see if she could see anything. Sr. Vitaline could not. The boys were becoming frustrated.

"How can you not see it?" Eugene cried out. "She is so brilliant. Can you see a triangle of bright stars?"

Everyone agreed that they could see three bright stars, which they had never seen before, and never saw again, except for that night.

"Well, the top of the triangle is where her head is, and the two stars at the bottom are at a level with her shoulders. Can you see that?"

No one but Eugene and Joseph could see the lady.

Mrs. Barbedette had heard the stories which had made their way up from the south of France about the two children from La Salette, and the little girl at Lourdes, who had claimed to have seen the Blessed Virgin. Perhaps this was the same, and only children could see the apparition. She took the nun with her, and together, they went back to Sr. Vitaline's school.

There were three children there. The nun asked them to come along with her and Mrs. Barbedette, to see if they could make out anything unusual in the sky. As they walked towards the home of the Barbedette's, one of the children, Francoise Richer, age 11, pointed up into the sky.

"There's something very bright above Monsieur Guidecoq's barn", she exclaimed. Mrs. Barbedette and the nun looked at each other.

As they got closer, both Francoise and a younger girl, Jean-Marie Lebosse, age 9, cried out, "Oh, the beautiful lady, with the blue dress and the golden stars". No one had said anything to these two. They had no idea of what they were supposed to be looking for. They had not spoken to the Barbedette boys as yet. But they saw the same thing that Eugene and Joseph had seen. The third child, however, saw nothing.

Word of the event spread through the little village rapidly. Soon, just about every resident of Pontmain was at the Barbedette barn, looking up into the clear winter sky, praying for a glimpse of the Lady.

She became enclosed in a blue, almond shaped frame, from which protruded four candles, two at the level of her neck, and two at the level of her knees. On her heart, a tiny red cross appeared.

The gathering took on the semblance of organization as the local priest, Fr. Guerin came upon the scene. The children reported that the expression on the face of the Lady had fallen into sadness. The priest ordered everyone on their knees in prayer. They began to recite the Rosary, the favorite prayer of Mary. The first of 5 changes began to take place.

As she listened to the earnest prayers of the people for peace, and for the safe return of their children, the visionaries saw her begin to swell in size. She grew to almost double her original size. The triangle of stars grew with her, but the rest of the stars made way for the magnificent visitor, queen of all the stars in the heavens. Some of the stars became enmeshed in her gown, while others positioned themselves at her feet.

A Sister Marie-Edouard, who was well known as a leader, began to lead the people in singing **THE MAGNIFICAT**. The children shouted out as a new development took place. A banner formed at the feet of the Lady, between her and the top of the barn. It was about the size of the roof of the barn, and as they sang, a word was formed on the top of the banner. It was **MAIS**, which means "**BUT**". As the hymn came to the end, the sentence was formed.

MAIS, PRIEZ MES ENFANTS
BUT PRAY, MY CHIILDREN

The children called out the sentence as it appeared. A shout of joy was sounded among the people. They began to pray the Litany of Mary. Another sentence appeared.

DIEU VOUS EXAUCURA EN PEU DE TEMPS
GOD WILL SOON ANSWER YOUR PRAYERS

As the children read out this sentence, the people began to weep tears of joy. It is Mary. She's there to help them. Praise Jesus! He allowed her to come again. As the assemblage wept and praised God and His magnificent mother, the Lady began laughing. The children shouted, "Look, she's laughing. . . . .Look, she's laughing!!" Soon, the people were affected by the laughter of the Lady. Everyone laughed with her.

They began to sing another hymn to Our Lady. Under the first sentence, a much larger letter began to be formed. It came to them in three stages. The first was

MON FILS—MY SON

It stayed like this until they began to sing the Salve Regina, at which point the next two words were formed.

SE LAISSE—ALLOWS HIMSELF

At the very end of the Salve Regina, the last word of the sentence was formed.

TOUCHER—TO BE TOUCHED

The entire sentence was

MON FILS SE LAISSE TOUCHER
MY SON ALLOWS HIMSELF TO BE TOUCHED

Another translation of the sentence is

MY SON IS WILLING TO HEAR YOU

In a small village in the middle of nowhere, at the very darkest hour, Mary, the giving Mary, the loving Mary, began a precedent which has stayed with us from that time until this. We can change His mind through His Mother. Tribulation and chastisement can be lessened, minimized, and very possibly done away with, through the intercession of the beautiful Lady who was given to us at the foot of the Cross.

They began to sing a hymn to Our Lady of Hope.

Mother of Hope
Whose name is so sweet
Protect our land of France
Pray, pray for us.

As the Lady heard this hymn, she raised her hands and moved her fingers in time with the hymn. The children shared this with the congregation. Everybody began to clap their hands in joy. The children's little voices cried out,

"Oh! She's lovely! She's lovely!"

In the midst of the hope and joy the townspeople felt, the vision changed again. A large red cross appeared in her hands, with the body of Her Son on it. At the top of the cross was a white stick, on which the words JESUS CHRIST appeared. Her face became deeply sad. Her lips quivered. She looked down at the figure on the Cross.

It was very obvious what Mary was saying to the people with this gesture. "I have given you this gift. I have promised you that your prayers would be answered. Do not forget my Son. Look at the pain and sadness on my face. It was put there by you. I love you unconditionally, to the point of having My Son change His Mind. Because of me, He allows Himself to be touched. Do not forget Him, or what He did for you. Don't give Him any more pain."

The young Barbedette boy, Joseph, recounted his feelings at that time.

"Her face was marked with a deep sorrow . . . the trembling of her lips at the corners of her mouth showed deep feeling . . . But no tears ran down her cheeks . . .

A few months later I saw my own mother overwhelmed with grief when my father died. One knows how such a sight can affect the heart of a child. Nevertheless, I remember thinking that my mother's sorrow was **nothing in comparison with that of the Blessed Virgin**, which came naturally to mind. It was truly the Mother of Jesus at the foot of her Son's cross."

From the bottom of the oval, where the stars had lined up at the feet of Our Lady, one little star began to move up towards a candle, lighting each of the four candles. Her sparkling eyes, happy again, followed the star as it went from candle to candle. Her hands returned to their original downward position. Everybody prayed.

At a given point, the group began to pray the evening prayers. It was about 8:30 at night. A large white veil appeared at the feet of Our Lady. Slowly, it ascended, covering her as it climbed up. Within a short time, it covered all of her except her face. It stopped for a beat, as she looked down at her children with so much love. Then it moved up over her face. to her crown, where it stopped. The crown could be seen for a moment, and then, it, too, vanished. It was 9 o'clock. She had been with them for three hours.

The Lady, that special Lady, had come down from Heaven to *give hope* to her children. From the description of the children, there is nothing to compare with the beauty of this Queen. We truly believe if we'd have asked any of them, Joseph, for instance, 60 years later, at the end of his life, what the Lady looked like, he would have been able to give us a perfect description. It never left him. She never left him.

She also gave them and us, an insight which has been repeated many times. *My Son allows Himself to be touched.* He will change His Mind if we change our ways. This message was repeated in Fatima in 1917, in Banneux in 1933, and most recently, in Medjugorje in 1981. His love is unconditional, but His intervention on our behalf is not. An action is required on our part. If we're willing to make the effort, He will move Heaven and earth for us, as in the instance of Pontmain. The actions on the part of the Prussian Army, as a result of this Heavenly visit, are unexplainable in human terms.

There was an entry made in the log of the Prussian Army for January 18, 1871. They had entered Laval, a short distance from Pontmain. The army was ordered to stop their advance, turn around and return to Paris. There was no reason given; the order was executed. The troops left the area. Within ten days, the war was over. An armistice was signed. All the soldiers from the little village of Pontmain were returned unharmed. The swift action of the Lord in honor of the request of His Mother, was realized.

Of the four children, the two boys, Joseph and Eugene Barbedette became priests. Francoise Richer spent her life as an assistant teacher. In her later years, she became the housekeeper for Eugene. Jean-Marie Lebosse joined the Sisters of The Holy Family in Bordeaux. There was much conflict in her life. At one point, she had great doubts as to whether she actually saw what she claimed she had. Our Lady won out, though. The apparition was authenticated by the local bishop on February 2, 1872, just a little over a year after Mary had come to Pontmain.

Of all Our Lady's apparitions, this one is our favorite, in that the Message is one of Great Hope, of Mercy. This is the Mary we know, the Mary of Hope. This is the Jesus we know, the One who wants to be touched, who wants to change His mind.

My Son Allows Himself to Be Touched

Our Protestant brothers and sisters reject the intercession of our sweet mother Mary. They must not know anything about the great love she has for her children. When Jesus gave us to her, and her to us, at the crucifixion, she took the mandate seriously. Have we taken it seriously? Mary loves us unconditionally. There's nothing she won't do for us, no way in which she won't help us. Can we say the same?

Knock, 1879: Listen With Your Heart

Ireland is a magical land, famous for its shamrocks and harps, leprechauns, shillelaghs, and green eyed coleens with skin as white as milk. It is called the Emerald Isle, and the national color is green; Ireland is lush green, almost tropical in certain areas. The national drink is Guinness, although he's a "damned Protestant". Ireland is not only a country; it's a state of mind, a way of life.

We think of the Irish people as being quite fanciful, partly because of Barry Fitzgerald, who gave us our unofficial description of what an Irishman should be, especially an Irish Pastor in the 1940's, when he made the film with Bing Crosby, **"GOING MY WAY"**. We find ourselves completely beguiled by their marvelous brogues, their limericks and folk songs, their grand tales of days gone by.

However, we find that the history of this dear little country is anything but gay. These people are a contradiction of their background. Theirs has been a tale of domination and persecution from the hands of their nearest neighbor, and all in the name of Jesus. Their major problems began when Henry VIII broke from the Church of Rome, and formed the Church of England, just so he could divorce his wife. Ireland would not go along with the disgrace of Henry, and the persecution began.

The situation was at its worst when the Penal Laws were instituted in 1691. These laws were designed to destroy Catholicism in Ireland. Those who remained loyal to the Catholic Church were denied their basic rights as citizens in an effort to keep them ignorant and impoverished. Those who chose to go over to the Protestant camp were rewarded, and lived the good life. Most Irishmen remained loyal to the Church. Their faith and their loyalty, in the face of great persecution, has been the mainstay of their existence during the dark years.

There is a beautiful Church in Dublin, called *"The Church of Adam and Eve"*. During the days of persecution, when it was illegal to practise their religion, the Church of Adam and Eve was a pub, called the Adam and Eve Pub. Dubliners frequented this pub by the droves, especially on Sunday. Irishmen going into a pub seemed a natural enough thing to the police, so they never questioned the crowds that went into the bar. The people walked in the front door of the Adam and Eve Pub, and out the back door, to an *underground Church*. Mass was celebrated under the guise of bringing the family to the local pub. It's very possible that after the Mass, they might have stopped off for a pint; as long as they were there, it would be a sin to waste the visit. They took their lives in their hands by disobeying the law in this way. But it was so important to these beautiful people, they took the chance, knowing He would protect them.

Although Ireland is a lush country, it is also very rocky. Many of the counties had very little farmable land, and yet agriculture was their main industry. The Great Potato Famine of 1845 almost dealt a death sentence to these people of faith. Between the economic situation and the persecution, many of them had to leave their homeland. They went to the New World, America, and today, there are more Irishmen, or rather people of Irish descent in the United States than in Ireland. A joke among Irishmen is that Boston should be made capital of Ireland, because there are more Irishmen living in that city than in all of Ireland.

County Mayo was one of the poorest areas in Ireland. The

land was completely rocky. Those who had left the country were not aware of it, but they made it more difficult for those who remained. The work became harder, because there were fewer people to do it. The strength of solidarity was lost with the mass exodus. The morale of those who remained was very low. With the ensuing famines of 1847, 1877, 1878 and 1879, the people were devastated. All they had to hold onto was their love of their country, and their Faith. They held onto both, with a passion.

It's necessary to give you this background to make you aware of what the Ireland of 1879 was like. We have to believe that Our Lord Jesus and Our Lady looked with great compassion on their faithful children in Ireland. The entire country was a giant *Biblical Job* holding onto, remaining faithful to, Jesus and Mary in the face of impossible odds.

August 21, 1879 was a rainy day in County Mayo, and particularly in the little village of Knock. The morning had given hope of a fair day; but as the afternoon progressed, the dark rain-clouds gathered over the little hamlet. Winds from the east whipped up, darting back and forth, bristling through the meadows and fields. The rains began, and hammered down on the little area.

We believe the preparations made in Heaven for this glorious day, 6 days after the Feast of the Assumption, were to give honor and recognition to the faithful children of Ireland. Mary must have looked down on this land from up above and decided that the poorest, most deprived area she could find was the windswept, rock-filled land of Knock. We have to think that the howling wind and black rain clouds were Satan's way of trying to prevent the visit from happening. By stirring up the weather, thus making it so miserable, no one would be able to go out to see her. We can be sure he was having a fit, in anticipation of Our Lady's visit to earth. She has always been his greatest enemy. He goes into a rage at the mere mention of her name.

She chose the side of a church, the village church in Knock. After the rains had started, one Margaret Beirne went over to lock up the church for the night. She noticed a bright light around the back of the church, and looked to see what was there. She saw what she thought were statues of Our Lady, St. Joseph, and a Bishop, standing alongside a new altar, on top of which was a statue of a Lamb with a Cross. Margaret didn't pay too much attention to it; she left the Church, and went home, not saying a word to anyone about it.

Satan must have been whooping it up in Hell. If this girl didn't tell anyone, no one would know about Our Lady's visit, and consequently, no one would come. His plan might have worked. Even the priest's housekeeper, Mary McLoughlin, passed by and noticed the apparition, but also thought they were statues. She went to the Bierne's home for a visit. So far so good for Satan.

But at 8 o'clock or thereabouts, when Mary McLoughlin decided to go home, the older Bierne girl, Mary, decided to walk with her *in the rain*. So here we have two Marys, walking in the rain past the church again. When they passed the apparition, Mary McLoughlin casually mentioned that the pastor must have bought some new statues in Dublin. But the other Mary, more inquisitive, decided to take a closer look. She jumped back with a start. *"They're not statues. They're moving. It's the Blessed Virgin!"* The two women didn't know what to do. Mary Bierne ran home to tell her mother and brother.

Rain or no, the people flocked to the church. Fourteen people in all came to witness the gift of Our Lady's presence on that brutal night. Their combined description of what they saw is as follows:

The entire back wall of the church was bathed in a brilliant light, which could be seen from quite a distance away. As they looked at the scene, everything was raised about two feet off the ground. There was an altar, on the top of which stood a Lamb with a Cross. The altar and the Lamb were surrounded by Angels, hovering above.

To the left of the Altar were three figures. On the left was

Mary speaks to the hearts of her people
Our Lady as she appeared in Knock, Ireland

St. Joseph; in the middle was Our Lady; to the right, closest to the Altar was St. John the Evangelist, his right hand raised, a book in his left. Our Lady was life sized. The other two were smaller.

Mary was lovely. She wore a white gown and sash. A veil flowed from the back of her head to her feet. On top of her head, above the veil, was a gold crown. Between the crown and the edge of the veil was a gold rose. She looked up towards heaven in prayer; her hands were raised to her shoulders, pointed inwards. She was almost iridescent.

At first, no one dared go very close to the images. They stood or knelt at a distance in the rain, becoming soaked, but not caring. One of the visionaries, fourteen year old Patrick Hill, gathered up courage to venture near to the apparition. He was able to get close enough to give a good description of what he saw. He could make out Our Lady's eyes, the pupils as well as the iris. He could see the smooth texture of her milky skin. He mentioned that St. Joseph's beard was grey. His head was bent slightly. He also saw lines on the pages of the book that St. John held. He reported that the three figures were full bodied, three dimensional, rather than images projected on the wall. He testified that they were a few feet out from the wall of the Church; but as he got too close, the images moved back, away from him. All the witnesses verified that the three figures moved during the hour and a half that they knelt before them. Patrick Hill also mentioned that he saw the wings of the angels fluttering.

Possibly because Patrick Hill had ventured so closely, and had not been struck dead by lightning, a lady gathered up enough courage to reach out to embrace Our Lady's feet. Mary moved back, and the woman felt nothing. All the witnesses stated that, although it was raining heavily, and the wind was blowing wildly, the ground under the images never became wet, nor did the side of the church where they appeared.

Judith Campbell was one of the visionaries. She had been adoring Our Lady and her heavenly entourage. She went back to her house at about 9 pm to see how her sickly mother was feeling.

Judith found her mother lying on the floor of the house. She thought the ailing woman had died, trying to go to the church. At about 9:30, all the people who were venerating the apparition were called to the house of Mrs. Campbell. They left the scene of the apparition, and ran to the Campbell house. However, when they arrived, they found that she was not dead, but had swooned. They stayed with her for a few minutes, then rushed back to the church. When they got there, the lights and images were gone. The apparition was over. They looked at one another. They didn't say much; they went to their homes.

The following day, the news had spread all over the area. A farmer, Patrick Walsh, claimed to have seen the great light from a distance. He didn't come to the church, but the next day, when he heard what had happened, he related what he had seen. His testimony was very important during the investigation, because it ruled out the theory of Mass Hysteria or Hypnotism. He had been nearly a mile away from the scene when he had seen the light.

Mother Mary never said a word. She didn't look at them. This caused many problems during the investigations which followed the apparition. It just didn't make sense for Our Lady to come, spend 3 hours with her people, and never acknowledge their presence in any way. It was very frustrating, to say the least. But again, we're thinking in human terms, not divine. We're trying to demand that Mary conform to our standards, rather than we to hers. We should be down on our knees in thanksgiving for *any* gesture she makes towards us. Indeed, her faithful people of Ireland did just that.

The Church has not yet officially approved the apparition of Our Lady at Knock. But Our Lady's visit has been venerated so sincerely by so many of our popes, we have to believe that officially or unofficially, Mary was there. It has also become a national shrine in Ireland. Perhaps the greatest endorsement of our Lady's visit to Knock, Ireland, came from His Holiness, Pope John Paul II in 1979, for the Centenary. He came as a pilgrim to Knock. He celebrated Mass in the Basilica, anointed the sick, and went to the Shrine to pray. He also presented to Knock Shrine a gold rose, in commemoration of the gold rose that Mary wore during her apparition.

The fact that Mary didn't say anything during her apparition was a problem in terms of authentication. But in terms of what *She may have been saying to the people of Ireland,* the door is wide open. There were no tears, as at La Salette. There were no recriminations, as at Lourdes, Fatima, Banneux and Medjugorje. Mary didn't impress on them the need for prayer, fasting and penance. In this, isn't it possible that she recognized that their entire lives were prayer, fasting and penance? Weren't they the suffering servants of Christ? Perhaps she was acknowledging their suffering.

There was peace and serenity at Knock. There was an altar, on top of which was the Lamb of God, the perfect sacrifice for remission of our sins, and the Cross. We believe very strongly that this symbol, was in honor of her Blessed Son, Jesus, in the Mass, and in the Eucharist. In the Mass, we reenact, in memory of Him, the Last Supper, Calvary, and the Resurrection. We are given the Gift, the ongoing gift of the Body and Blood of Christ, for our nourishment and salvation. In the apparition at Knock, Mary, St. John, and St. Joseph were not the center of attention. They stood off to the side, while the Lamb of God, the Cross, and the Altar, captured our attention immediately. She always does this. From the days when Jesus and Mary were with us on earth, she always deferred to her Son. At all the Marian shrines in the world, she takes second place to Jesus. Knock was no different.

Another aspect of this apparition is that St. John and St. Joseph were with her. St. Joseph is Jesus' foster father. During the life of Our Dear Lord, St. Joseph was His mentor, His teacher. They had to have been very close. Then there is St. John, beloved of Jesus. While Peter was the right arm of Jesus, His strength on earth, St. John was His heart. If Jesus ever had a brother, it would have been John. It was to John that Jesus gave His Mother. It was to His Mother, through John, that Jesus gave us, the Church.

There have been reports in 1984–5–6 that Our Lady has appeared to different people in various parts of Ireland. At a little shrine devoted to Our Lady of Lourdes in Cappoquin, Waterford County, which we visited a year before the reported apparitions, Our Lady allegedly complained about the loss of faith that was being experienced by the people in Ireland. We are not going to attempt to speculate as to the veracity of these reports. We will say, however, that if they were true, they give more credence to the silent, approving apparition of Mary at Knock in 1879.

She was not upset with her Irish children in 1879. She was proud of them. She felt compassion for them. In the 100 years that have lapsed since that time, Satan has been able to accomplish something with a small box, containing a picture tube, that he was not able to accomplish with 300 years of Persecution. American television has come to Ireland, and not the best, but the worst. They are a beautiful people, for the most part. They are trying to hold on. They are still one of the few countries in the world where Divorce is outlawed.

Miracles began to take place at Knock as early as ten days after the Apparition. A young girl, Delia Gordon, had experienced deafness and pain in her left ear. While visiting the place of the Apparition, her mother put a small piece of cement from the wall of the church, into her ear. Afterward, during the Mass, Delia experienced an excruciating pain in her ear. It was followed by complete healing of her deafness; the pain never returned. She lived out her life in good health. When she died in 1930, in San Francisco, California, the same piece of cement which her mother had placed in her ear in 1879, was buried with her.

In A Centenary issue of the Miracle of Knock, by Fr. Tom Neary, 687 cures are chronicled from 1879 to 1880, the span of a year. Our Lady used the faith of the people and the cement or grouting from the back wall of the Church as a means of healing. This presented a slight problem to the Pastor of the Church. Every pilgrim who came to Knock wanted some of the gravel or cement. This meant that the walls would have to come tumbling down;

there was just so much material there. Wooden planks were put up, so that the cement could not be pulled off the walls, in an effort to save the Church from being ripped apart by zealous pilgrims.

From the days when Our Lord Jesus walked the earth, *spiritual* healings were more important than *physical* cures. He told the people *"Your sins are forgiven."* before He said *"Take up your mat and walk"*. The same applies to the healings at Knock. For every account of physical cures, there are twice as many reports of conversions, reconciliation, and return to the Church and the Sacraments. Our Lady was able to touch her children through this apparition. She wanted the lost sheep back, and back they came.

The people of Ireland had been waiting for hundreds of years for a sign. Knock became that sign. In a very short period of time, the floodgates were opened. Pilgrims poured into Knock by the thousands, and tens of thousands. At first they were from Ireland, but very quickly, the rest of the British Isles followed suit. Then Europe began to come, pilgrims from France, Italy, Germany, and finally, a pilgrim group carrying a large flag with the Stars and Stripes emblazoned on it from the United States. The world was paying tribute to Mary at this special place.

One has only to go to Knock Shrine to be aware of the devotion of the people of Ireland to Our Lord Jesus and His Mother Mary. Every parish in the country makes at least one Pilgrimage a year to this shrine. There is such reverence here! The great number of pilgrims outgrew the little shrine area in the original church, and in back of the church where Our Lady appeared to the people. A resplendent church was built to accommodate the pilgrims, which was later raised to the level of a Basilica.

There is a grand Mass every day, a healing Mass. All the sick are anointed at that time. There is never ending faith and hope at the Shrine. Our Lady never said a word to the visionaries at Knock, yet *they know* just what she wants here. Every day there is the Stations of the Cross. People can pray the Stations inside the main Basilica, or at the shorter Way of the Cross, between the old Church and the Basilica. There is **PERPETUAL ADORATION OF THE EUCHARIST** in a special Chapel, as well as monthly all night vigils. How were these dear people able to hear and act on the words of Our Lady if she said nothing to them? Why has Knock Shrine become a worldwide place of Pilgrimage, of healings and conversion?

The people Our Lady chose to gift with her presence at Knock were *simple* people. It's hard to believe that they could have made up such a story, and if they had, why didn't they embellish it with great conversations with Mary, as many other reported visionaries have claimed? One of the greatest hindrances to the authentication by the Church of the Apparition of Mary at Knock was that she said nothing. *But did she really say nothing?* Again, we find ourselves limiting my dear Lady to human equation. The only means of communication we know are sounds that go from the mouth to the ear to the brain. But is that the only way to speak to people? What about words that go from one heart to another, one spirit to another spirit?

How did these dear people know to put cement or gravel from the walls of the church on the affected parts of their bodies? Who told them to institute Healing Masses, Eucharistic Adoration, the Way of the Cross, and All Night Vigils? I believe it was Mary. She speaks to all of us at various times in our lives. Don't wait to hear with your ears. Your ears may be stuffed with the world's wax. Listen with your heart. And when you feel a very special presence trying to reach you, you can be sure she is talking to you. She loves you very much. Trust her.

Fatima, 1917: My Immaculate Heart will Triumph

Portugal is a very special place in the hearts of Our Dear Lord Jesus and His Mother Mary. It has been consecrated to Mary for as long as anyone can remember. The History of Portugal is filled with kings making petitions to Our Lady which were always answered, and promises which were always kept.

The area in and surrounding Fatima has been particularly blessed by Our Lord Jesus through our loving Mary. In Bathala, about 20 miles from Fatima, a promise was made to Mary that a great Church would be built in her honor if she would help the Portugese people win a battle against Spain, which took place on the day before the Feast of the Assumption in 1385. The splendid Basilica rises majestically towards her in Heaven as a tribute to and in thanksgiving for, the victory granted. The Church is called appropriately, **OUR LADY OF THE VICTORIES**.

In Alcobaca, closely connected geographically and spiritually with Fatima, a beautiful monastery was built in honor of and in thanksgiving to Mary for enabling the Portugese to recapture the important city of Santarem from the Moors in 1152. Santarem is situated about halfway between Fatima and Lisbon.

It is the site of a great Eucharistic Miracle which took place in the early 13th Century. The miracle is ongoing in that the Sacred Blood of Our Lord Jesus is still in liquid form for the faithful to venerate and marvel.

In our research and study about the various shrines throughout the world, *we use the term cluster*. In the sense to which we apply the term, we mean *groupings of places, villages, cities, all in the same geographical area*, where the Lord has given great gifts or special favors to the people. Look at a map of Portugal, particularly at the area around these small towns we've mentioned. Look at their proximity to one another. Each of these towns has become very important to us as Catholics.

Let us go back in time to the Spring of 1916. The world was in turmoil. A World War was devastating Europe. Bodies were strewn all over the farmlands of France and Germany. The winter had been hellish, slowing troop movement to a virtual standstill. Because of the terrible weather, soldiers of both sides were pinned down in foxholes for months at a time; all in feeble attempts to control small patches of land. Mustard Gas, the Agent Orange of the early 20th Century, was ripping out the lungs of those who breathed it in. Humanity had absolutely no regard for his brother and sister.

In Russia, a monster was being created which would cast its hideous, godless shadow over the entire world. The Bolsheviks were not involved in the World War. They were too busy destroying their own brothers and sisters, in purges that would parallel the outrages of Adolph Hitler and his gang of perverts some 20 years later.

The tiny country of Portugal was having its own problems, mostly financial. They had only established a republic some 6 years before, which had not quite worked. In the hundred years prior to the creation of the republic, Portugal had lost most of its colonies in South America. No one knew how to run the government wisely, and so the country fell into chaos and disorder. In a very brave, but very unwise move in 1916, they declared war on Germany, and sent troops into France to fight the Huns. The effect of this on the homefront was disastrous.

We mentioned that the history of the country was filled with tales of kings making pledges and committments to Our Lord Jesus and Our Lady. The attitude of the new leaders of Portugal was just the opposite, not unlike those of other newly formed republics. They equated the Church with the Monarchy. Portugal had thrown the Monarchy out in 1910, and was now persecuting the church, in an attempt to throw *it* out of the country.

The one power they had not taken into consideration in their harassment of the Church was its head, **JESUS CHRIST**, a faithful God to a sometimes unfaithful people. They had forgotten about the strength of His Love, His Patience, His Adeptness at changing people's hearts, and His Mother, my Mary. They were so sure they could succeed without God, they ignored the Source of their well-being. They were children playing in the adult world, without knowing what they were doing. Fortunately, Jesus cannot resist caring for wayward children.

We can't help but wonder why Our Heavenly Family bothers with us. We continue to make the same mistakes, commit the same outrages that began with the murder of Abel by Cain. Thank Jesus for His Mother Mary. She is so *touchable*. It's that one teardrop she sees falling from the eyes of a mother whose baby has been killed, whose husband has been dragged off, screaming into the night, never to be seen again. It must be these outrages against humanity, which have gone on since the dawn of creation, that propels her into action. We had great need of Our Lady's help in 1916. There were no kings left in Portugal to plead the cause of the people. So, it was up to the mothers to pray to Our Lady for peace. She heard these prayers, and answered them, as only she could.

A great plan was conceived in Heaven. It began to make itself known in a very small way to three little shepherds in the remote little farming village of Aljustrel, in the **Spring** of 1916.

It was still early in the season, the rainy time, before the weather warmed up. That morning, Lucia dos Santos, and her cousins Jacinta and Francisco Marto, had led the sheep to the Cabeco to graze. The ground and the grass were wet from the morning rain. They could feel the moisture on their feet, through their little sandals. Drizzle began to fall gently from the sky. The children ran up a hill to a cave where they could shelter themselves and their sheep until the rain stopped. They ate their lunch in the cave; and although the rain stopped, and the skies cleared, they stayed there, playing a game with pebbles.

The early afternoon was very calm, very still. The children became mesmerized by the game they were playing. *Suddenly, a powerful blast of wind ripped through the trees, bending the branches as it whipped around the little cabeco, breaking the still of the day.* The children snapped out of their lethargy. They jumped up like a shot, looking around frantically to find out what was causing the abrupt change in weather. All at once, their eyes zeroed in on a bright light off in the distance, approaching them. It drew closer to their little cave. As it moved closer, it became larger. They could make out the transparent figure of a person. Their hearts pounded. They were too frightened to speak. Closer and closer the vision came, until it was almost on top of them.

It was a beautiful young man. His long mane of blonde hair blew in the breeze. There was a sensitivity about him, almost contradicted by a forceful strength. His eyes were cobalt blue. When he looked at the children, they could feel his stare to the depths of their souls. While they were frightened of this majestic figure before them, they couldn't take their eyes off him. He spoke to them.

"Do not be afraid. I am the Angel of Peace."

From this title by which the angel called himself, we can be fairly certain it was the beloved of Mary, **St. Michael the Archangel**. Although the angel never actually called himself by the name of the Prince of the Heavenly Hosts, scripture and the Litany of St. Michael gives him the title, "Angel of Peace" among many other equally important honors. It has also been handed down in Church tradition and Marian devotion that wherever Our Lady is, St. Michael is sure to be found close by.

The Angel continued: "Pray with me". He prostrated himself on the ground, and said the following prayer.

"My God, I believe, I adore, I hope, and I love You. I ask forgiveness for those who do not believe, nor adore, nor hope, nor love You".

The children, in a state of shock, followed suit. They put their heads to the cold stone, and repeated what they heard the Angel say. He repeated the prayer three times. They did the same. Then he stood up again. He seemed to be nine feet tall. He looked at them. "Pray in this way", he told them. "The Hearts of Jesus and Mary are ready to listen to you." Then he took his leave. A gust of wind followed him as he turned into a bright light again, becoming smaller and fainter as he drew away from them. Finally, he was gone.

SILENCE. The sound of silence was so strong, it completely overpowered them. They looked at each other. No one said anything. They were dumbfounded. For the rest of the day, they thought of nothing else. They didn't play anymore. They stayed off by themselves, each separated from the other. Every now and then they would look at one another. They were incredulous. It was never even considered by any of the three that they tell anyone what had happened. It was too intimate. They quite honestly didn't even know how to describe it. There were no words.

The plan was in motion. Ponder in your hearts for a moment the words of the Angel. "I ask forgiveness for those who do not believe, nor adore, nor hope, nor love You." Who was he talking about? Was it the leaders of this country who had rejected Our Lord Jesus in the Blessed Sacrament, His Mother Mary, and all things the people had always held dear? Were they trading Jesus in for something *better*, and if so, what? The words fit the pattern of what the official attitude of the country towards the Church had become. They certainly had stopped loving Jesus. *Adoring Him* was out of the question, and they seemed to have lost *hope* in the ability of their God to provide for His children. But whatever they had hoped to receive in return for their betrayal was not forthcoming. The government of Portugal continued to be extremely poor, up until the present time. Judas got 30 pieces of silver for his treachery. These wretches did not even get that.

Could it be that Mary was looking into the future, to that fateful day in January 1973, when the Supreme Court of the United States ruled in favor of Abortion, opening the door to wholesale murder in our country of yet unborn American Citizens, and future exploitation of the fetuses for Nazi-type experiments? The atrocities of the concentration camps appear like fairy tales in comparison to the slaughter and ghoulish experimentation on unborn citizens of our "Free" society. Did she watch in tears as an entire generation of Americans was murdered by Abortion and Drug abuse? Can she see into the 1990's, and the turn of the century, as the impact of that lost generation will be felt in our country?

The second apparition of the Angel set the tone for what was to come a year later. We were in serious times. There was a great urgency for return to prayer, penance, sacrifice and mortification. It was the *Summer* of the same year, 1916. Portugal, and especially the Serra, where the children lived, became unbearably hot. The flocks were brought out in the pre-dawn hours to graze while there was still a cool breeze in the air. Later, they would be kept out of the hot rays of the sun until evening, when the weather cooled off again.

During this time Lucia and her cousins tended sheep in back of Lucy's house, near the well. It was here that the Angel came to them a *second* time. It was the lunch hour. All the sheep had been put away to protect them from the hot sun. The children were sitting under some trees near the well. The angel did not make an entrance the way he had the first time. One moment, they were alone; the next, he was there. His manner was one of impatience.

"What are you doing?" he said. *"Pray! Pray! The hearts of*

Jesus and Mary have merciful designs for you. Offer your prayers and sacrifices to the Most High."

Lucy asked him "How are we to make sacrifices?"

The Angel responded *"In every way you can, offer a sacrifice to the Lord, in reparation for the sins by which He is offended and in supplication for sinners. Thus you will bring peace to our country. I am its Guardian Angel, the Angel of Portugal. Above all, accept and bear with patience the sufferings which the Lord will send you."*

The Lord gave the children very important messages through the Angel. For one thing, it was determined that they would be sacrificial lambs. They were required to suffer and do penance for the sins of many others. When the Angel asked them to "above all, accept and bear with patience the sufferings which the Lord will send you", the message was reminiscent of that given to Bernadette at Lourdes, when Our Lady told her "I cannot promise you happiness in this world, but in the next".

In another part of his message to the children, he told them "In every way you can, offer a sacrifice to the Lord. . . . in supplication for sinners." We can't help thinking of "The Little Way" of St. Therese of Lisieux, the Little Flower. She never did anything spectacular in the world. When she died, nuns in her own community didn't know who she was. But in her life story, "Autobiography of a Soul", she tells us that everything she did, every little thing, she offered as a sacrifice to Jesus for the conversion of sinners.

It was after this second apparition by the Angel that we learn that Francisco had never heard the words of the Heavenly visitor. As in the previous vision, the children were completely stunned by what had happened. They couldn't talk about it. Francisco had a burning desire to know what had been said. First he asked Lucia. She was not able to talk. She told him to wait until the next day, or ask his sister, Jacinta. Francisco went to his sister. She, too, was unable to put into words how the Lord had touched her in the deep recesses of her soul. She told him to wait until the next day.

The next day, Lucia told him what the Angel had said in both apparitions. He didn't understand all the big words that were used. Lucia explained their meaning as best she could. His tiny heart was filled with love of Jesus and the Angel. He thought of nothing but the Angel and his visit.

From that time on, the children prayed all the time. They found themselves shying away from the other children of the village. They had been just like the others before the Angel's apparition. Now, their entire beings were taken up with matters of the spirit.

In the *Autumn* of 1916, the Angel of Peace, Blessed Michael the Archangel, visited the children once more, in a most dramatic way. They were at the Loca de Cabeco again, caring for their sheep. Suddenly, he appeared above them, holding a *Host in one hand, and a Chalice in the other. Drops of Blood fell from the Host into the Chalice.* He looked at them with an expression that was gentle, yet serious. This was a very important visit.

The Angel prostrated himself on the ground, leaving the Host and Chalice suspended in mid-air. He began to pray.

"MOST HOLY TRINITY, FATHER, SON AND HOLY GHOST, I ADORE YOU PROFOUNDLY AND I OFFER YOU THE MOST PRECIOUS BODY, BLOOD, SOUL AND DIVINITY OF JESUS CHRIST, PRESENT IN ALL THE TABERNACLES OF THE WORLD, IN REPARATION FOR THE OUTRAGES, SAC-RILEGES AND INDIFFERENCE BY WHICH HE IS OF-FENDED. AND BY THE INFINITE MERITS OF HIS MOST SA-CRED HEART AND THROUGH THE IMMACULATE HEART OF MARY, I BEG THE CONVERSION OF POOR SINNERS"

He remained in the prostrate position for a time; then rising, he took the Host and Chalice into his hands. He gave the Host to the older of the three, Lucia, and the Blood of Our Lord Jesus to Francisco and Jacinta.

Jacinta and Francisco
Marto
Lucia Dos Santos
The Children of Fatima

Take and drink the body and blood of Jesus Christ horribly outraged by ungrateful men.
The Angel and the Seers at Loca da Cabeco, Autumn, 1916

As they drank from the Chalice, he said *"Take and drink the Body and Blood of Jesus Christ, horribly outraged by ungrateful men. Repair their crimes and console your God"*.

After this, the angel prostrated himself on the ground once more, and repeated the prayer he had said to the Trinity at the beginning of the apparition. The children prostrated themselves, and prayed with him. Then the angel rose, and looked at the children. They could feel a tingling inside of them. They were not sure if it was because of the unwavering stare of the angel, or the burning of the Eucharist they had received inside their bodies.

After what seemed an eternity, but was actually a matter of seconds, the angel slowly disappeared. The wind whistled through the Loca de Cabeco. It was beginning to get cold, but the children could not feel it. They were flushed by the Eucharist inside them and the angel's presence. They stared for a long time into space. They could not speak.

We have to stop here again to try to understand the full impact of what the angel was saying in his prayer, and what was really happening. We mentioned that in his first two apparitions, he prayed regarding *"those who do not believe, nor adore, nor hope, nor love You."* In this apparition, He used words such as *"outrages, sacrileges and indifference"*. The Lord was angry. Mankind was on the verge of **The Lord's Wrath**. He had reached the proverbial *"Last Straw"* with us. Tribulation was on its way.

To an outsider, it would seem that in the next six months, the effects of the magnificent gift of the angel visiting them had worn off the children. They appeared to be back to their old ways. They were involved in matters of "little people". But the seed that had been planted in their hearts remained throbbing, waiting for the right moment to bloom, the moment *chosen* by the Queen of the World. When it bloomed, the most beautiful rose in creation would appear, never to die.

The chosen time, the day when the seed was to open into full bloom was May 13, 1917. It was a Sunday. The cold winter had taken its toll on the world, on Portugal and the little farm country of the Serra in particular. Its people were ready for Spring. They needed the *newness* of it. The buds of the trees were showing their heads to see if it was warm enough to come out. The grass was being nourished by the sun, bringing forth the beautiful shade of green that tells the world "Have hope, it's a brand new day."

Our three shepherds had gone to Mass this day, and then brought their flocks out to the Cova di Iria, a distance from their home in Aljustrel. But the weather was so beautiful. There was not a cloud in the sky, no fear of rain. They began to play as they tended the flock.

We want to fantasize for a moment, what might have been happening up in Heaven at about this time. Jesus is angry with the world, with good reason. The people He died for, whom He had protected for almost 2,000 years, had a history of being completely unfaithful. He was disgusted with us. His mother, the eternal optimist, pleaded to give us one more chance.

"Son, let me go back down there. I want to make them aware of how they've hurt you."

"It's as much for you Mother, as for me, that I'm angry. They have defiled you and ignored you so many times in so many ways. I'm God, and so I expect it. People always blame God when things go wrong. But why you? You've never been anything but loving and caring to them."

She looked at Him in the same way she did at Cana, and countless times before and after. He probably smiled and said,

"Mother, how can I possibly deny you anything?"

As the word "Yes" formed in His mind, the curtain of the fourth dimension, separating Heaven from Earth, tore open. A bolt of bright light shot out. With St. Michael the Archangel in the lead, his red cloak flowing behind him, a choir of angels on either side of him, and completely surrounded by the angels and the brilliant light, the Queen of Heaven and Earth, of all the Angels and the Saints, my Mary, made her way back to earth *one more time.*

The children saw what they thought was a flash of lightning streak across the sky. They were sure it meant that rain was coming. But it was followed by complete silence. No wind, not even a breeze broke the calm and quiet of the moment. They were confused. There were no clouds in the sky. But it must have been lightning. They had better get the flock to safety. Another burst of light flew by them. They couldn't move.

Then, gently, quietly, what seemed like a bubble of light rested on top of the holmoak tree in front of them, and Mary was there. The most powerful message Mary had ever given the world was beginning. Years later, Lucia described the scene,

"It was a lady, clothed in white, brighter than the sun, radiating a light more clear and intense than a crystal cup filled with sparkling water, lit by burning sunlight."

To anyone analyzing the visits of Our Lady to earth, it becomes immediately obvious that she had an urgency this time that we've never seen before. On that first day, she gave these little children, who could not possibly understand, **HER KEYNOTE MESSAGE OF FATIMA.** Everything she wanted to communicate to the people on earth was touched on in that first apparition.

Mary opened the conversation. "Do not be afraid. I will not harm you."

Lucia asked her "Where do you come from?"

Our Lady answered "I come from Heaven". Then she pointed to the blue skies above.

Lucia asked her "What to do you want of me?"

The Lady responded "I have come to ask you to come here for six months on the 13th day of each month, at this same hour. Later I shall tell you who I am and what I want. And I shall return here yet a seventh time."

Lucia asked "Will I go to Heaven?"

Mary smiled at her and answered "Yes, you will."

"And Jacinta?"

"She will go too."

"And Franciso?"

"Francisco too, but he will have to say many rosaries first."

Lucia then asked about two girls who had died recently in her village. One was in Heaven, and the other in Purgatory, Our Lady told her.

Mary got back to the point of her visit quickly. "Will you offer yourselves to God, and bear all the sufferings which He sends you, in reparation for the sins which offend Him, and in supplication for the conversion of sinners?"

Lucia answered "Yes, we will."

Our Lady continued "Then you will have much to suffer, but the grace of God will be your strength."

Lucia described what happened next.

"As she pronounced these words, she opened her hands and bathed us in a very intense light; it was like a reflection coming from her hands, which penetrated our hearts to the depths of our souls, so that we saw ourselves in God, who was this light, more clearly than in a mirror. Then by an impulse which came from our hearts, we fell on our knees in unison, and repeated inwardly: *"O Holy Trinity, I adore You. My God, My God, I love You in the Blessed Sacrament."*

Then Mary said, "Say the rosary every day, to bring peace to the world and the end of the war."

Enough! Our Lady wanted to tell them all that she would share with them over the next six months, but knew that she had better stop now. After all, this trio consisted of a 10 year old, an 8 year old, and a 7 year old. How much could their little minds absorb?

The Lady from Heaven slowly ascended. The bubble of light enveloped her; she moved slowly to the east, back to from where she had come, and finally out of sight. The children watched until there was not a sign of her left in the sky.

On their way back to their homes, they made a pact that they would tell no one about what they had seen. There was no way that this would happen, however. They were so filled with joy, they were about to burst. Lucia was able to maintain the discipline they had vowed to keep. Francisco went off by himself to try to sort out what had happened. Keep in mind that on this first apparition, he did not see the Lady. He saw the light, and knew that something important was happening. On the way home, he heard Lucia and Jacinta talking about the most beautiful lady, but *he* had not seen anything.

Jacinta, for her part, might just as well not have made any promise. First off, she looked for her mother, who had not as yet returned home. Determined to tell her as soon as she saw her, Jacinta waited outside the house for her parents to come home. Spotting her mother in the distance, she ran to her, and told her all that had happened. This was the beginning of the childrens' suffering.

Mary had told the children many things that first day. When she told them she was from Heaven, they automatically assumed she was the Blessed Mother. She asked them to come to the Cova da Iria for the next six months.

She asked them to bear the sufferings the Lord would send them. This has become almost a tradition in our Faith Belief. Does this sound familiar? Our Dear Lord Jesus suffered and died for the sins of man. Throughout our Church History, we learn about the suffering servants of Christ. St. Paul tells us *"I bear the wounds of Christ."* Bernadette Soubirous, Francis of Assisi, Rita of Cascia, Catherine of Siena, Teresa of Avila, Therese of Lisieux, most recently in our time, Padre Pio, plus many many others have been given the gift of suffering for the sins of men. Were these children being asked to suffer as a means of turning men back to God?

Redemption is through the Cross. *"Take up your cross and follow Me."* Our Lady knew that if these children were to accept the gift of her physical presence, they would experience suffering. She asked them up front to accept the inevitable.

"The Grace of God will be your strength." Again, we go to St. Paul, who tells us that the grace of God was enough to handle the sufferings he was given. We are given strength *not only by not*

sinning, which is a negative, but *by doing something*, receiving the Sacraments. We need that nourishment, that grace that comes from reception of the Sacraments.

"My God, My God, I love You in the Blessed Sacrament." That tells it all. How can we really know God? While it's true that He exists in all His creation, in the trees, and the fields, and the wind, and most especially in His inspired Word, what can be more powerful than in His Body and Blood, the Blessed Sacrament?

The last important thing she told them that first day was **"PRAY THE ROSARY EVERY DAY, TO BRING PEACE TO THE WORLD"** In Medjugorje, Our Lady tells us to say 15 decades of the Rosary every day. In 1986, in the Phillipine Islands, during the revolution against Marcos, the people walked through the streets with the Rosary in their hands, to fight off the tanks, and they were victorious. What weapon do you and I, the little people have, against the satanic forces of war mongers, armed with nuclear weapons? **PRAYER!!** We have nothing else, and there is nothing stronger than the power of prayer. Mary was trying to tell us that through these children in 1917.

From May 13 to June 13, speculation about what might be happening at the Cova da Iria spread among the people of the village. It really never went very far beyond Fatima. But in a close knit community like Aljustrel, all the emotions of the entire world could be found, and were indeed manifested towards the children and their families. Anger, envy, jealousy, and disbelief spit its poison out on one hand; love, happiness, great hope and joy poured out on the other. Unfortunately, the anger, envy, jealousy and disbelief, far outweighed the love, happiness, hope and joy. The children became immediately aware on a small scale what the suffering Our Lady spoke of might be like. Both families were split as to who believed and who thought the children were lying or fantasizing. Snide comments from neighbors, like "The mothers and fathers can't take care of their own children." and "If they were my children, I'd know how to stop them from spreading these lies."

June 13 was the Feast of St. Anthony. Most of the world

honors this great Franciscan saint as St. Anthony of Padua, Italy, and while St. Francis is the Patron Saint of the country, St. Anthony is by far the most popular saint in Italy. In Portugal, however, it's a different story. He is a **NATIVE SON** *of the Portugese, and is called St. Anthony of Lisbon, which is where he was born and raised. So for the people of Portugal to go all out for this most famous saint is justified. They even try to outdo the Italians on this day.*

For the people of the combined villages of Fatima, the feast day was an occasion for dancing, singing, a special Mass, and games. It was a community event which no one ever missed. However, the Lady told the three children to come out to the Cova da Iria on June 13th. Their parents were sure the prospect of the Feast would dim their zeal for going to the Cova. They could not have been more mistaken. The children were up at the crack of dawn to go to the Cova.

It was an even more difficult decision for Lucia to make. June 13 was the day that her First Holy Communion Class was having a reunion in Fatima. She wanted to go there badly, and indeed, did go. But instead of becoming preoccupied with the reunion, all her classmates asked if they could *join her* at the Cova da Iria at the time of the Apparition. So they all went together.

There were about 50 people at the Cova da Iria that day. When the time came and Mary appeared to the children, it felt to them like their entire existence from May to June was just in anticipation of this time. She was so warm and loving. The conversation that we're aware of, was very similar to that of May 13th.

MARY -"I want you to come here on the 13th of next month. Say the Rosary every day, and after each mystery, pray **'O MY JESUS, FORGIVE US AND DELIVER US FROM THE FIRE OF HELL; TAKE ALL SOULS TO HEAVEN, ESPECIALLY THOSE WHO ARE IN MOST NEED.'**"

Lucia asked for the cure of a sick person who had asked for Our Lady's intercession. Mary responded that if the sick person were to convert, she would be cured within a year.

LUCIA—"Will you take us to Heaven?"

MARY—"Yes, I shall take Jacinta and Francisco before very long, but you will stay a little longer. Jesus wishes to use you to make me known and loved. He wishes to establish in the world devotion to my Immaculate Heart."

LUCIA—"Must I stay here alone?"

MARY—"No, my child. Do not be sad because of this. You will never be alone. My Immaculate Heart will be your refuge and the way which will lead you to God."

In this apparition, Our Lady opened her hands and enclosed the children into the light that surrounded her. Lucia said that Jacinta and Francisco were in the light that was of Heaven, and she was in that which was poured into the earth.

Bystanders, including Ti Marto, the father of Jacinta and Francisco, testified that they heard what sounded like a rocket off in the distance at the time the Apparition was over. They could see a little cloud a few inches from the tree; it rose very slowly and went off towards the east. Senor Marto also said he could hear a buzzing sound during the apparition, like a bee.

The 30 day period between June and July brought the apparitions from the level of a local phenomenon to a national curiosity. It was also the time the children learned the meaning of the Scripture Passage of Jesus "NO PROPHET IS ACCEPTED IN HIS OWN HOME TOWN. Anyone who has ever accomplished anything, gained any degree of acceptance in the national or world community is just about shunned by his own. Close friends become very distant, almost strangers. The easiest way to become invisible to those you love in your hometown, is to gain recognition outside the community. You just about don't exist any more. It's not easy for anyone to accept, but we believe it must be easier for an adult to understand, than for children. It must have been devastating for these beautiful young people to experience.

By and large, the people of Fatima scorned the children and were ashamed of what was happening. Lucia, Jacinta and Francisco became the brunt of very cruel jokes. Adults, whom they had looked up to, yelled at them, and cursed them. The locals were annoyed with the visitors from all over Portugal, who were descending on their quiet village, and creating such a commotion over these *"little brats"*.

Lucia went through a particularly bad time. Her parish priest had a meeting with her. He all but convinced her that it was not Our Lady from Heaven who was visiting her, but the devil. For a ten year old, whatever a parish priest said was akin to Gospel Truth. This little girl didn't have the inner strength of Bernadette at this time in her life; but keep in mind that Bernadette was older than Lucia at the time of the apparitions in Lourdes. Also, these little ones were being given a series of the most serious messages Our Lady had ever given the world; therefore, it was understandable that the attacks would be greater.

As the time for the July 13 meeting approached, Lucia had decided not to go back to the Cova da Iria. She was convinced she was being assaulted by the devil himself in the form of this beautiful lady. The other two couldn't understand Lucia's logic. For them it was impossible that it was anyone other than the Queen of Heaven. So much good was going on at the Cova. It was a contradiction of what satan would have wanted. But they couldn't budge Lucia. Brave little Jacinta said that if Lucy didn't go, *she* would speak to the Lady, though she was frightened out of her mind.

On the day of the apparition, Lucia hid out from everyone. She was determined to stay away. But she didn't stand a chance against Mary. We're told that Lucia had an irresistible urge to go to the Cova that morning. She couldn't control herself. She knew she *had to go!*

This time there were about 2,000 people at the Cova da Iria. The word had spread all over Spain and Portugal. While many were praying near the holmoak tree, others just wandered around, curiously trying to see what was going on. However, once the children arrived, order was maintained immediately without anyone having to be a policeman.

The messages given to the children at this meeting, were the heaviest to share with such little people. We have to believe that at this time, Lucia, who was to bear the burden of telling the secrets to the world at the proper time, did not understand the real meaning of what the Lady was saying to her. These were powerful messages.

Mary spent a lot of time with Lucia at that meeting, before she gave her any messages. She had to convince the child that she was from Heaven. She had to soothe her and comfort her because of all the pain Lucia had suffered, the hell she had gone through from June to July. Mary knew that this was just the tip of the iceberg, the beginning of years of suffering the child had to look forward to. But this was the first real attack. Lucia needed the reassurance and attention, the love and support from this most Splendid Lady.

After Lucia was confident that she was being honored by the Queen of Heaven, the conversation assumed an almost ceremonial form. Lucia asked Our Lady what she wanted from her. The Lady repeated her request that the children return on the 13th of the following month, and say the Rosary daily. The only difference this time was *"Continue to say the Rosary every day in honor of Our Lady of the Rosary to obtain the peace of the world and the end of the war, because only she can obtain it. . . ."*

LUCIA—"I would like to ask you who you are and if you will do a miracle so that everyone will believe that you appeared to us."

MARY—"Come here every month and in October, I will perform a miracle so that everyone can believe."

Then Lucia asked for cures and healings for the many people who had asked for favors over the month. The list was getting very long. Mary smiled, and said that some would be healed, and others would not. She made a very important condition, however. *"All would have to say the Rosary as a general condition for the reception of grace."*

Then the great Secret was revealed to the children, of which two parts have been revealed to the world, and the third part is in the hands of the Pope.

First, she said to Lucia, "Make sacrifices for sinners, and say often, especially when you make a sacrifice,

O JESUS, THIS IS FOR LOVE OF THEE, FOR THE CONVERSION OF SINNERS AND IN REPARATION FOR SINS AGAINST THE IMMACULATE HEART OF MARY".

After this, Mary opened her hands and pointed down to the earth. The brilliant light opened the earth, burrowing deep into the bowels of the Underworld. The children were given a vision of Hell. They spoke about a sea of fire, filled with devils and the souls of people, black or bronzed, burning fiercely, ghastly screams of indescribable pain coming out of them, being carried down a river of fire, like molten lava, embers flying off their charred bodies. The demons could be distinguished from the people in that they looked like ghoulish, deformed animals. The grotesque vision would have bristled the hair on the necks of the strongest adults. These innocent little children were petrified.

Mary spoke to Lucia. "You have seen Hell where the souls of sinners go. To save them, God wishes to establish in the world devotion to my Immaculate Heart. If you do what I tell you, many souls will be saved and there will be peace. The war will end, but if men do not cease to offend God, another worse one will begin."

The following is part of what Our Lady told Lucia, but it was not revealed until the time of the Second World War.

"WHEN YOU SEE A LIGHT LIT BY A STRANGE UN-KNOWN LIGHT, YOU WILL KNOW THAT IT IS THE SIGN THAT GOD GIVES YOU THAT HE IS GOING TO PUNISH THE WORLD FOR ITS CRIMES BY MEANS OF WAR, HUN-GER AND THE PERSECUTION OF THE CHURCH AND THE HOLY FATHER. TO PREVENT IT, I SHALL COME TO ASK FOR THE CONSECRATION OF RUSSIA TO MY IMMACU-LATE HEART AND THE REPARATORY COMMUNION OF THE FIRST SATURDAYS.

IF MY DESIRES ARE FULFILLED, RUSSIA WILL BE CONVERTED AND THERE WILL BE PEACE; IF NOT, SHE WILL SPREAD HER ERRORS THROUGHOUT THE

WORLD, CAUSING WARS AND PERSECUTIONS OF THE
CHURCH; THE GOOD WILL BE MARTYRED AND THE
HOLY FATHER WILL HAVE MUCH TO SUFFER, VARIOUS
NATIONS WILL BE ANNIHILATED.

BUT IN THE END, MY IMMACULATE HEART WILL
TRIUMPH!

THE HOLY FATHER WILL CONSECRATE RUSSIA TO
ME AND SHE WILL BE CONVERTED AND THE WORLD
WILL ENJOY A PERIOD OF PEACE. IN PORTUGAL, THE
DOGMA OF FAITH WILL ALWAYS BE CONSERVED. YOU
MUST NOT TELL THIS TO ANYONE EXCEPT FRAN-
CISCO."

LUCIA—Do you want anything more?

MARY—No, today there is nothing more.

The people heard a clap of thunder, followed by a rumbling
vibration, like an earthquake. The little cloud moved eastward
again, and the apparition was over.

It appears that on each successive visit from Our Lady to the
children, she was preparing them more and more for this, the
most important message that could be given them. Could you
picture any adult giving this kind of information to three children,
completely uneducated, the oldest of whom was 10 years old?
Obviously, Mary had great faith in the power of Our Lord Jesus
to open their minds, so that His work could be accomplished
through them.

If we've ever had a complaint with Mary, other than that she
chooses the most remote places to visit us, it's that she has always
given us a way out of praying. If only she had left out *But in the
end, my Immaculate Heart will triumph. The Holy Father will
consecrate Russia to me and she will be converted and the world
will enjoy a period of peace.*

This apparition, the third from Mary to Lucia, Jacinta and
Francisco, is really the climax of her visit to Fatima. On August
13, the children were kidnapped by the Mayor of the town, in an
effort to show his superiors that he was doing something about
"this farce in Fatima, which has gotten completely out of hand."

It was a stupid attempt on his part. The crowd at the Cova da Iria heard about it, and marched en masse on his office. It could have been a very ugly incident; however, the Lady, she who was in charge of all that would happen, came to the aid of the mayor, and he survived the incident unscathed.

She then came to the children 6 days later at Valinhos, a short distance from their homes, very close to the Loca da Cabeco. On this visit, she reiterated that in October, she would perform a miracle that everyone could witness. Possibly the most important aspect of this visit was that her mantle left her fragrance on the branch of a tree, above which she stood. Lucia cut the branch off, and let her mother smell it. The Heavenly aroma melted the mother's heart; finally, she became a supporter of Lucia and the children.

The crowds grew larger from one apparition to the next. By the 13th of September, 25,000 people were gathered at the Cova da Iria. Unquestionably, there was a mix between believers and curiosity seekers, but the fervor of the faithful, the manner in which they behaved, the prayers and reverence to Our Lady before, during and after the apparition, was a beautiful tribute to the Heavenly Visitor.

The ritual that Lucia and Mary had developed was the same this day.

LUCIA—"What do you want?"

MARY—"Continue to say the Rosary every day for the end of the war."

Then Our Lady repeated all that she had said in August, that they were to come on the 13th of October, when they would see St. Joseph and the Holy Child, Our Lord Himself and the likeness of Our Lady of Dolors and Our Lady of Mount Carmel. She also said, "God is content with your sacrifices, but does not want you to continue to sleep with the rope. Wear it only during the day."

LUCIA—"I have many petitions. Will you cure a little deaf and dumb girl?"

MARY—"She will improve during the year."

LUCIA—"And the conversions and the cures?"

MARY—"Some will be cured; others will not. Our Lord does not trust them all."

Our Lady shared with Lucia that the obstacle to miracles occurring for some would be the lack of faith and prayer on their parts. For others, Mary said a healing might jeopardize their souls; sickness would be better for them than a cure.

LUCIA—"The people want to build a chapel here."

MARY—"Use half the money which you have received up to the present for Pedestals (Columns), and place on one of them the statue of Our Lady of the Rosary. The other half of the money may be used to build a chapel."

LUCIA—"Many people say that I am deceiving people and that I should be hanged or burned. Will you do a miracle so that they may believe?"

MARY—"Yes, in October I will perform a miracle."

Then Our Lady disappeared. There is a beautiful eyewitness account written by a priest, some 15 years after this day. He had been to the Cova da Iria on the 13th of September, 1917. His name is Monsignor John Quaresma.

"At midday, there was complete silence. One only heard the murmur of prayers. Suddenly there were sounds of jubilation and voices praising the Blessed Virgin. Arms were raised pointing to something in the sky. 'Look, don't you see? 'Yes, I do . . .' I too raised my eyes and scrutinized it in case I should be able to distinguish what the others, more fortunate than I, had already claimed to have seen . . . with great astonishment I saw, clearly and distinctly, a luminous globe, which moved from the east to the west, gliding slowly and majestically through space. My friend, (a priest), also looked and had the good fortune to enjoy the same unexpected and delightful vision. Suddenly the globe, with its extraordinary light, disappeared.

'What do you think of the globe?' I asked my friend, who seemed enthusiastic at what he had seen. 'That it was our Lady', he replied without hesitation."

October 12 was a night filled with rage. We can picture in our mind's eye, the powers of Heaven and Hell, battling violently for possession of the earth and its inhabitants. Satan had his way with the weather. He created a vicious storm over the entire continent of Europe. He didn't want to take chances that anyone would come to Fatima on that fateful day. God, for His part, filled His children with such a burning desire to witness the promised miracle, that nothing could stop them. They were willing to die for the privilege of whatever the Mother Of God had in store for them.

There were reports that the villages in the surrounding area, indeed as far as a hundred miles away, were deserted. All the inhabitants had left to go to the little Cova da Iria in Fatima. The roads, which Lucifer had turned to mud, were filled with peasants, some walking, others trying to ride bicycles, a favored few with horses, automobiles and motorcycles. Torrents of rain pelted the pilgrims. Everyone who came had to sleep out in the open, because there were no facilities in this little farming village. They tried as best they could to protect themselves from the satanic attack of weather. They were committed. Their eyes looked straight ahead to their final destination. Their mouths uttered silent prayers of the rosary, their rosary beads slowly cascading from their soaked fingers.

The estimate is that anywhere between 70,000 and 100,000 people came to Fatima that day. There was a great contrast in attitude between the pilgrims to the shrine and the local people of Aljustrel, in particular Lucia's mother, who didn't share the faith of the thousands that Our Lady would keep her promise. She wasn't even that sure that the Lady had ever come. She was sure that she and her family, Lucia in particular, and her niece and nephew, Jacinta and Francisco, would all be killed when the miracle *did not* take place. However, something told her to be with her child, so she went to the Cova da Iria that day, confident that it would be her last.

Considering the enourmous amount of humanity at the

cramped, little area of the Cova, the behavior was outstanding. For the most part, there was peace and tranquility about everyone who came. They didn't speak to each other very much. They mostly prayed. These were the serious pilgrims. They had a reason to be there. They had struggled and sacrificed to come. They were not about to let anything interfere with their goal. In addition, there were indeed the non-believers, the doubting Thomases; we are certain that deep down in their souls, they desperately wanted to believe. They just had to be shown. Why not? Aren't we all that way? Don't we all need the sign and symbol?

There were newspaper reporters from all over Portugal. They were here to see the children fall flat on their faces. They wanted to be able to write about the *hoax* of Fatima firsthand. They believed that would be the greatest news story of all. What they were given was a much greater story, one that would continue to be told for the next 70 years, and then some.

With all of the above, it becomes increasingly clear why this was such an important day, and why the battle raged between the powers of light and darkness to have their way. This was an opportunity for great conversion. It was also a tool for Lucifer to cause Our Lady and the Church to suffer a crushing defeat. Because of this, Satan used every trick he had at his disposal. Rumor has it that there was not one demon left in hell that cold, rainy October day. They were all in Fatima, trying to turn the tide, and create disaster. Rumor also has it that every guardian angel in Heaven was working a double shift that day, with St. Michael in charge, moving at lightning speed from place to place, and person to person, to foil every attempt of his deadly enemy, Satan, to ruin the day.

Lucifer's wicked weapon of weather continued on, pounding the entire assemblage with great torrents of rain, right up to the last minute. There is also a story of a man believed to be a priest, who had stationed himself near the place of the Apparitions the night before. When the children arrived at the appointed time, the man kept looking at his watch. He asked Lucia what time Our Lady would come.

She answered "At Midday."

He replied, "It's past noon now. Our Lady would not tell an untruth."

He then tried to push the children out of the place, telling them to go home, that the charade was over. At that instant, Lucia pointed to the east, and exclaimed: **"LOOK, SHE'S COMING NOW!"** The man disappeared, and was never seen again.

Everybody went down on their knees. The now familiar flash of lightning streaked through the sky. The little cloud moved slowly towards the holmoak tree. *She was here!*

The Lady spoke first to Lucia, telling her to continue saying the rosary every day for the end of the war, and to have a chapel built in this place. But she was really here this time for the people. This was her greatest opportunity.

At a given point, Our Lady raised her hand in the direction of the sun. The brilliant light emanating from her hand shot up into the sky. As if the clouds were the curtains of a great stage, they parted, revealing the brilliant sun. Lucia shouted **"LOOK AT THE SUN"** It turned from a blinding gold to a dull silver. It began to dance in the sky. It twirled uncertainly on its axis. Then it began to descend on the people. It grew bigger and bigger as it came down on them. Streaks of varied colors shot out like sparks from a wheel, covering the people, causing changes of color on their faces and clothes. Reds, yellows, blues, greens hurled down onto the little Cova. **"IT'S THE END OF THE WORLD" "FORGIVE ME MY SINS"**. There were reports of open confessions, shouted at the top of the lungs of the sinners. They thought the Lord was taking His final vengeance on them.

And then it stopped. A command was given from Heaven; the sun moved slowly back, up into the sky. It returned to its proper place in the atmosphere, and at once turned from dull to brilliant. The pilgrims could not look directly into it again. A

Lucia shouted "Look at the Sun"
The Miracle of the Sun,
Fatima, October 13, 1917

In the end, my immaculate heart will triumph
The Basilica of Our Lady of Fatima Chapel of Apparitions in foreground
Fatima, Portugal

great hush took place on earth. The 70,000 were stunned. They had been *saved*, but they weren't quite certain about it yet. Then they began to look around them. Their clothes, soaking wet moments before, were completely dry. The mud which had caked on them, was gone. They were clean. Then from various parts of the assemblage, voices rang out, "I CAN WALK!!" "I CAN SEE!" The blind opened their eyes; the lame threw down their crutches. Others went down on their knees in tears of reconciliation. Mass miracles, cures and conversions took place in a period of minutes.

The children didn't actually take part in this miracle. They were being given special gifts from Our Lady. They saw St. Joseph with the Child Jesus, Our Lady of the Dolors, Our Lady of Mt. Carmel with the Scapular hanging from her hands, and Our Dear Lord Jesus blessing the people at the Cova da Iria. The children were saved. Our Lady, as usual, had kept her promise, and more. The number of conversions due to this miracle, called **THE MIRACLE OF THE SUN'**, is beyond comprehension.

Lucia looked around her, noticing for the first time all that was happening at the Cova. She could hear the sobs of joy, the shouts of thanksgiving from those cured of illnesses and deformities. She turned quickly towards Our Lady, who was beginning to fade away. Their eyes met that one last time. A sweet smile broke out on the face of the Lady. Lucia began to cry. Without saying a word, just by looking at Lucia, Mary told her it was not over for them. In that final exchange of glances, their bond was sealed. They would see each other again. Then she left. The little cloud slowly moved back toward its final destination. Lucia watched every movement of the cloud, hoping Mary would come back again, though she knew she would not. A single tear ran down her face. Then she smiled. She knew.

The finale of this great series of Heavenly apparitions by the Queen of Heaven, under the title of the Queen of the Rosary, catapulted into motion, a movement which, though slow in beginning, has emcompassed the entire world. The message of the children of Fatima, the pleas of Our Lady, and the promises of Fatima have been repeated to and embraced by everyone she has touched. A new generation of believers, people like us who were not born when Our Lady gave us this gift, have become completely enthralled by the power of Jesus and the love of Mary, as revealed to us at Fatima.

We thank you, dear Mary, for the sign you gave us here at Fatima. We thank you for telling us that no matter what we do, *"Your Immaculate Heart will triumph in the end"*. We thank you for it, but we wish you had kept it to yourself. Perhaps we would have prayed a little harder, fasted a little more, and sinned a little less. Maybe we could have avoided World War II. Perhaps through Medjugorje, we can avoid World War III.

Beauraing, 1932: Do You Love My Son?

Mary's appearance to 5 children in Beauraing, Belgium, in November and December of 1932 has always fascinated us. There are so many aspects of the visit from Our Heavenly Lady that we don't quite understand. But we know there was a need for Mary to come to our aid in this place at this time. Nothing is by coincidence with her. Every time she comes to us in an apparition, she has to upset the balance of nature, break through the dimension separating Heaven and Earth, just to make contact with us. Then she has to condition the minds of the seers and us, the people for whom she comes to earth, to accept the supernatural, that which cannot be explained.

She knows that a battle will ensue between the power of light and the power of darkness, which has to cause her some anguish. There are so many who won't believe that she has actually come. The authenticity and sincerity of the visionaries is always seriously questioned. They receive no support from the Church. Actually, because the Church has to take on the role of Devil's Advocate, it becomes the most difficult obstacle to overcome. Also, she never picks anyone whom we would expect to be the natural choice. Would we doubt an apparition by Our Lady to Mother

Teresa, or Pope John Paul II? But that would be too easy. There's no challenge to our faith in that.

Mary appeared to five children almost every day, sometimes two and three times a day, for over a month. There were *33 apparitions* in all. The bulk of her message was very little. People constantly tried to build things into each of the messages, but the children were firm that the short two and three word messages were all that had been given to them. Her message was strong, but the words were few. We had to strain our spiritual consciousness to grasp the meaning of her words. There was nothing really to grab onto. In many *claimed* apparitions of Our Lady in this century, she reportedly goes on and on for volumes, talking to the *alleged* visionary. Yet in this apparition, approved by the Church, she gave us little gems to ponder on.

Beauraing was and still is an unassuming little village in Southwest Belgium, about 4 miles from the French Border. One would never consider it a candidate for a visit from the Greatest Lady who ever lived, either then or now. At the time of the apparition of Our Lady, the total population was about 2,000 inhabitants. The downtown or main area of the village consisted of three or four blocks. There was no great industry in Beauraing. They were victims of the Great Worldwide Depression as was the rest of the world, but their needs were not as great as others, consequently they seemed to be able to survive with what they had. Dainty suppers were a normal part of their diet. No one ate meat every day of the week, or every week of the year. They didn't have to concern themselves with change of wardrobe every season, and hand-me-downs were always in style. It was not necessary to keep up with the Joneses, because the Joneses were in the same financial condition as everyone else.

The two families involved, the *Degeimbres* and the *Voisons*, felt the sting of doing without, much more than they had ever felt it before. They had to learn to do without even the *little* to which they had become accustomed.

GERMAINE DEGEIMBRE was a widow. She had been born

in Beauraing, and married a local man. Her first two children were born in the town, but the family moved away when her husband was given a job taking care of a farm in Voneche, some miles distance from Beauraing. They stayed in that place for 13 years. Upon the death of her husband, however, she and her children returned to the town of her birth. At the time of the apparitions, they had only been back in Beauraing for 2 years.

Germaine was a very strong woman, and very personable. She was a single parent, which was more difficult in those days than it is today. However, for her, there was a peace and security in her hometown. She regarded her neighbors as family; she could count on them for help. She had three daughters, *Gilberte, 9, and Andree, 14*, to whom Our Lady appeared, and Jeanne, 17, who had nothing to do with the apparitions. However, in her anger and disappointment at not being a visionary, Jeanne voiced the slanderous opinions about the children and the apparitions that many of the townspeople *thought*, but didn't say out loud.

Germaine was an outgoing woman. She was very sociable with her friends. Her home was a meeting place, where the laughter never stopped, and the coffee pot was always ready. She was known to have a calm, reasonable disposition. She was able to size up problems and come up with solutions to situations that some families with both a husband and wife were not able to cope with. She never got ruffled. All of the above traits have to be prefaced with *Before Mary*. Once the apparitions began, everything that had been normal to that time became completely abnormal.

HECTOR AND MARIE LOUISE VOISON were the parents of the other three visionaries, *Fernande, 15, Gilberte, 13, and Albert, 11*. Hector was employed by the Railroad, for which he was thankful, but he didn't earn enough on his salary to support his family. To augment his meager income, he and his wife opened a shop on the main street in town, selling wallpaper, pastes and assorted items for the home. This took away from Marie Louise's time as a mother, but all understood that it was needed.

When Hector came home from work, he took over at the store while his wife made supper for the family.

Both the Voisons dabbled in the Socialist Party. Hector spent most of his free time at the Socialist Party headquarters, where he was respected and liked. He was one of the guys, and that was more important to him than the frowns of some neighbors, and the official disapproval of the Church. Neither he nor his wife had been to church for years, but all their children had been given at least the basics of a Catholic upbringing. There were two good Catholics buried deep beneath exteriors which had been wounded by scars of war and poverty, but it would take a *miracle* to pull them out.

We have to take some time out here to explain the political-religious situation in this part of Belgium during the early 1930's. The Wall Street Crash of 1929, and the Great Worldwide Depression which followed in its wake, had turned many people away from *Capitalism*. It had failed them badly. They were the victims of its excesses. The Bolsheviks, Communists, and Socialists put out their helping hands, and they were accepted by the people.

No one would actually own up to not being Catholic anymore. They just didn't have time for church. Trying to survive was enough of a struggle. The whole thing was God's fault anyway. Sure, why not? Never mind that he had delivered these dear people from the hands of the Germans not 20 years before. Was the First World War his fault, too? One would think that their reaction would have been just the opposite, that they would have turned back to God in thanksgiving for their deliverance from the First World War. But that was not the case.

A new phrase was coined, *Cultural Catholics*. We find this all over Europe in our travels. Countries that have been stalwarts of the Faith, 95% Catholic from the Middle Ages, are now known as Cultural Catholics. They were born Catholics. They will die Catholics. They were baptized, received First Holy Communion, Confirmation, were married, and buried in the Church. They may even have gone to Mass at Christmas and Easter Time, but that's where the similarity ends. They knew very little about our religion. Their children were sent to Catholic Schools, but with very little example in the home to back up the teachings of the good sisters; all that was taught the children was generally lost shortly after they left school to go into the *"Real World"*. Attendance at Mass and the Sacraments by adults was very thin. Obviously, Our Lady's reasoning for visiting Beauraing at that time was *not* in Thanksgiving for the veneration afforded her or her Son.

Such was the condition of Beauraing, on November 29, 1932 a little town tucked away in the southwest corner of Belgium, that no one knew or cared very much about. Because of our human limitations, we cannot see into the dimension of God, and neither could the inhabitants of Beauraing. If we were able to, we might have seen a transluscent curtain being lifted, high in the Heavens, and a single figure, small in stature, very beautiful, dressed in white, appear and descend towards the earth once again, accompanied by a legion of angels, in an attempt to shake up her children, and straighten out the mess we had made.

She knew that a great monster was looming not far from this place. The pestilence of Adolph Hitler was spreading all over Europe. They had just gotten over World War I; the Germans had marched through this little country on the way to France, and had taken it over with ease. The memory was still strong in their minds, but they prayed that nothing like that would ever happen again in their lifetime, or that of their children. Our Lady may have been coming to prepare them for another, more fearsome plague than the first. They would need the strength of Jesus to carry them through the days ahead. Great storm clouds were gathering over Germany, and threatening to embody the entire continent of Europe in its wake.

November 29, 1932 was a cold and windy night. There was a chill in the air, which gave the promise of an early and bitter winter. The Degeimbre family was huddled around the kitchen, the warmest room in the house. Two friends of Germaine's had dropped over for coffee and conversation. The children were eating supper.

There was a commotion outside of feet running up the steps. Andree and Gilberte knew who it was; they jumped up from the table. Fernande Voison and her brother Albert were calling for them to join them. Together, the four children went to the local school, run by the nuns, to pick up Gilberte Voison, who was finished for the day at 6:30 in the evening. Her father, Hector was supposed to get her, but a tradition of sorts had been established. The two Voison children met her when the father was working, or when they could talk him into letting them go, which was as often as possible. They always called for Andree and Gilberte D (Degeimbre), and the foursome would frolic on their way to the school, meet Gilberte V(Voison), and continue playing until they reached home.

As far as anyone could tell, this evening was to be no different from any of the others when they had played out this ritual. But they were not able to see the Lady descending upon them from far up in the heavens. They walked from the Degeimbre house towards the school. They played their pranks on the way. This was actually the highlight of the whole affair. If they just had to go and pick up Gilberte V and come right home, it would have been boring. But the little games they played, ringing doorbells, then running before they were caught; these little adventures made it worthwhile. There was a very special adventure awaiting them, much greater than they had ever expected.

They walked down the block, and turned the corner to the street on which the convent and school were located. Meanwhile, up above them, the Lady was approaching, a short distance from their view. The children passed a little grotto, which was a shrine to Our Lady of Lourdes, and turned into the entrance of the convent. Albert ran up to the door and rang the bell. The three girls genuflected in front of the statue of Our Lady of Lourdes.

Albert danced up and down the steps of the stoop of the

**Do you love me?
Do you love my Son?
Sacrifice yourself for me.**
Statue of Our Lady of
Beauraing, Belgium

**Will you always be
good?**
The Visionaries
Beauraing, Belgium

convent, waiting for the sister to open the door. The girls climbed the steps and faced the door. All of a sudden, Albert exclaimed excitedly, "Look, the Virgin, dressed in white, is walking on the bridge."

The girls paid no attention to him. But then Fernande turned around, partly because of the way Albert's voice sounded, and partly because of the expression on his face. She looked up and froze in her tracks. The other girls, meanwhile, were still facing the door. "It's only the light of an automobile, silly" they said.

Albert was having none of it. He made them turn around. As they looked up, they all went into shock. There she was, above the bridge. *They all saw* the greatly illuminated figure of a woman in white, wearing a long flowing gown. She seemed as though she were walking on a cloud. They were able to distinguish that she was bending her knees, walking on air.

They didn't know what to do. They did know they needed an authority figure, an adult, at once. Albert rang the bell of the convent. The girls began pounding on the door for all they were worth. They yelled and cried at the same time. Sister Valeria answered the door, but upon seeing that it was the children, she turned and went to fetch Gilberte V. This was the wrong thing to do. They needed her outside. While Gilberte V put on her coat and hat, Sister Valeria took notice of the great commotion going on outside the open door. The children were clamoring inchoherently, and pointing in the direction of the apparition. She asked them what was wrong. They all yelled at once.

"Look, Sister, the Virgin is walking above the bridge."

"She's all dressed in white."

"We're afraid."

The good nun could sense their anxiety. She tried as best she could to see what they were talking about. She looked in the direction to which they pointed. She couldn't make anything out. She thought perhaps they were referring to the statue of Our Lady of Lourdes in the Grotto. She turned on a light, so they could see better.

"It's only a branch in the wind." she said. "Statues don't walk."

The children insisted the Blessed Mother was walking above the bridge. She was plain as day. The sister strained her eyes, but could see nothing. About this time, Gilberte V walked out the door, and immediately saw the vision. She exclaimed in wonder: "Oh, Look!"

The children were in a state of panic. They wanted to get home. They wanted their mother.

"Let's go home." they said. "We're afraid."

The nun dismissed them with a comment about their being silly children, and went inside. She couldn't help but notice how differently they behaved from the other times they had come to pick up Gilberte V. They were normally playful, mischievous children. This time, however, they looked as if they had seen a ghost. It was equally strange that Gilberte V had taken part in this nonsense. She had been inside with Sister Valeria just minutes before the incident, and seemed very calm and normal. However, the minute she walked out the door, she began to act like the others.

Sister Valeria related the story to the Mother Superior, Sister Theophile, and the rest of the community at dinner that night. She met with strange looks, and a curt comment from Sister Theophile. "Oh sister", she said, "How can you tell such a story? You sound as *childish* as those children." The words spit out like a machine gun. Sister Theophile was angry. Sister Valeria dropped the subject. She felt a flush of embarrassment rush to her face. The Mother Superior had made her positon on the matter very clear. Sister Valeria wondered why her superior was so angry. However, prudence dictated that the younger sister not get involved in it any further.

Meanwhile, the children ran down the streets towards the Degeimbre house, as if they were possessed. They passed a man on the street. From their expressions, he thought there was a fire somewhere. "What's happened?" he asked.

Without skipping a beat, or slowing down for an instant, one of them yelled "We saw something in white."

When they arrived at the Degeimbre house, Germaine was still sitting at the table with her two friends, Raymond Gobert and Jules Defesche. It seemed to her that the children had just left the house. She knew immediately that something was wrong with them. Their faces were flushed. They were completely out of breath. They were in a state of shock. They all spoke excitedly at the same time, in between trying to catch their breath.

"I think we saw the Blessed Virgin!"

"We saw a man in white!"

"I think it was the statue that moved!"

"The Blessed Virgin was walking!"

The reaction from the adults was typical, and one which we'll see more of as we delve into the apparitions of Mary. The first blush of shock was followed by total disbelief, coupled with annoyance, which finally turned into *downright anger*.

The Mother: "Be quiet, you silly children. Before long you'll have us believing that a stone statue can move."

The older Degeimbre daughter, Jeanne, set a pattern from the outset, which was to continue throughout the apparitions. She said what everyone else thought. She lashed out angrily at her sisters. *"You two see the virgin? Now if I had seen her, that would be different. But you two! You're not good enough."*

Germaine gave them a brisk dismissal, sending her two girls off to bed. Then she tried to sweep the whole incident under the carpet. Using her harshest tone, she turned to the three Voison children. "Now listen to me, you children. Don't tell any of this foolishness to your parents."

Fernande, the oldest, spoke for the rest. "Of course we will tell them, Germaine, just as we told you."**AND IT BEGAN!**

What occurred that night of November 29, 1932, in the house of Germaine Degeimbre, was exactly what continued to happen over the next 34 days, and for many years to come, only on a much larger scale. The children faced great opposition from all sides. Actually, they were all alone, with the exception of their Heavenly visitor, Mary. Their parents, their friends, their teachers, the local priest, the Mother Superior, the police, the civil authorities, all of them badgered the five brave little soldiers, in an effort to get them to renounce the "lies" they had been telling. But the children could not renounce them, because they were *not lies*.

In front of them at all times, from their waking hours to the time they were finally given the respite of sleep, the haunting image of the unbelievably captivating face of the Lady was imprinted on their hearts and minds. She had picked them out of all the children in the world to visit. The strength they derived from the smile she gave them, the radiance of her eyes when she looked at them, was enough for them to go through fire for her. And that is exactly what they did do.

Our Lady didn't really help them out very much with their opposition. For the first three days, she said absolutely nothing to them. The local people, the skeptics and their parents asked them "What did she say?" Their reply was "Nothing". Then, on Friday, December 2, in response to questions the people had prodded them to ask Our Lady, she replied:

To the Question, "Are you the Immaculate Virgin?", she nodded her head and opened her arms.

To the Question, "What do you want of us?", she spoke for the first time. "ALWAYS BE GOOD".

They answered her "Yes. We will always be good."

The response from the unbelievers was "That's it? That's all she said?" The sweet, innocent children thought this had been fantastic. "Yes!", they replied excitedly, "that's what she said." We can see here the attitudes of the pessimist and the optimist. Is the glass half empty or half full? To the children, it was half full.

The following day, Saturday, December 3, they repeated their questions.

To the question, "Are you really the Immaculate Virgin?", she nodded her head in assent.

To the question, "What do you want of us?", her response was "Is it true that you will always be good?"

Their response, in unison, was a resounding "Yes! We will always be good."

We have to get into values here. What would have been the easiest thing for the children to do? The curiosity seekers and various doctors who interrogated the five children endlessly, wanted to *hear* something. It was not too difficult even for their young minds to grasp what the people *wanted* to hear. There is no doubt that their lives would have been a lot less complicated had they just given everyone what they wanted. But what was the value in that? To the outsiders, what had happened was not enough. Throughout the apparitions, there was not enough sensationalism. Even a priest, asked to comment about our Lady's first message, commented that it was too trite a statement to have been made by the Mother of God. Where were the miracles? Where were the signs? What was she saying that was momentous? **"BE GOOD ALWAYS".** What was that?

Well, if you're trying to "Be Good Always", you know what a challenge that statement is. *"Being"* is so much more difficult than *"Doing"*. To many, however, that just wasn't enough.

But to the children, the great miracle was that she had appeared to them in the first place. They were given the gift of *near ecstasy*, just being in the presence of Mary. This was the greatest miracle they would ever experience. Why embellish it? But the rest of the world was not privy to their gift. They had no way of knowing what this radiant visitor from Heaven was bestowing on these young people. They were looking at it from the eyes of the world, rather than from Heaven. There was no miraculous, healing spring, as in Lourdes. There was no Miracle of the Sun, as in Fatima.

A battle began that November day in 1932. The forces of evil attacked from the outset. *Good people* were saying *bad things*. People that you would expect to come to the aid of the children became their greatest enemies. Outside influences, mostly in the form of outrageous fabrications from the Socialist Press, and well known anti-Catholic writers mocked the visit by Our Lady to Beauraing. There wäs such a spewing of venom on this apparition that it seemed like satan was in a mad rage, and had taken possession of the souls of everyone in the country. He must have known that something extremely important was to come from this place which would have a devastating effect on him and his followers. He had to stop it at all costs. From the reports we've read, which began almost immediately after the first apparition, never has there been such an outpouring of hate and accusations against the children, beginning with their parents, continuing onto the Sisters of the community, the Church, and including members of the government. Hate and anger are like a buckshot blast. The spray wounds everyone in its path. Lucifer shot off a crippling round of hate and anger.

But then there is the other side of the coin. Praise Jesus, there will always be the other side of the coin. Good things, great things happened in Beauraing, again, almost from the very outset of the apparitions. They were subtle, not as noticeable as the raging campaign of hate. Suddenly, the church had more participants at Mass than before. The mothers of the two sets of visionaries, Germaine Degeimbre and Marie Louise Voison, had asked for a Mass to be said to Our Lady, so that if what their children were experiencing was not from the Lord, Mary would put an end to it. The day chosen for the Mass was December 8, the Feast of the Immaculate Conception, a powerful day. The two mothers and the children entered the Church on that day for the Mass. Marie Louise Voison received the Eucharist for the first time in ten years. Her husband followed her soon thereafter. They both embraced Mother Church.

The Church became the center of the life of the town. For the longest time, it had been the place to drop off the children for Mass and learning, but not for *adults* to get involved with the Sacrifice of the Mass. It had lost importance in the family. But a revival began taking place. The Parish priest, Fr. Leon Lambert, had kept a very low profile during the early stages of the apparitions. He had a great devotion to Our Lady, however, and never ruled out the possibility that She had chosen Beauraing as the place to give the world an important message. He was not able to make a public statement regarding the authenticity of the apparitions, but he prayed privately that Our Lady protect the Church and the children, if it were not truly her doings in his little town; and that if she truly *were* appearing to the children, that she give them the strength to bear up under the pressure to which they would be subjected.

On Thursday, December 1, the Blessed Virgin appeared to the children for the *first* time on the Hawthorn tree inside the grounds of the convent. From that time on, it was to be the place where she would visit with them.

On Sunday, December 4, they asked her to cure some sick people in the crowd. She did not respond. They asked her the same question they had asked repeatedly before.

"Are you the Immaculate Virgin?"

She nodded "Yes" again.

Then they asked her, "What day should we come?"

She answered, "The Day of the Immaculate Conception".

They also asked her "Should we have a chapel built?" (This was in response to questions people wanted to have asked, to determine if this was truly the Blessed Mother)

Her reply to them was "Yes".

Our Lady specified December 8, the Feast of the Immaculate Conception as a day that the children should return. Because of this, the entire town construed it to be a sign that a great miracle was to happen on that day. The sadness of it is that, in looking for a big, spectacular miracle with lights and fireworks, they missed out on a beautiful miracle. Shall we call it a *little* miracle? I don't think there are such things as little miracles.

The gift was to the children. For the first and only time during the *33 apparitions*, she allowed them to go into complete ecstasy. They became completely oblivious to everything and everyone around them. Doctors had come into the picture by this time. They observed the children during this apparition, noting their behavior while Our Lady was with them. On this particular day, flashlights were shone in their faces. Matches were lit under their fingers and hands, with absolutely no reaction from the visionaries. They were pinched hard and often, but the trance could not be broken. During these periods of torture, they were noted to be smiling as they all looked in the direction of the Hawthorn Tree.

The great sign was given. The miracle was performed for the people as they had expected. But it was not what they had envisioned, or what they had wanted. It was not enough. So they said no sign or miracle had occurred. They wanted her to act according to a script they had written.

For many, however, the miracle of the Feast of the Immaculate Conception was a turning point in their believing. Mother Theophile, superior of the convent, who had been the most vocal in her condemnation of the Apparitions, seemed to be softening. The priest, Fr. Lambert, gave an interview to a Catholic Newspaper from Namur. While he remained very cautious, he conceded that the children seemed sincere, and that their individual stories *confirmed* what they said as a group.

On the other hand, the enemy of *Doubt* crept into the proceedings. Mother Theophile put a St. Benedict's medal on the Hawthorn tree on which our Lady appeared to the children. For reasons only known in Heaven, Mary did not come back again for the next four days. Someone pointed out that Our Lady never appeared to anyone at night, and yet in this instance, Mary always came to the children in the evening. At the prompting of the doubting Thomases, the children asked Mary if she would come at an earlier time, during daylight hours. She told them to keep coming at the same time.

To make matters worse, a series of hysterical people claimed to have apparitions of their own in different places on December 8, while the children were waiting for Our Lady to come. They claimed to see her on the mountains. Some saw rays coming out of her head, others claimed to see a ball of fire. Their allegations were determined to be unfounded, but again, a *shadow of darkness* fell on the authenticity of the apparitions.

We can't help but ask ourselves WHY? There was so much doubt to begin with, why did Our Lady allow all of this confusion to continue? At that time, it was thought that the evil powers were trying to interfere with the Apparitions. But now, some 50 odd years later, after the Church has authenticated the apparitions as being genuine, we have to wonder if it wasn't Mary all the time, testing. How much do you really love me? Can you stand up against all of this obvious opposition, and still believe? Who says that the gift has to be a handout? If we really want Mary, and she is willing to perform the miracle of coming to us, why can't we work for it? It's never easy on the visionaries. They become sacrificial lambs. Why can't we take a little of the suffering on our own shoulders? In this series of apparitions, Mary made it difficult for us to believe. We had to rely more on faith than on external signs. Why, we wonder did she force this on us? There is an answer.

There is no indication that the children ever waivered in their belief in what they saw. They were put under excruciating pressure due to the never ending flow of questions by everybody from doctors to government officials, to judges, to priests and bishops. The doctors came first. It was decided the visionaries were to be questioned after each apparition, unless there was nothing new to report. By this we mean that very often, actually more times than not, Mary would just look at the children and smile. She followed them as they recited the rosary, but didn't join in. If she said nothing, that meant there was nothing to report, and the children could go home.

The children defended the reports they gave, from the very first day, against all opposition. Their parents, whom they loved, were greatly affected by the apparitions in a negative way. The little shop of Hector and Marie Louise Voison became the target of curiosity seekers who wanted to know about their children.

There was no room for customers. Business fell off drastically, and they had to close the shop. Hector became the laughing stock of his Socialist Party Club. This had been a very important part of his life. It appeared that all the things the Voisons held sacred were being taken away from them. On the plus side, but not right away, Hector did come back to the Church after an absence of many years. He received the sacraments, and became a staunch supporter of the apparitions and the children. But this was a hard time in coming.

At the beginning, all five had seen and heard the same thing during each apparition. Their reports matched almost perfectly. As part of the pattern, each time Our Lady came to the children, they all went down on their knees as if they had been pushed down by a strong force. There were those who commented that the noise made from their knees hitting the ground made enough pressure to break the kneecaps of other people. Yet the children never felt pain from it. Also, each night prior to the Lady's appearance, the children prayed the rosary in a natural voice. However, once she arrived, their voices took on a very high tone. They also prayed much faster.

Then things began to change. All the children did not see the lady each time she appeared. She spoke to some of them, and not to the others. On two separate occasions, she spoke only to one of them, which had the others upset. In hindsight, and after having studied the apparitions at Fatima and Medjugorje, these variations don't bother us at all. But at that time, when most people were looking for flaws in their stories, reasons *not* to believe, all this caused confusion at best, and in some instances, turned people away from the apparitions.

There's an important key to the outcome of the apparitions in that on two separate occasions, Our Lady spoke only to one of the visionaries. The child was Fernande Voison. There was a reason for this, which we will see later on. Fernande became very self conscious about this. She was afraid that people didn't believe her when Mary spoke to her alone. She felt they thought she was making up stories to get more attention. She could also feel the resentment of her fellow visionaries during these times. Fernande made it obvious to everyone that she didn't like when Our Lady spoke to her alone.

On Sunday, January 1, 1933, Fernande did a foolish thing. The tradition had become that when Our Lady moved her lips to speak, the children would stop praying so that they could hear her words. During the apparition of January 1, when Mary began to move her lips to speak to the children, Fernande was afraid that she would speak to her alone, so she continued praying and lowered her eyes so that she could not hear what Our Lady wanted to say. Two days later, she would be extremely sorry she had done this.

On Wednesday, December 28, Our Lady told the children that she would stop coming to them very soon. This made the visionaries extremely sad. They had always known it was coming, but never wanted to think about it. Now it was to become a reality.

On December 29, as Mary was giving her farewell to the children, she opened her arms to expose a brilliant gold heart. This was the first time she had done this. Because of this, she has been given the title of **THE LADY WITH THE GOLDEN HEART**. Obviously, she was making reference here to the Immaculate Heart of Mary.

On December 30, she showed her golden heart to the children again. She told them **"PRAY! PRAY VERY MUCH!"**

On December 31, she revealed her golden heart once more to the children.

On January 1, 1933, she said to the children **"PRAY ALWAYS."** She also told them that she would not see them again after the 3rd of January.

A great crowd assembled on January 3 for this final apparition. They knew something spectacular was about to happen. The children had mixed feelings. They felt a deep sadness to think that they would never see this beautiful Lady again. But they, too, were filled with anticipation that something special would happen on this day, perhaps something which they could carry with them for the rest of their lives. No one quite expected what was to happen to Fernande.

It was very difficult for the children to get to their places for the apparition, because of the great swell of people. Finally, however, they reached their places, and began to pray. After a short time, they fell to their knees, all except Fernande. She looked around in amazement, then slowly went down on her knees for a few seconds. She got up. Her face was distraught. She was in tears. "I can't see her".

The Lady was there! She was more beautiful than they had ever seen her. She was brilliant. Her eyes, her lips, everything about her glistened. She spoke first to Gilberte D.

"This is between you and me, and I ask you not to speak of it to anyone".

Mary then gave her a secret, and said "Goodbye".

Next, she spoke to Gilberte V. "I will convert sinners". She then gave the child a secret, and said "Goodbye".

Then she spoke to Albert. She told him a secret, and said "Goodbye".

Finally, she spoke to Andree. "I am the Mother of God, the Queen of Heaven. Pray always." Then she said "Goodbye" and disappeared.

During this time, Fernande prayed for all she was worth. She shut her eyes hard, prayed, and then opened them. She could see nothing. She looked at the expressions on the faces of the other children. She knew Our Lady was speaking to them. There were tears in their eyes. Fernande was in a state of panic.

The children began to rise. The crowd started to disperse. Fernande stayed on her knees. She looked around, bewildered. Someone suggested they say another rosary. Perhaps Our Lady would return. The children went down on their knees again, and prayed the Rosary. The Lady did not return. The children got up and walked towards the grotto to pray.

Fernande cried out "I want to see her."

She was all alone on her knees, praying. The crowd began to thin out. They bumped into Fernande on their way to the Grotto, in pursuit of the other children. We can only assume what might have gone on in the mind and heart of Fernande as she knelt there praying.

"Please, please come back to me. Don't leave me this way. I'm sorry. I'm sorry for not letting you speak the other day. I love you. You promised me a secret. It can't end this way. I need you. Please! Please!"

A crack of thunder shot through the evening sky, followed by a ball of fire, which landed on the hawthorn tree. Everyone could see it. The crowd froze. They turned their attention back to the Hawthorn Tree. Fernande broke into a great smile. **SHE WAS THERE!!**. Those eyes, those radiant eyes, rested on the face of the child, enveloping her in their warmth. Fernande cried great tears of joy. She couldn't stop. Mary waited a moment, then spoke to her.

"Do you love my Son?"

"Yes" she cried out.

"Do you love me?"

"Oh, yes."

"Then sacrifice yourself for me".

Fernande wanted to keep her there. She had many questions to ask. But the Lady opened her arms, shone more brilliantly than ever before, and exposed her Golden Heart. She looked at Fernande lovingly, and said "Goodbye". Then she left. Fernande collapsed in tears; her entire body shaking from uncontrollable sobbing.

And those three short sentences, my brothers and sisters, constitute the Message of Beauraing. She made us wait to the eleventh hour. She had us straining at the bit. Every word, every gesture was analyzed in an effort to determine what she was trying to tell us. According to man's logic, we almost didn't get the message. But she would never let us down. She would not fail us. She knew what was to come in a very short time to this little country, to the continent of Europe, and to the entire world. She was preparing us for Holocaust.

Mary had a purpose, a very definite reason for appearing to her children in Belgium, TWICE within a period of SIX WEEKS, in two different locations. We truly believe that the apparitions by Our Lady, sweet loving Mary in Beauraing and Banneux, Belgium in 1932/1933 have a very strong connection. After the chapter on Banneux, we will share what we believe Our Lord Jesus and His Mother Mary were asking of us in these two places at this point in history.

If we were able to see with the eyes of God, we'd see Jesus and Mary, our Guardian Angels, plus all the angels and saints, surrounding each of us all the time. It's just that when it's really important that they bring home a message to us, when they have an urgency to help us in a very unique way, they move Heaven and Earth to come down to us in miracle form.

We thank you, dear Lord Jesus, and our most beautiful Lady, for loving us so much that you just can't stay away from us. Please, don't ever stop.

DO YOU LOVE ME?
DO YOU LOVE MY SON?
THEN SACRIFICE YOURSELF FOR ME.

Banneux, 1933: Believe in Me . . . I Will Believe in You

Twelve days after Our Lady with the Golden Heart said "Goodbye" to the five children in Beauraing, Belgium, she made her presence felt again in Banneux, Belgium, some fifty miles to the northeast. Mariette Beco, an 11 year old girl, saw a beautiful young lady, dressed in white, standing above the ground outside her house. It begins again. **OR does it continue?**

Mariette Beco's background and personality could be considered at best to be coarse, or basic. At 11 years old, the eldest of seven children, she was not intelligent, yet she was not stupid. She was a very outspoken girl, to the point of being offensive. But it was not intentional; this was the way she was. She had no inkling or sensitivity for spirituality, or for religion. She had no interest in her religious training; therefore, she did very badly in Catechism Class. She had stopped going for First Holy Communion instructions.

She was a product of her environment, which was, in a word, hopeless. Her father was an unemployed wiremaker. He had a house, so we can assume that in better days, he was a successful worker. But this was the time of the Depression. Nobody was successful. We don't know for sure that he blamed God for his predicament, only that he had no use for God or the Church. He was born a Catholic, but that was a long time ago. He hadn't been near a church for years. Unlike the residents of Beauraing, who insisted that their children receive a basic Catholic education, Julian Beco couldn't care less that his eldest daughter had given up her religious training. His attitude infected the household. There was nothing in the house of a religious nature. His wife, Louise, followed his lead, for whatever reason. Traditionally, the wife and mother is the member of the family who encourages attendance at Mass, reception of the sacraments, and religious training. If the mother is not active in fostering these virtues, they usually are missing in the home.

The winter of 1933 had turned extremely bitter. The eerie sounds of the wind wailing through the trees, bending the branches in a contest of strength, created a deafening din inside the house. Drafts blew through the open cracks under the doors and in the window frames. The flames in the fireplace flickered wildly, as they battled the cold winds blowing down the chimney. It was dark, around 7 in the evening, on this freezing night. Mariette sat by the front window of her house, looking into the black of night for some sign of her brother Julien, who was late returning home. As she opened the curtain to look out, she saw a Lady standing in their front yard, surrounded by a bright light. The Lady was short, about five feet tall, and exceptionally beautiful. Mariette had never seen anyone so lovely before. She was not dressed like any of the ladies from the village. She wore a long white gown with a blue sash. One of her feet could be seen. She was barefoot, with just a gold rose in between her toes. In this kind of weather, she should be freezing. Mariette noticed that she stood just above the ground, sort of on a cloud. She didn't seem to be cold at all.

Mariette had a very logical mind, even at age 11. The scene she saw before her eyes didn't make sense. It was probably the reflection of the oil lamp. She took the oil lamp from the table, and put it in another room. Then she went back to the window

**She's beautiful, Mama.
She's smiling at me.**
Statue of Our Lady
Banneux, Belgium

**Mariette Beco sat at the
bay window of her
home, looking out
the window**
Banneux, Belgium,
January 15, 1933

and looked out. The Lady was still there. She resorted to the next natural course of action. . . . she called her mother. Mariette explained what she was looking at, to her mother. Louise Beco responded in a natural way also.

"Rubbish", she said.

Mariette was a very persistent girl. She described what the Lady looked like. Her mother replied jokingly,

"Perhaps it's the Blessed Virgin."

The child was insistent that her mother come over to the window and see for herself. After much persuasion, but feeling very foolish, Louise went over to the window and looked out. She did indeed see something, a white shape, but she couldn't make out any figures.

"It's a witch." she said, and let the curtain fall, blocking the image from Mariette's eyes. The child opened the curtain again.

"She's beautiful, mama. She's smiling at me." The mother ignored her eldest daughter.

The child noticed that the Lady had a rosary, hanging from the blue sash. The cross was the same color of gold as the rose between her toes. Mariette went to a drawer, and rummaged through, looking for a a rosary she had found outside on the road. When she found it, she began to pray. The Lady's lips moved, but she didn't say anything that Mariette could hear. After a few decades, the Lady raised her hand, and motioned with her finger for Mariette to come outside. The young girl told her mother what the Lady had wanted, and asked permission to go outside.

"Lock the door." Her mother replied.

By the time Mariette returned to the window, the Lady had disappeared. She could not get the vision out of her mind. She kept going back to the window to see if the beautiful Lady had returned, but she had not. Pretty soon, her brother Julien came home. She told him what had happened while she was waiting for him at the window. His reaction was similar to that of his mother's, only a little more vocal. His comments ranged from "You're a fool" to "You're crazy".

The next morning, Mariette told her father. His initial response was "Nonsense. You're crazy." But his curiosity had been aroused. His reasoning was pure logic, however. She was not the type of child who lied. She had no *reason* to lie. She never feared repercussion for her words or actions. Also, she never had flights of fantasy. She was a very down to earth girl. After she left for school that morning, Julien asked his wife to show him the exact spot where she had seen the white shape. Then, that evening, he tried various ways to recreate the conditions of the previous night to come up with some logical explanation for what his daughter claimed to see.

He moved the oil lamp in various positions, but the light never shone on the garden, only on the road. He then threw a bucket of water on the spot where his wife and daughter had seen something. After it had frozen over, he tried to get the oil lamp to reflect off the ice, but he was not able to duplicate what Mariette and the mother had seen.

On that same day, Monday, January 16, Mariette told a girl friend at school what had happened. The girl told her she had to tell the priest. Mariette was afraid, but with the encouragement of her friend, the two of them went to the priest's office. Mariette backed out at the last minute, and ran off. The girl friend told the priest, Fr. Louis Jamin, what Mariette had said. The priest was sure Mariette was influenced by the recent reported apparitions in Beauraing, and paid no attention to it. He cautioned the girl friend, however, not to tell anyone about Mariette's reported apparition.

For the next two days, Monday and Tuesday, the Lady did not return. However, that one visit had a deep effect on Mariette's spirituality. She returned to her Catechism class on Wednesday, embracing the material with a *renewed* enthusiasm. She knew her lesson perfectly. This amazed Fr. Jamin, because Mariette had always been the worst student in the class.

After class, Father asked her why she had run away on Monday without telling him what she had seen. By this time, the child had had time to reflect on the possibility of what had happened. She was not frightened anymore. She spoke very calmly to the priest, telling him exactly what she had seen. He, for his part, did not treat her as a child, or belittle what she claimed. He only told her to pray to Our Lady for guidance.

That night, Wednesday, January 18, was the first time Mariette actually had contact with the Lady. It was cold, well below freezing. The ground outside the house was frozen like rock. Mariette knelt down at around 7 o'clock, and began to pray. Her father watched her from inside. Then, after a time, she opened her arms. The Lady returned like a shooting star, appearing at first very small off in the distance. As she moved through the sky, she became larger, the closer she got to Mariette. She moved silently between two trees and came to a halt in front of the child. A dazzling brilliance emanated from her. Mariette could feel the warmth of it from where she knelt, a distance of about 5 feet from the Lady.

The father came outside, and tried to speak to the child, but she did not seem to hear him. When she opened her arms, Julian Beco realized she was having another apparition. He got on his bicycle, and rode to the town to get the priest. He couldn't find him, so he asked a practising Catholic acquaintance to come back to his house. As they approached, they saw Mariette walking away from the house, as if being guided to a particular place.

"Where are you going?", he cried out to her.

"She's calling me." the child answered, without stopping.

Mariette knelt a few times on her way, and then went over to a stream. She knelt in front of it. The Lady stood opposite her on the other side.

"Plunge your hands into the water." Our Lady requested.

After the child had obeyed, Mary spoke again.

"This spring is reserved for me. Goodnight. Au revoir."

Our Lady rose into the air, and proceeded to return to Heaven. She became smaller and smaller, until finally she disappeared out of sight. Her eyes never left the child the entire time.

When Fr. Jamin returned to the rectory, he was advised of Mr. Beco's excited call. He knew what it was about, and after enlisting the aid of another priest and a friend to join him, he went to the Beco's home. By the time he reached there, Mariette was in bed asleep, so he spoke to the father. Julian explained all that had happened in the course of almost an hour that the Lady spent with the child. At the end of the interview, the priest asked Mariette's father if he believed the child's claim of what she had seen. His response was *"Yes, I do, and to show you how deeply I believe, I am coming to Church tomorrow to make a Confession. I would like to receive Communion again. It'll be the first one I will make since my First Holy Communion as a boy."*

The immediate reaction to Our Lady's visit to Banneux was powerful. In all the research we've done on visits by Our Lady to our troubled world, we've never seen such sudden conversions. After the very first visit, the girl was converted. Her father, who had been the dominant force of apathy, or rebellion against the Church, experienced change on the spot. Not in Lourdes, or Fatima, or Beauraing, did the changes come about so quickly. The parents of Bernadette Soubirous and Lucia dos Santos didn't come around to accepting the apparitions until well after they had ended. Yet, here in Banneux, Our Lady's power was felt and acted upon immediately.

The priest, Fr. Jamin, held his reserve for some time before he publicly admitted his belief in the apparition. His was a difficult position. The child in his parish was making claim to a Heavenly visit right on the heels of another claim in the same country in the same month. He knew comparisons would be drawn. He also knew that the eyes of Belgium, and possibly the whole of Europe would be on him, and his behavior. We have to believe that a great factor in his accepting the apparitions was the immediate fruits that surfaced.

The Lady's visit to Mariette Beco on Thursday, January 19, was of particular importance. She gave the child her title, which is so apropos for the time and the country. She called herself

"THE VIRGIN OF THE POOR. How well-chosen it was for her to give herself that title. How many poor wretches were there in the world in the winter of 1933? POOR was a multi-faceted term as it applied to the world of 1933. There was the very obvious poverty caused by the devastation of the Great World War, followed closely by the Worldwide Depression. Those who *had* had, were having great difficulty adapting to not having. Those who had *never* had, were feeling the pressure of being totally destitute.

There is also the poverty of not having the gift of Faith. When these dear people gave up on Jesus and the Church, they gave up on the very beautiful gifts He showered on them. They gave up everything. They put their trust in a system, a form of government, people. People will always fail you, even the best of them. They may not want to. They can't help it. They're victims of Adam and Eve. I will fail you. I certainly don't want to. I pray constantly for the strength not to fail my brothers and sisters. *Jesus* will never fail you. *Mary* will never let you down. The *Angels* and *Saints* are our best friends. With them as a support system, we are so rich. If we walk away from them, we are truly the poorest of God's creatures.

A nun spoke to us on the phone recently. She was in tears. She quoted Mary as having said in Medjugorje that this is the last time she will come to us on Earth. I told her that Mary may have said that. It's true that it's part of the message of Medjugorje. But Mary is Mary. She's **MOTHER OF US ALL**. As long as we're here, as long as we need her, as long as there are three or four good people left on the earth, she will always be with us. It's one of her predictable traits.

And so we believe that Banneux was an example of *Mary Working In Our Lives*. She called herself "The Virgin of the Poor", and we, all of us, who had turned our backs on her Son and herself, were the poor for whom she came.

The Lady, Our Lady, then led Mariette to the Spring again. Mariette questioned her. "Beautiful Lady, you told me yesterday this spring was reserved for me. Why for me?"

Mary looked lovingly at the child, and laughed. Mariette had obviously misunderstood the message of the day before. The Lady clarified the statement.

"This spring is reserved for all nations." She stopped for a moment, then continued. "To relieve the sick."

We have to take a minute again to determine who Our Lady meant by *"all nations"*, and "the sick". There is the apparent meaning in the literal sense of what she said. Almost immediately, within a few months of the apparitions, many physical cures were recorded at Banneux. Pilgrims flocked from all over Europe, and then eventually from every corner of the world. There are even reports that during World War II, Nazi soldiers came to both the shrines of Beauraing and Banneux, praying to Mary for cures, conversions, and deliverance.

But we have to look for deeper meaning to her words. She came to give hope to "all nations". Shortly after this time, all nations would be embroiled in the war against Nazism and Fascism. Many of the nations were to be put under the crushing heel of the Third Reich. The rest of the nations were to fight the battle to stop the satanic onslaught of the Hitler Gang. Could these not have been the nations Our Lady spoke of to little Mariette Beco on that freezing January evening?

Mary said to the child, *"To relieve the sick"*. If we are to believe that Our Lady's visit from Heaven twice in one month to two different locations within Belgium was for a greater reason than the obvious, isn't it possible she was trying to prepare her dear children for what was to come? The next twelve years were to produce tens of millions of "sick" in mind and body. Lives would be uprooted, ripped apart at the seams. Families would be separated and destroyed. *"Whole nations will be annihilated."* In a time of hopelessness, could she not have been trying to give us a moment of hope? When all around you is being devastated, when you see your entire life crumbling between your fingers like so much dust, where can you turn? *"Mama!"* The words are instinctive. And she is always there, arms open, waiting to bind up

the wounds, nurse you, console you, and give you new beginnings. We believe that was what Mary was doing at Banneux in
January of 1933.

Our Lady said many important things to Mariette Beco during her visit to us in Banneux. She said something very unusual,
very demanding, possibly very threatening. On February 15,
when Mary came to the child, Mariette said to her, embarrassedly,
"The priest told me to ask you for a sign."

Mary smiled, but did not answer for a long time. What must
she have been thinking? How many times, how many signs do
you need? When will you stop asking me for signs? How much
change will take place, and for how long, if I give you a sign? Is
the extent of the belief based on the greatness of the sign?

Her eyes never left the child. Her smile never left her face,
but her eyes became very serious. Finally, she spoke to Mariette
what we believe to be the Keynote of her Message at Banneux.

"Believe in Me, I Will Believe in You."

The parish priest, Fr. Jamin, was incredulous when Mariette
repeated the message of Our Lady.

"But that's impossible." he said. "She said 'Believe in me',
but why would she have said 'I will believe in you.'"

I say **WHY NOT?** How long has she been bending to our
whim, giving us signs, proving to us that it's really her? And how
have we reacted? Have there been mass conversions, as at Guadalupe? Have we all gone back to the Faith, in thanksgiving for
the gifts she's given us? Why do you think she comes back so
often? Is it possible it's because we didn't pay attention to her the
last time, or the time before that? Or is it as Jesus prophesied in
the Parable of the Sower of Seeds in Luke 8:5–8?

*A farmer went out to sow some seed. In the sowing, some
fell on the footpath where it was walked on and the birds of the
air ate it up. Some fell on rocky ground, sprouted up, then with-
ered through lack of moisture. Some fell among briers, and the*

thorns growing up with it stifled it. But some fell on good soil, grew up, and yielded grain a hundredfold.

When we wrote about Our Lady's apparitions at Fatima, we said that we believed Fatima was **NOT** a failure. But it was not a great success. More attention has been paid to the Fatima message in the last 35 years than the 35 years immediately following the Apparition. Anyone who had been alive in 1917, and had witnessed the great **MIRACLE OF THE SUN** would have bet their very lives that the entire world would convert to Mary. Yet it did not happen.

So here we are in 1933, barely 15 years after the Miracle of the Sun. Mary returns, a faithful Mother to such unfaithful children, and we *Dare To ask for a Sign.* Perhaps it was time for the tables to be turned. She had reached out to us unconditionally for centuries, asking for, but never demanding, our faith, our belief. Maybe for the first time in 1933 years, she was putting a condition on her gifts. Might she not have been saying,

BELIEVE IN ME, and I WILL BELIEVE IN YOU
or
IF YOU BELIEVE IN ME, I WILL BELIEVE IN YOU

We've never had a personal appearance from Mary, and we don't believe we ever will. We're sure that if we were ever given that gift, we'd have a heart attack and die on the spot. Perhaps that's why she appears only to children. Their hearts are stronger than us *old folks.* But not ever having been given that gift, our speculation on what she may have really been saying at this time is just that, pure speculation. Or perhaps Divine Inspiration. We won't know for sure until we finally meet her face to face in heaven.

That message **BELIEVE IN ME, I WILL BELIEVE IN YOU** may very well be the most important message she has given us in this century. It requires a call to action on our part. She has always bailed us out in the past. In Fatima, when she spoke about Russia, and the devastation that would be caused if we did not pray for Russia's conversion, she gave us an out.

"But in the end, my Immaculate Heart will triumph. Russia will be converted, and there will be a period of peace."

On February 15, 1933, Mary knew what was going on even at that very moment, what satanic forces had already been unleashed in Germany, less than 100 miles from this little hamlet. She knew how they would build in the years to come, and overtake Europe like a giant Tidal Wave. She gave us the gifts we would need to get us through that time, but she also gave us a mandate, an action. **BELIEVE IN ME, I WILL BELIEVE IN YOU,** not with your mouth, but with your actions. Many people understood, and acted on that word of knowledge. Others did not.

Mary believes in us, even when we don't believe in ourselves. Could she have been giving us the gift of self worth? Was she telling us not to limit our horizons to our environment or background. **BELIEVE IN ME, AND NOTHING IS BEYOND YOU. BELIEVE IN ME, AND YOU CAN SOAR TO THE HEIGHTS OF HEAVEN, ACHIEVE THE IMPOSSIBLE DREAM, BECAUSE I BELIEVE IN YOU.** She knew how her children would be degraded to the level of animals in the next 12 years. Perhaps she was trying to give them the faith, the hope, and the strength they would need to survive the war years.

If only her children had acted on her words. That message was not only for that time and place. It was for the Jews in 1947, trying to create a home of their own, a country, Israel. It was for the black Americans of the southeastern United States in the 1960's. Were not Martin Luther King's words, **I HAVE A DREAM** the message of Mary at Banneux? She is trying to give strength to the victims of Apartheid in South Africa. It was for the members of Solidarity in Poland in the 1970's. Listen to her. She is pleading with you. **BELIEVE IN ME, I WILL BELIEVE IN YOU.**

Each time Our Lady left Mariette, the child was devastated. However, she had the memory of the visit, and the anticipation of the next visit to give her strength. But in the recesses of her mind, deep in her subconscious, she knew that eventually her time with Mary would have to come to an end. We believe she secretly dreaded this time. On March 2, that fear was to become a reality. It rained so hard that it seemed even Heaven was crying because the end was at hand. Mariette came out, covered by a shawl and umbrella, and began to pray. Soon the rain stopped. The clouds parted, revealing the stars and the heavens. Through the opening in the clouds the Queen of Heaven and Earth came for the last time to visit the little child of Banneux, and for the last time in a long time to her children on Earth.

She was more beautiful, and more majestic than she had appeared in previous visits. But she did not smile. Her face was very serious. Perhaps she, too, was sad for the end to have come. She said to the child, **I AM THE MOTHER OF THE SAVIOR, MOTHER OF GOD. PRAY A LOT. ADIEU.** With that, she blessed Mariette, and left. As she departed, the clouds covered the heavens again, and the rain continued to pour down relentlessly. Mariette was unaware of the heavy drops pounding on her face and body. She collapsed in a heap on the ground, crying convulsively, repeating Hail Marys as she cried.

As always, Mary was true to her word. Almost immediately, miraculous cures and conversions took place. As a matter of fact, the great number of miracles that took place at the little shrine was so overwhelming, it took the local Church by surprise. The poor Bishop had to determine the authenticity of the apparition of Banneux in the shadow of Beauraing. Perhaps Our Lady graced Banneux *more* at the outset because of the growing skepticism that had taken place during and immediately after the visits by Mary. For a time, it appeared that Mary at Beauraing and Mary at Banneux were *both* competing for recognition. She took care of that, also. In 1949, both apparitions were approved by the Church, Beauraing on July 2, and Banneux on August 22.

The little chapel she had requested was built, and pilgrims from all nations flocked to the shrine. In a few short years, the need for this place of hope became all too apparent to the people of Belgium, and all of Europe. After the war years, the shrine of Banneux was greatly enlarged. A basilica was built, although the original, tiny chapel, built on the spot where Our Lady first appeared, is still the main attraction to pilgrims who come here. Down the road, about 150 yards, is the statue of Our Lady of Banneux, **THE VIRGIN OF THE POOR**, standing above the spring which she reserved for all nations, to relieve the suffering of the sick.

Believe in Me, I Will Believe in You

What if we just once took her at face value, and did the things she asked of us? What if we believed in ourselves as much as she believes in us? What cures and conversions would we experience? How great would be the marvel? What if we were really strong enough to achieve world peace? What if?

Epilog On Beauraing and Banneux

Our Lord Jesus and our Sweet Mother Mary are always teaching us. We felt we had come up with a connection between the apparitions by Our Lady at Beauraing in December 1932, and Banneux in January 1933. There had to be a connection. Nothing like this had ever happened before.

We assumed it had to do with the onslaught of World War II. This dear little country, Belgium would soon be under the Iron Fist of the Third Reich, as, indeed, would be the entire continent of Europe. Belgium, however, was in a direct line from Germany to France. The Germans would need easy access to the French border, and Belgium provided the way.

In Beauraing, the main message given to the young girl, Fernande, was **DO YOU LOVE MY SON? THEN SACRIFICE YOURSELF FOR ME.** At first, everyone believed this statement was an afterthought, just for the girl. Then, after all the persecution the children had to endure in defense of the apparitions, the belief was that Our Lady was trying to give them strength.

In Banneux, the overpowering message was **BELIEVE IN ME, I WILL BELIEVE IN YOU.** There was, and is, much speculation as to what she meant in that statement. We've suggested many possibilities, any or all of which may be correct.

At first, it was assumed that these were two distinct messages, completely independent of each other. But with the holocaust of World War II, many believed that Our Lady was trying to prepare Europe, the whole world, for that matter, for the dark days to come. There was not much to hold onto, or believe in, for the victims of Europe. We believe she was trying to build strength, in them in anticipation for that time. **DO YOU LOVE MY SON? THEN SACRIFICE YOURSELVES FOR ME—BELIEVE IN ME, I WILL BELIEVE IN YOU.** Together they form one powerful teaching.

Prepare yourselves for days of darkness. You will have much to endure. But know that I am always with you. Believe that you are beloved of God. If you can love yourself, I can love you. With the strength of that love, all things are possible. We can change the world.

Our Lady was most definitely coming to the aid of her children of 1932/33, preparing them for the worst, which was to come. But were those combined messages just for that time? Read them. Try to understand what she was saying. Do they apply today as much, or even more so than in 1932? Why do women abort their children by the millions? Why do young people, people of all ages, for that matter, abuse their bodies with drugs and alcohol to the point of death? Why do young people, and all people, commit suicide in staggering proportions today? Why are we, as a

My angels she said. You are my angels.
Our Lady of Medjugorje, Yugoslavia

The children ran to the church to hide from the police
St. James Church—Medjugorje, Yugoslavia

civilization, hellbent on torturing and killing our brothers and sisters? Why are we, as a world, determined to destroy ourselves?

DO YOU LOVE MY SON? SACRIFICE YOURSELF FOR ME
BELIEVE IN ME, I WILL BELIEVE IN YOU

Medjugorje, 1981–(?): Our Lady of the Apocalypse?

Author's Note:

As of the writing of this book, the Apparitions of the Mother of God, Mary Most Holy, in the Parish of Medjugorje, Yugoslavia, have not yet been approved by the Church. The information given here is based on the following: our own personal experiences at Medjugorje in 1985–1986, a videotaped interview we made with Fr. Svetozar Kraljevic, a telephone interview with Fr. Robert Faricy, and three books on the subject, written by Fr. Svetozar Kraljevic, Fr. Joseph Pelletier, and Fr. Rene Laurentin, priests who are authorities on the apparitions. Also, we were given information by lay people, in particular, Stan and Marge Karminski, of Pennsylvania, who have dedicated their lives to spreading the word of Medjugorje. *WE WANT TO MAKE IT CLEAR THAT WE ARE NOT PREJUDGING THE CHURCH. WE STAND OBEDIENT TO THEIR FINAL DECISION ON WHETHER OUR LADY IS TRULY APPEARING IN MEDJUGORJE.*

This is the first and only reported apparition we have written about, *which has not yet been approved by the Church.* We are obedient to the Holy See. If it is ever determined by our Holy Father that Mary did not appear to the children at Medjugorje, we will humbly submit.

Medjugorje is a personal experience. It may always be a personal experience. But for me personally, Mary is back, pleading with us for our own survival, and the survival of the human race. We're at the edge of Apocalypse. This is terrifying clear. If you cannot believe in the apparition, believe and act on what is being taught there.

Medjugorje is one of, if not **the most exciting** place on earth today. The name of the village, which was a tongue twister 5 years ago, is on everybody's lips. The great question being asked is **IS OUR LADY APPEARING TO SIX TEENAGERS IN MEDJUGORJE, AND IF SO, HAS IT REALLY BEEN GOING ON SINCE 1981?**

Pilgrims by the thousands, and tens of thousands, arrive every week, especially during the summer. The official Church has made no comment on the authenticity of the apparitions; yet many priests have made what they call private Pilgrimages. They've brought groups on what is termed *Fact Finding Missions.* They come back to the United States, filled with the Holy Spirit, and the love of our Lady. The answer to the question *"Is She really there?"* has to be a personal one. Most of the clergy we have met, or heard, begin their talks with *"I'm not speaking for the Church, but for myself. I know personally, that Our Lady is appearing to her children at Medjugorje. You have to determine for yourself whether Our Blessed Mother is speaking to you there."*

Mary gives us miracles at Medjugorje. She shows us signs of her presence, and her power. There are healings and conversions. There is reconciliation, change of attitude towards self and neighbor. There are so many things going on in Medjugorje, as a result of the Miracle of Mary, I don't know where to begin. I keep picking out bits and pieces. Let me begin at the beginning, the beginning for me.

My Own Experience

On June 28th of 1985, four days after the 4th Anniversary of the First Apparition of our Lady in Medjugorje, we brought a group of Team Ministers on what was to be a Fact Finding Research Journey. On this visit, I received special spiritual gifts which caused me to believe that Mary was in Medjugorje. It is true that my own desires and feelings were involved, and I don't want to make any special claims, but these experiences were the *beginning* of Medjugorje for me, and I would like to share them before outlining the basic history of Medjugorje in general.

I don't think I ever doubted that Mary was there in Medjugorje. I have believed all my life, however, that I have a very close relationship with her. Much to my shame, I even believed that if she would come to *anyone*, she would come to *me*. If I went to Medjugorje, and something special didn't happen to me, it had to be because she wasn't there.

I gave her some very strict conditions. I fantasized, that as I waited outside the rectory where she appeared to the children, one of the visionaries would come out the door during the time Our Lady was with them, and say *"Is Bob Lord from California here? Our Lady would like to speak to him"*. I didn't think I was testing Mary, but really, I was.

I saw many things that first day. I spoke to Fr. Svetozar Kraljevic, a Franciscan priest who has written a book about the Apparitions. We made a videotaped interview, in which he talked about the fruits of Medjugorje, which were conversions, reconciliation, and a return to the Sacraments. He has experienced a great sadness because of the many who will not accept Our Lady's appearance at Medjugorje. In his talk, he asked us to look around at what is happening in Medjugorje. "Don't concern yourself with the question of whether or not Our Lady is appearing here. Look at the fruits. The church is packed with people day and night. The field outside is filled with priests hearing the confessions of all the people who come here. There's not enough room in the Church. Teen Agers, young people in their early 20's can be found all over the grounds. They practically live here. The nightly Mass is so crowded we had to put loudspeakers outside, so that those who cannot get into the Church can hear the Mass."

The Day the Sun Danced

At the time of the Apparitions, on June 28, I stood outside the rectory, watching the window from below, *waiting for Mary to call me*. The assembled group prayed the rosary in many languages. At the time when Our Lady was to appear, everybody ran to the left of the rectory to look at the sun, poised in the sky, between the church and the rectory. I wasn't about to follow them, but some of the children from our group called me over. There was an urgency in their voices. I ran over to where the crowd was, and looked up at the sun. Though it was a clear day without clouds, I could look right into the sun without being blinded by its brightness. It moved; it danced; it whirled. It shot out bolts of various colors, blue, green and yellow. It seemed to become larger. Then it stopped. It moved back to its original position. It became too bright to look into it, as it had been before the movement had begun.

As I returned to the rectory, to continue praying, I said to myself, "I'm not getting into that. This is too much like what happened at Fatima". I considered myself the victim of hysteria, and let it go at that. However, the next day, when Fr. Svetozar was giving us a talk on Medjugorje, a priest asked him to comment on the fact that **OVER 250 PEOPLE HAD SEEN THE SUN DANCE AS I HAD**. Fr. Svet answered that this phenomenon had happened many times since 1981. But they don't like to talk about signs. It confuses the true message of Our Lady.

Getting back to that first night; after the phenomenon of the Sun, which I did not consider a sign, I waited for someone to invite me into the room. No one did. Our Lady had done nothing special for me, so I thought. I went back to the hotel angry, frustrated and disappointed. On the outside, I said I didn't believe, but inside, I was hurt. I thought she just didn't love me enough.

Mary Answers Me

The following morning, Fr. Svetozar had arranged for us to celebrate Mass in the room where Our Lady had appeared over 1,000 times to the children, off to the right of the main altar of the Church. There were about 50 Irish Charismatics, and our little band of 12. It's a very tiny room, so we were packed in like sardines. I had been helping the priest prepare the altar for the Mass. When the crowd came in, I found myself pinned against a wall. I couldn't move. Penny was way over on the other side of the room, squeezed in with the rest of our group. During the Mass, before the priest asked us to present our petitions, he prefaced it by saying that *whatever we asked our Lady for in this room would be granted us.* I asked for the release of the 39 hostages from the TWA Hijacking, which had occurred in Athens two weeks before.

It was June 29, 1985. I was not to find out until two days later in Italy, when we called our Ministry office in California, that my prayer had been answered. The Hostages had been released Sunday, June 30. Luz Elena Sandoval, who heads up our Hispanic Ministry, was in tears of joy. She said everybody was amazed that the hostages were released, because on Friday, the 28th, President Reagan had said something negative about the hijackers, or the negotiators, and as a result, all negotiations were broken off. She didn't know how it happened, but on Sunday morning, they were released. Everybody in the United States was in a state of shock, but also in a state of great joy. Now, we know that thousands, probably millions, of people had prayed for the release of those hostages. I don't make any special claim that it was *my* prayer that did it. But we prayed for the release of the hostages on *Saturday*, and they were released on *Sunday.* If everyone was shocked by their release, it is perhaps because they didn't know what we know. They didn't know who the real power was.

I knew that day, that Mary had heard me in Medjugorje, had added my prayers to millions of others, and had acted in a way which showed her love for me. She had treated me in a very spe-

cial way, but her way, not mine. I was reminded of her visit to Juan Diego in 1531, when the Bishop requested a sign. Mary gave him the Miraculous Tilma of Guadalupe, but not what the bishop had asked for. I'm also reminded of Our Lady's appearance to Bernadette Soubirous in Lourdes in 1858, where Cure Peyramale asked for a sign, and Our Lady gave Bernadette the words "I am the Immaculate Conception", which the child could not begin to understand, but the priest did. As an added gift, she gave us the Miraculous Spring, which has been running since 1858.

I have known Mary for so long, and studied her ways so much, I can't understand why I expected her to do *what* I wanted, in the *way* that I wanted. She's so much more generous. I asked her for a bone, and she gave me meat. Yet, I was upset that she hadn't given me the bone!

A Third Miracle from Medjugorje?

We had made a decision right then, after hearing about the release of the hostages, that when we returned to the United States, we would write about Medjugorje, show the videotape we had made, and spread the message Our Lady had given us in Medjugorje. But we had another month to remain in Israel and Europe, and two more Pilgrimages to lead. Early in July, our grandson, Rob, who has asthma, became afflicted with allergies. The pollen was running rampant in Italy. By the time we reached Fatima, he was extremely sick. We called his doctor in Encino, California, who prescribed Prednisone. The next group who came across brought the medicine. By the time we got the medication, we were in Jerusalem. The prescription called for 6 tablets every six hours, or a *total of 24 tablets in 24 hours*. This is an extremely heavy dosage, but the doctor had treated Rob since he was an infant, and Rob was now 18 years old. We trusted in his judgment.

Rob's allergies stopped, but he became seriously ill. He was so sick he could barely lift his head, or talk. We asked our spiritual director on the pilgrimage, a beautiful, spirit-filled Mexican priest, Fr. Alejandro Burciaga, to pray over Rob. About six of us gathered in our hotel room. The priest prayed. We all prayed. At one point in our praying, Fr. Alejandro said, *"I can see Our Lady. She is holding Rob in her arms."*

I immediately thought of Our Lady of Medjugorje. I said to her, "Dear Mary, we're already committed to spreading the message of Medjugorje in the United States, but wouldn't it be wonderful if we had a **THIRD MIRACLE** to tell them about?"

The priest said, *"Let everything that is not of Jesus come out of him"*. The praying ended. We all went to bed. At one o'clock in the morning, the phone rang. It was our daughter, Sr. Clare, calling from San Bernardino, California, to tell us that Rob was *allergic to Prednisone*. When the phone had rung, Rob woke up and went into the bathroom. I scolded my daughter for calling at such an ungodly hour, that she had awakened Rob, and he was sick. He, in the meantime, proceeded to have diarrhea and vomit at the same time. **EVERYTHING CAME OUT OF HIM.** When he was finished, he crawled back into the bed, barely able to move. The next morning, he awakened as if he had never been ill. Everything that was not of Jesus had come out of him. Had Our Lady at Medjugorje done it again?

We did as we had promised. We promoted the word of Medjugorje, as told to us by Fr. Svetozar. We made copies of his videotape, and sent them out wherever people were interested in seeing them. The reception was outstanding. It was the first time that we had shown a videotape, 45 minutes long, of which 32 minutes was a talk by a priest, where the people were glued to the television set.

We made Medjugorje an optional extension to any pilgrim who wanted to go personally, on some of our Pilgrimages for 1986. It became one of the most requested shrines. It seemed that all was working according to the plan of Our Lady, until the outburst of terrorism overseas began. Frightened people canceled in droves. There was no way that we could convince them that Our Lady would protect them on a Pilgrimage to her shrines. The struggle began. But the struggle was good. Medjugorje is struggle. If we were not willing to accept, no, *embrace* struggle, Medjugorje could not have the meaning that Mary has planned for us there. So our groups were small, but special.

Every pilgrim who journeyed in faith with us was hand picked by Our Lady for a special reason. We didn't know why they were picked. We feared that some of them would not be able to adjust to the poverty and austerity of Medjugorje. How little we trusted in Mary. How little we had learned over the course of the year. Everyone who went with us was touched in a way that will never leave them. There are some families who go on Pilgrimage with us every year. They have been blessed financially by the Lord; they want for nothing material. We wondered how they would be affected by Medjugorje. We all stayed in private homes, less than a half mile from the church. The rooms were small. We had to share the hall bathroom. It didn't bother any of them. Dear Lord, how we were blessed.

Then there was the greatest gift for me, the sign which I can never forget, the responsibility I can never deny. The following reflection was begun by me on July 5, 1986, in Medjugorje, and finished on the plane from Amsterdam to Los Angeles on July 19. I had such an urgency to write it, I took every spare moment I had, including the hours from 11 pm to 12:30 am every night in our hotel room, very often writing in the bathroom, so as not to awaken Penny. The gift I had asked for in 1985, the condition I had set for Mary, was given to me unconditionally in 1986.

I was in the room during the apparition of Our Lady
Saturday, July 5, 1986

Tonight, I stood in the room with the visionaries during Our Lady's visit from Heaven to Medjugorje. At the time I was in a state of shock. I still find it hard to come to terms with exactly what gift my sweet Lady and her dear Son Jesus have given me.

The only people allowed in are priests, sick children, and friends of friends. I didn't fall into any of the three categories, with possible exception that my friend might have been the visitor from Heaven. By all that is logical, I should not have been there. I should have been outside with the crowd, singing "Ave, Ave", praying the rosary, and wishing I could be there in the room.

My darling wife knelt on the gravel, outside the rectory, praying, from the moment I walked up the stairs to wait at the doorway. There were some French priests who seemed to know everybody. There was a persistent Italian priest who managed to get two young men up the stairs. The guard at the gate drew the line when he tried to get a third, a woman up the stairs. The two young men and I were the only ones not dressed in clerical black and white. The guard must have left the gate for a moment, because all of a sudden, a mob of people charged up the steps, jamming together. The guard came up and chased everyone down the steps. He looked at me, and told *me to go*. I pointed to my priest, and said weakly, "I'm with him". The man looked at me. My heart pounded. Then he walked away from me. I looked down at my wife. She was still on her knees, only now she was crying.

We waited for what seemed like hours at the doorway. I tried to be as inconspicuous as possible. My mind raced feverishly. I didn't want to move, for fear someone would realize I was there, and shouldn't be, and throw me out. But I wanted to look around to see the visionaries as they came up the stairs, so I could take pictures of them. Every time I looked down towards the people, Penny motioned me to turn around and hide.

People kept going in and out of the house. Franciscans, Sisters, friends, friends of friends, the parade never ended. Every time someone came up the steps, I knew it was to tell me to leave. But they didn't. I looked down to Penny. She jumped up off her knees, ran over to the steps, and handed her pilgrim's cross up to me. I almost couldn't reach it. She's only 5 foot tall. It was her way of going into the room with me, (as she said), in my pocket. Finally, after an eternity, the door opened for us to go inside.

My actual movement inside the room is hazy. I can recall passing from one place to the next. But I don't remember actually

walking, only moving. I didn't know what to expect from the
room, or where to stand. I had never been in there before, nor had
I seen pictures of it. It was a typical priest's room. It was very
small, perhaps 15' x 20', full of furniture. There was unopened
mail on a table, and chairs scattered about, all in all, a very un-
pretentious room. There was a bed on either side, a cot against
the window, and a fold out bed against the wall. Above this bed
were shelves with books and videotapes stacked high, in no particular order. Above the book shelves was a blank wall, except for
a crucifix and a plaque of praying hands. Against this wall, Mary,
my Lady, the Mother of Our God, comes to visit her children
every night at about 6:45 pm. And on this one very special night,
July 5 of 1986, I was there when she came.

We began the rosary. The time flew, and yet I was in that
room forever. It was very warm, because the summers are brutal
in Yugoslavia, and because we were jammed into this little space.
I found myself looking at the room, trying desparately to commit
it to memory. Then I saw a priest remove the cross he was wearing, and place it on the bed. That was the first time I noticed that
there were bags full of rosaries and religious medals on the bed.
In a soft whisper, Our Lady reminded me of our Pilgrims's
crosses. I was wearing mine, and Penny had given me hers. I took
hers out of my pocket and tried to take mine off my neck. There
was a great struggle. It had gotten caught in my camera strap. The
more I fought with it, the more entangled it became. The more
difficult it was, the more I knew I had to get it off my neck, to put
both crosses on the bed. I didn't know how much time I had,
because the rosary was coming to an end. In a fit of frustration, I
took everything off my neck. A man standing next to me held my
camera while I untangled the Pilgrims's Cross. Our priest gave
me his, as did our teen aged pilgrim, Jennifer. I took all and
placed them on the bed.

A few minutes later, Marija and Jakov got up, went over to
the bed, and knelt near where I had placed our crosses. They
prayed, but I couldn't understand their prayers. Suddenly, they

stopped, and looked up at the wall, above the book case, where the crucifix hung. Their eyes were fixed. They were frozen. Their lips moved rapidly, as if they were speaking very quickly, but no sounds came out of their mouths. Time stood still. The whole world stopped. I looked at them, then at the wall, then back to them again. I closed my eyes. There was not a sound. Even the sick children were still. **SHE WAS THERE.** I know she was there. I didn't *see* anything. I didn't *hear* anything. I can't even say I felt a physical presence in the room. I felt, what can I say? Peace? Joy? Security? A blanket of protection? All those feelings, and more. It's not explainable in human terms. My vocabulary is too limited to describe a sensation such as I have never experienced before, and will never experience again. I do know that at one point, there was no one in the room, or the whole world, except Mary and me.

As quickly as it had begun, it ended. The seers dropped their heads and prayed aloud for a few moments. Then they got up and left the room. Their faces were expressionless, as if they were not aware of what had just happened. There was a mad dash to follow behind Marija and Jakov. I waited. Silence blanketed the room. It was empty now except for me, and so quiet. But there was something I can't describe, in the walls, in the beds, in the air. There was a sweetness about the air, a fragrance of cleanliness, of purity. Anita, an Irish girl who works at the shrine, came in to tell me to leave. Our eyes met. She smiled, turned around and left. She knew I wasn't ready yet. I'm sure she has seen the expression I was wearing on many faces over the years. *In that room, at that time*, I felt a closeness to Mary that I had never felt. I had to savor as much of the experience as my senses could absorb. I knew that my dear wife, who had struggled and sacrificed so much for me to go into that room, was waiting for me, to hear what I had to say. That's what finally moved me out of the room.

A soft breeze caressed my face as I walked out into the hot Yugoslavian evening. It enveloped me, and cooled me. A great peace had come over me, but also a numbness. My mind went blank. I wasn't quite sure what I would say to Penny, or the rest of our group. I didn't know exactly what had happened. I still don't. With each passing day, more and more is revealed to me. All I could say was *"She was there. She is there."*

We're reminded of the words of St. Paul, after having been given the privilege of a vision of Heaven. He said, *"Eyes have not seen, ears have not heard, what God has in store for those who love Him."*

That was the high point of Medjugorje for our family. Admittedly, it is an emotional account, but **HOW *CAN* I SPEAK OF MEDJUGORJE?** My story had to be based on what happened to me. But it isn't necessary to rely on my personal experiences in forming your own conclusions. We're not trying to *convince* anyone to believe, or not to believe in Medjugorje. The story of Medjugorje is much greater than what I have shared.

Our Lady Comes to Medjugorje

There are six main characters in our account of Mary's visit to Medjugorje, beginning on June 24, 1981, and ending. . . . ? They are, in the order of their appearance, MIRJANA DRAVI-CEVIC, IVANKA IVANKOVIC, VICKA IVANKOVIC, (NO RELATION TO IVANKA), IVAN DRAVICEVIC, MARIJA PAVLOVIC, and JAKOV COLO. The oldest at the time was 17, and the youngest, 10. Because the full names of the young people sound like the cast of a Russian drama, we will limit ourselves to their first names. There were two other children involved the first day, IVAN IVANKOVIC, and MILKA PAVLOVIC, Marija's sister. But they only saw the Lady on the first day. The other six have been recipients of the gift of Mary from June 24 onwards.

June 24, 1981—The Beginning

Summers are extremely hot in Yugoslavia, especially in the area of Medjugorje. Relief doesn't usually come until late afternoon. School and work go on, however. Late in the afternoon of June 24, 1981, Mirjana and Ivanka were taking a walk in the little

Mary speaks to her children
July 5, 1986
Marija and Jakov, Visionaries at Medjugorje, Yugoslavia

Pilgrims carry crosses up the Hill of the Apparitions barefooted
Medjugorje, Yugoslavia

village of Bijakovici, near their homes. It had begun to cloud up, but there were no cool breezes to give them relief from the heat. Ivanka looked up at Mount Podbrdo. She saw a bright light, and what appeared to be the figure of a young woman suspended in the air. She nudged Mirjana. She said, "Mirjana, look! It's Our Lady". Mirjana's response was natural. "Give me a break. Would Our Lady appear to us?" She never looked up at the mountain. They continued walking. This seems strange, that Ivanka would just walk away without saying anything, or looking back; and that Mirjana never bothered to look at the mountain. We have to believe that they were frightened. We thank Our Lord Jesus for giving His Mother such patience. She's been through this with us every time she comes to visit us. She waited.

The girls returned along the same path later in the afternoon with Milka, who was looking for sheep. This time the three of them saw Our Lady at the same time. They went down on their knees immediately. Another comrade, Vicka (pronounced Viska) was not with the two girls, but was told where they could be found. She came out from the village to meet them. When she arrived at the place where they were, she saw her friends on their knees, praying. Mirjana said to Vicka "Look up there. Our Lady". Panic set in. Vicka didn't look up the mountain. She ran for her life. She lost her shoes in the process.

Along the road, she saw the two Ivans picking apples. She told them what was happening, and they decided to have a look. Perhaps because men were now going, Vicka went back to the place where she had run away from her friends. But as soon as Ivan Dragicevic saw what was going on, he turned tail and ran away. Now, Vicka and the older Ivan (20 years old), knelt with the three girls and prayed.

They all saw Our Lady on the mountain. All said that she was holding something, but they could not agree on what it was. Ivanka thought it was the Child Jesus. Mary waved for them to come up the mountain to her, but they were too frightened to move. (The feeling was similar to that of the children of Beauraing, who ran to their homes screaming after they had seen Mary. But they couldn't wait to see her again.) These young people were frightened, but also in awe. Even from that distance, they could tell the Lady was beautiful.

They didn't know what to do, so they continued to pray for about 40 minutes. Then Mary disappeared. The girls stayed there a little longer. It began to drizzle. This brought them out of their trance. They all went home.

They couldn't contain themselves when they returned to their homes. They had to tell their family and friends what had happened. Naturally, they were ridiculed, called crazy. It didn't seem to bother any of them. There was not much sleep that night. Although they hadn't seen the Lady that closely, their hearts pounded with the splendor of her. They had felt so peaceful with her. Would she come back again?

Mary Comes a Second Time—Thursday June 25, 1981

The best way to describe that second day was *excited anticipation*. The young people tried to go about their normal duties, but in the front of their consciousness was the mountain where they had seen the Lady. They were trying to make excuses to return. As soon as their work was over, the three girls, Ivanka, Mirjana and Vicka headed back to the spot where they had been the day before. They agreed that if the Lady came back, Vicka would run to get Marija and Jakov, two of their friends who had not seen the vision on the previous day.

Ivanka walked ahead of her two friends. She couldn't contain her enthusiasm. Some of the townspeople followed along, out of guarded curiosity. Suddenly, Ivanka cried out "Look! There she is!" Way up, farther up the mountain than before, the same vision that they had seen yesterday, was there, looking at them. Vicka went to get Marija and Jakov. Our Lady waved to them to climb the mountain to her. They ran so quickly up the mountain, it seemed to them and the onlookers as if they were flying. Vicka recalled being barefoot. She thought for sure she would be full of cuts and scratches, but there was not even a nick on her legs or hands. As they approached the place where Mary was waiting, they all felt themselves thrown down to the ground on their knees. Jakov was thrown into a thorned bush, but he wasn't hurt at all.

Any fears, any doubts that they might have had as to who she was, melted away as they found themselves in the warmth of her presence. Indescribably beautiful is the best description they could give of her. She had a beauty that was not of this world. The most expressive part of her that they could remember were her eyes, those radiant eyes. They burrowed deep into the souls of the young people. There was a warmth and peace that stayed with them.

The children asked why she had come. She told them that this area was filled with people of faith. She was asking for peace and reconciliation. Ivanka had lost her mother a few months before. She asked about her. The sweet Lady told her not to worry about her mother; she was happy with her. Mirjana shared a little about how the people in the village were calling them crazy. Mary just smiled.

Day Three—Friday, June 26

We can picture Our Lady up in the heavens, watching the proceedings in the little village of Bijakovici that first Friday. As the afternoon wore on, and the appointed hour of 6 p.m closed in, great crowds converged on the hill of Mt. Podbrdo. They came from as far away as Citluk, and Ljubuski. The word had indeed spread throughout the countryside. There were a reported 3,000 spectators and believers on the hill that day. They came to see, or to touch, or to be touched, by the most powerful, yet loving woman the world has ever known. Our Lord Jesus might have stood by her side, and said, "It's good. It's just the beginning, but it's good."

The question on everyone's lips and minds was, **IF IT'S REALLY MARY, THE MOTHER OF GOD, WHY HAS SHE**

COME? WHAT IS SHE TRYING TO TELL US? IS THE END OF THE WORLD AT HAND? The situation in the world was tenuous, at best. We were sitting on a fire keg. The slightest sneeze in the wrong direction could mean mass destruction. Was she here to tell us that? Propaganda on both ends of the world had the people of the Communist Bloc countries believing that all Americans were satans, ready to destroy their peace loving world at a moment's notice. Americans were made to believe that every citizen of a Soviet Bloc country was a spy, working feverishly for the government in an effort to overthrow our country and our way of life.

We have to go back to Mexico City in the year 1531, to get an inkling of what Our Lady might have had in mind. Mary had to use Juan Diego, the least likely candidate, to bring about peace and harmony between the Spanish and the Indians, on the eve of massacre. IT HAD TO BE DONE THROUGH AN INDIAN. Was she doing the same thing here in this Communist country? Was this her way of bringing the whole world together in this barren land, with an eye towards peace, before nuclear holocaust could obliterate civilization as we know it? Nobody knew.

Three lights were seen on the horizon. It had been established that this was Our Lady's sign that she was coming. Everybody could see it. Marinko Ivankovic and some friends cordoned off the young people from the onrush of humanity that hit the hill.

The visionaries saw Mary on the hill, much higher than she had been the day before. Each day, she made herself more unattainable. They had to climb greater heights to reach her than the previous day. They began to run to her. This time, they didn't fly up the hill as they had done yesterday. The boys were faster than the girls, who needed help from Marinko to find their way up. They found her standing on a cloud. *This has since become the symbol of Our Lady of Medjugorje.*

We're sure that Mary was amused at the rituals the children performed, which had been done by their predecessors at

Lourdes, Fatima, Beauraing, and on and on. Only the faces change. Vicka was the one with the holy water this time. She sprinkled it on Our Lady, saying,

"If you are Our Lady, stay with us. If you are not, go away." Mary smiled tenderly. That being over, the children breathed a deep sigh of relief, and began asking her questions.

Mirjana asked about her grandfather, who had died the year before. Mary said, *"He is well."*

Ivanka asked again about her mother. Was there any message for the family? Our Lady answered her, *"Obey your grandmother and be good to her, because she is old and cannot work."*

Ivanka then asked her the question that was on everybody's mind. *"Why have you come here, and what do you want?"*

Our Lady answered, **"I HAVE COME BECAUSE THERE ARE MANY BELIEVERS HERE. I WANT TO BE WITH YOU TO CONVERT AND RECONCILE EVERYONE"**

This message turns out to be the keynote of her entire message at Medjugorje, **PEACE THROUGH CONVERSION AND RECONCILIATION WITH GOD AND NEIGHBOR.**

It was extremely hot that day. Even though Our Lady came at the coolest hour of the day, the heat, coupled with the closeness of the thousands of people assembled, was too much for the girls. All the girls but Marija fainted. They had to be carried down the hill.

Our Lady told them she would return the next day. She ended her visit with the words, *"Go in the peace of God."*

As Marija was walking towards the village, she saw a multicolored cross. In front of it, Our Lady stood, crying. This cut Marija to the heart, seeing the Blessed Virgin crying. Mary said to Marija, **"PEACE! PEACE, PEACE! RECONCILE YOUR-SELVES."**

It was as if Our Lady felt she had not gotten her message across strongly enough on the hill; she reiterated it in a powerful way, crying, and showing Marija the cross.

Day Four—Saturday, June 27

On the fourth day, the Pastor of St. James Church, Fr. Jozo Zovko, who had been away in Zagreb, heard about the apparitions. He had an interview with the young people in the morning.

The authorities from Citluk couldn't help but be aware of the commotion going on in the little village five miles from their town. They brought the children in for an interrogation that afternoon, and consequently, sent them to a doctor for an examination. By the time they were finished, they had to take a taxi back to Bijakovici to be there in time for the visit from Mary. Only Ivan did not go back with them. He was taken home by a relative. He also did not go to the Hill of the Apparitions that night.

The estimated crowd of pilgrims was 15,000 on the fourth day. We're reminded of the words of St. Peter on Mount Tabor, as Our Lord Jesus showed Himself in His divine state. **Lord, It Is Good for Us to Be Here!**

Marinko Ivankovic, who had befriended the visionaries, and gained their trust, wanted to try something different that night. He got them to agree to break up into two groups. Jakov and Marija waited at the foot of the hill for Our Lady to make herself known to them. The other three girls, Ivanka, Mirjana and Vicka, went up the hill to where Mary had appeared on one of the other days, and waited.

An uncanny thing happened. They saw the light, and Our Lady, way up at the top of the hill. Marija began to run at breakneck speed. No one was able to keep up with her. She felt as if she were being pulled up the rocky hill to the place where Our Lady waited for her. But when she arrived, Mary disappeared. The young girl was bewildered. Soon the others joined her.

The children felt themselves being forced to their knees. *She was there.* When the crowds saw the light which preceded Our Lady, and the children fall to their knees, they descended like locusts on the place. This caused another unusual occurrence. They crowded in so close to the children that they were stepping on Our Lady's gown. The visionaries tried to get them to back off, but nobody listened to them. Mary disappeared.

She came back again. A young man stepped on her veil; she disappeared again. Finally, Marinko and some of his friends formed a circle around the young people, so that no one would step on the veil of Our Lady.

She returned to them a third time. They began asking questions. Vicka asked her to prove to the people that she was there. Mary replied that they should believe as if they were seeing her themselves.

Mirjana said that people were calling them drug addicts and epileptics, especially her. Couldn't Our Lady do *something* that would make the people believe they were not crazy. Mary said there had always been injustice in the world, and not to pay attention to it. This reminds us of her words to St. Catherine Laboure in the Chapel of the Miraculous Medal. "My grace will be enough for you." In retrospect, she's always right. But it's **SO HARD** when you're going through it.

Ivanka asked her who she was. She replied,

I AM THE BLESSED VIRGIN MARY

They asked if there was a message for the Franciscan priests of the Parish of St. James. She replied,

THE FRIARS SHOULD BELIEVE FIRMLY

Mary disappeared again, but she had not given them the blessing she normally gave when she left them, so they were sure she would come back again. They waited and prayed, but she did not return. They started down the mountain. Then, suddenly, they broke away from the crowd, and yelled "THERE SHE IS!!" Marinko and his friends formed a protective cordon around them. Our Lady looked at them with an outpouring of love. She said to them, **"MY ANGELS, YOU ARE MY DEAR ANGELS."** *Then she*

told them to return the next day at the same time. As she left them,
*she said, "**GO IN THE PEACE OF GOD.***"

If you remember, we told you that Ivan was not with the other visionaries at the Hill of the Apparitions that day. He was feeling the pressure of the disbelievers, as were his parents. When the visionaries were called to the police station, his parents asked him to stay away from the hill for a while. He was sad at not having seen the beautiful Lady that day, but he felt uncomfortable with all the attention they were receiving. He walked alone on the road after the apparitions had taken place. Our sweet Lady had not forgotten him; she was aware that he had not been with the other five this day. She came to him on the road. She told him to be at peace, and have courage. As she left him, she smiled that smile which melts all hearts. Needless to say, Ivan rejoined the group.

Day Five—Sunday, June 28

The crowds reached record proportions this day. It was estimated that 15,000 pilgrims came to the little village of Bijakovici, to see, to hear, to be in the presence of Mary.

When we talk of Lourdes and Fatima, or Guadalupe, 15,000 people is respectable, but not overwhelming. However, for a small village like Medjugorje, it boggles the mind where 15,000 might have fit. We know they were all centrally located on the Hill, or near the Hill. It's a miracle in itself for that many people, that many cars and buses, to have been able to get anywhere near the little town. But for Mary, nothing is impossible.

For the first time, priests were in attendance. Fr. Zrinko Cuvalo was the Devil's Advocate at the beginning of the apparitions. However, he was to become a staunch defender of the children. With him was a Fr. Viktor Kosir.

Maria and Jakov went ahead of the others. They shouted, "LOOK! LOOK, LOOK!" They ran up the hill. According to eyewitnesses, including Fr. Zrinko, Marija ran so fast, she looked like she was flying. When the other young people reached the place where Marija and Jakov were, they knelt down. They began speaking to Our Lady.

They asked Mary many questions. The young people did not make these up in their heads. They were given these questions by many people, priests, villagers, their parents and others. They were the same things that Our Lady had heard so many times before in so many places. But she has such patience with her children. She smiled at them patiently, and answered everything.

They asked "What do you want of us?"

She replied **"FAITH AND RESPECT FOR ME"**.

Their next question was "Dear Blessed Virgin, what do you want of our priests?"

She looked very seriously at them. **"THAT THEY BELIEVE FIRMLY"**.

Then they asked "Dear Blessed Virgin, why don't you appear in the church so that everybody can see you?"

Her response was **"BLESSED ARE THEY WHO HAVE NOT SEEN AND WHO BELIEVE"**.

They knew that she reacted favorably to prayer and hymns. They asked her "Dear Blessed Virgin, do you prefer that we sing or pray?"

She smiled broadly at them. **"DO BOTH, SING AND PRAY"**.

They asked about the great number of people present. "Dear Blessed Virgin, what do you want of these people gathered here?

She looked out over the huge crowd, and somehow you could be certain that she knew each of them personally. She looked back at the visionaries. **"THAT THEY BELIEVE WITHOUT SEEING"**.

She disappeared. They were sure she would return. They began singing "Mary, Mary, how beautiful you are". She came back. She smiled at them very lovingly, and said **"MY ANGELS, MY DEAR ANGELS."**

"Dear Blessed Virgin," they repeated, "What do you want of these people here?"

She said "THAT THOSE WHO DO NOT SEE ME BELIEVE LIKE THE SIX OF YOU WHO SEE ME."

They had been holding their big question for last. "Dear Blessed Virgin, will you leave us some sign here on earth that will convince these people that we are not liars and that we are not playing games?"

She looked at each of them individually. She didn't speak for a moment. She smiled at them. "GO IN THE PEACE OF GOD", she said. Then she left them.

As the thousands of pilgrims left the Hill of the Apparitions, the message of Our Lady at Medjugorje began to make itself known. The villagers came out of their homes, offering to share whatever they had to drink with the thirsty people who had been on the Hill for such a long time. They didn't charge them anything. They didn't think of profit.

Day Six—Monday, June 29

The harrassment from the authorities continued. The six young people were sent for a psychiatric examination. They were kept with the doctor until late afternoon. He could find nothing wrong with them.

They had to rush back to Medjugorje to be there in time for their appointment with Our Lady. The crowds were greater than the day before, if that was possible. They had to struggle to get through. But Our Lady waited for them.

There were many questions, and many answers that day. Mary asked for *firm faith* and *confidence* from those who came to this hill.

From the questions asked, it was obvious that the young people were extremely concerned about their ability to hold up under the pressure that was being put on them. At one point, they were reported to have said, "THE ONLY ONES WHO DON'T BELIEVE US ARE THE CHURCH AND THE GOVERN-MENT". However, in addition, there were innuendoes from the local people, and snide remarks made under the breaths of many skeptics.

The seers asked Mary if they would be able to endure the persecution, which seemed to get worse, not better. She looked at them with the *Love of a Mother for Her Children*. Then she said, **"YOU WILL ENDURE IT, MY ANGELS"**.

There was a woman, a doctor, whom the authorities had sent to observe the goings on. The children asked Our Lady if the doctor could touch her veil. Mary replied **"THERE HAVE AL-WAYS BEEN UNFAITHFUL JUDASES. LET HER COME"**. As the woman touched her veil, Our Lady disappeared. The doctor didn't feel anything in her hands, but she went down the mountain visibly shaken.

The children prayed. Our Lady returned. The next question showed the tension the children were under from those who wanted favors from Mary. The visionaries almost begged for a positive response. This is how it went.

Seers: Dear Madonna, will this little boy, Daniel, ever be able to speak?

Please make a miracle so that everyone will believe us.

> These people love you very much.
> Please Madonna, make ONE miracle.
> SHE IS LOOKING AT HIM!
> Dear Madonna, say something.
> SHE IS LOOKING AT HIM!
> Dear Madonna, say something, we ask you!
> Say something, we ask you!
> Say something, dear Madonna!

Finally, she answered them.

"LET THEM BELIEVE THAT HE WILL BE HEALED

Then she said, **"GO IN GOD'S PEACE"**. She left them.

As a special gift from Our Lady to the visionaries, the boy

began to talk that day. He was not completely cured for some time, but eventually, the healing was complete. It helped their credibility a little with some, but not with others.

We have to go back here to the question of their ability to withstand the cruel things that were being said of them. This is the second time in the first week that this was brought up, again by Mirjana. She shared a little with Fr. Vlasic after the apparition how disgusted she felt about what they had "been put through" at the psychiatric clinic. She talked about having been taken to a MORGUE, where they were with LUNATICS. It's not likely that they went to a morgue, but probably a prison for incorrigibles. She, the second oldest of the group, was having great difficulty with this. Most likely, they were all feeling the pressure from the interrogations, but Mirjana voiced it more than others. After the grueling session they had gone through that day, Mirjana told Fr. Vlasic she most likely would not go back to the Hill of the Apparitions ever again.

However, the next day, she was there with the rest. When asked why she changed her mind, she said that as the time approached, she had an overpowering urge to be there. Nothing could have kept her away.

Day 7—Tuesday, June 30

Today was the turning point for the seers and the apparitions. We see how God accomplishes His goals. He uses anyone or anything for His Plan. No one is beyond the strength of the Lord.

The police sent two women to gather up the visionaries from their homes and take them away from the area of Medjugorje. They reasoned that if the children were not there, and there was no show for the pilgrims, the people would be disappointed, leave the Hill, and the whole *charade* would come to an end. Of course, they were using man's logic, and Jesus and Mary are not restricted to man's limited resources.

Ivan was not with the group again this day. The government women drove the five children all around the surrounding villages. When the time approached for the rendezvous with Our Lady, the seers were about three miles away, at Cerno. They talked the women into stopping the car. They got out and prayed on their knees. They were able to see Mt. Podbrdo from Cerno, and the thousands of pilgrims on the Hill, waiting for them and the Mother of God.

A great light appeared on the mountain. The visionaries could see it from three miles away. The two women from the government could also see it. The light moved from the mountain to the place where the children were praying. The government women saw that, too. Mary came to the children.

They asked her if she minded visiting them here, rather than on the mountain. She said she did not mind.

They asked her if she minded if they didn't go back to the mountain, but met with her at the church. Our Lady hesitated for a minute, then said **"I WILL NOT MIND, MY ANGELS."**

After this, Our Lady left them. She said her words of departure, **"GO IN THE PEACE OF GOD"** When she left them, however, she faded slowly. As soon as she was gone, they all saw a light on Mt. Podbrdo. The government women brought them back to Medjugorje. Then they went back to Citluk, and resigned their jobs. They had been touched that day. They were never the same.

When the young people returned to Medjugorje, they went to visit the pastor of the Church of St. James, Fr. Jozo Zoko. They suggested having the apparitions at the church, but he was noncommital. The visionaries wanted to go up on the hill to tell the people what had happened. It was decided, however, that it was best for the people not to see them that night.

When they arrived home, they were told that Marinko Ivanovic had been arrested. He was charged with "concocting the whole Apparition hoax". They all went to the police station to vouch for Marinko. By the time their day had ended, it really contained only 30 minutes which they would have considered pleasant, the time Our Lady came to visit them. But that 30 minutes gave them the strength they needed to endure all the persecution the rest of the day held for them.

Their lives became a series of pressure points and releases. The pressure points were all they had to endure from the Church, in the form of questions, and the government, through accusations and threats of many kinds. In addition, there were the non-believers who took pleasure in poking fun at them. It hurt the most when they were attacked by people of their own age and from their village. Their only releases were the apparitions by Our Lady.

Day 8—Wednesday, July 1

The power of the Lord manifested itself mightily on this little communist country this day, and nothing and no one was able to withstand it. His plan was to influence the local government of Yugoslavia, let them be the *instruments* to bring Our Lady's appearances and the pilgrims into the church, where He wanted them in the first place.

The authorities had tried a low key approach to stop the young people and the pilgrims from going to Mt. Podbrdo. They were unsuccessful. Their doctors refused to pronounce the children insane, or mentally unbalanced. The lady doctor who had been sent to spy on the apparitions, went back a changed woman. The two women the authorities used to keep the children away from the shrine, saw the light travel from Mt. Podbrdo to Cerno. They quit their jobs. It was time for a more direct approach. When in doubt, make a show of force. This is exactly what Jesus and Mary wanted.

Police were sent in to Bijakovici to disperse the crowds, block the entrance to the Hill of the Apparition, and grab the children. The visionaries panicked, and ran from the village, with the police in hot pursuit. They even changed clothes, in order not to be recognized.

This day was also a major day for Fr. Zoko, the Pastor of St. James Church. His was a very delicate situation. He personally wasn't sure of the veracity of the childrens' stories. Even if he were convinced that Our Lady was appearing to the visionaries, he had no right to make a stand for the Church. He could personally feel whatever he wanted, but when it came to his position as pastor of a Catholic Church, he was obliged to wait and obey his superiors. That decision was taken out of his hands, however. To quote Fr. Svetozar, in our videotaped interview with him,

"Fr. Jozo said he couldn't put his faith in the stories of the children. He had to get his answers from God. He opened the Bible to Moses' problem with the Jews, the pressures that were being exerted on him for having taken them out of Egypt. Moses asked for God's help, and received his own answers.

Fr. Jozo asked for the same, for God to give him the answers. The Lord said 'GO AND PROTECT THE CHILDREN'. *Fr. Jozo went to the door of the church. He met the children at the door. He brought them to the rectory, and they had a vision in the rectory.*

It was a decisive moment. The hill was not the place to organize prayer. But the priest's quandry was how to bring the people from the hill to the church. Up to that point, no one had paid any attention to the church.

The government forced the children from the hill. The people came to the church, not for the church, but after the children. The children were the center, not the church.

Fr. Jozo didn't know what to offer the people, so he gave them the only thing he knew, what the Church has given for years. He celebrated the Mass. He preached the word of God, and celebrated the Eucharist.

The first Mass was celebrated in the evening of the seventh day after the apparition, and has been celebrated every evening from that time to this. The government forbid people to climb the hill. They put guards there to keep the people off the hill. God, through the government, brought the people to the church, which became the center. The hill should not have been the center. The church was the center.

In Medjugorje, Mary is saying the same thing she did at Cana in Galilee. DO WHATEVER HE TELLS YOU. She's putting herself in between God and the people. She's leading the people to her Son. She's also reversing the process. She's telling her Son to do something for these people. They're in such trouble.

God is serious. God is telling us, 'It's not too late yet'. Do something. Mary, through Medjugorje, is calling the people, the priests, the whole Church to do better what we are called to do, to be better Christians. . . .

...Mary is offering us her Son at Medjugorje.

...If you want to know more about what Mary is saying at Medjugorje, open your Bible and read it. You'll know everything.

...Mary asked the children to go to convents and monasteries to be priests and nuns. But she leaves it up to them.

...In the same way, she asks us to fast on bread and water, but it's up to you to determine your own way of fasting and penance.

...God is not trying to scare us at Medjugorje. He is trying to **teach** *us, to make us aware of the reality of life. On the Hill of the Apparition and the Mountain of the Cross, humanity and Divinity have an opportunity to touch. Humanity is taught by the Divine as a result of this hardship. We open ourselves up to listen to God.*

...The Journey to the Hill of the Apparition and the Way of the Cross is not in place of the church—It is an extension of the church—but as you can see, even looking at it from a geographical viewpoint, THE CHURCH IS THE CENTER."

On the eighth day, a new age began, a Marian age, possibly the Medjugorje age.

The Medjugorje Experience

Medjugorje is a hard place, There are absolutely no frills here. This hamlet is farm country, as are the surrounding villages.

But it's not even good farm country. It's rock, with rose colored soil beneath. The local farmers dig up as much rock as they can, to give themselves the best possible chance at making a go at farming. Tobacco is the major crop. It's planted on every postage stamp sized plot available, and yet it's barely enough for the local residents to squeeze out a living.

For me, once I accepted Medjugorje, it became a *special* place, one that I would savor like the bouquet of a prize wine. It became very personal, my own private place. Our group stayed at the homes of the local residents, so that we could walk to the church each morning. I remember Penny and I sneaking out of the house early, just as the dawn was breaking, so as not to have to share that time with anyone.

The morning fog hugs the trees in Medjugorje. It looks like God is smoking His pipe on the mountain. Early morning is quiet time. The only disturbance is the occasional far-off cry of a rooster, waking the world to a new day. Early morning is a time for listening, for meditating, for getting in touch with Jesus through His Mother Mary, for asking her why she has summoned us here to this very foreign land.

The magnetism of the now familiar looking church of St. James draws us to it. It's the hub of everything in Medjugorje. There's nothing else there. There are some interesting things about the church we'd like to share. It took 31 years to build it. Work was begun in 1937, and it was finished in 1968. When it was completed, the complaint was that it was too big for the amount of villagers in the area. Why did they have to build such a large church for such a small community? Now they can't fit a fraction of the people who go there, into the church. Mass is piped into loudspeakers so that those outside, who can't fit into the church, can take part in the Liturgy.

A cool, gentle summer morning breeze caresses our faces, cheeks and mouths. We can feel the loving embrace of Mary in the wind. She gives us many messages other than those we receive through the seers. We have to step back to understand them. They don't come right away. Sometimes, we have to leave Medjugorje to understand why we're there in the first place. But once the message comes through, she doesn't let us rest until we get to work.

As we walk alone in the early morning, our eyes focus in on the sights we have heard of, perhaps seen in pictures or videotapes brought back by other pilgrims. But now they're *real*. We're here. The first recognizable shrine after the church is the big cross on top of the mountain, Mt. Krizevac. It was erected in 1933 in tribute to Our Lord Jesus in commemoration of the 1900th anniversary of His death. There was never the slightest thought that Mary would grace the village with her presence some 50 years later. But why not? What a loving and faithful people they had to be to build that monument to Jesus. If anyone is worthy to receive this special gift from Mary, why not the children of these faith-filled people?

The next important place is more difficult to locate from the church. Looking off to the left of the church, into the mountains above the houses, we scour the heavy vegetation for a path that resembles a vein or artery, cut into the bush. Finally, our eyes zero in on it. It's rose colored from the dirt of the road. If the day is clear, we can make out what appears to be tiny crosses to the right of the path. In actuality, they are very large crosses, carried up the hill by pilgrims, usually bare footed. This is Mt. Podbrdo, the Hill of the Apparitions.

The Franciscans at the Church recommend that each pilgrim make *both* journeys, one to the Hill of the Apparitions, and the other, the Way of the Cross, to the top of the mountain. Both should not be done in the same day, except possibly by the very young. In the summertime, each should be done in the early morning while there is still coolness in the air. Good walking shoes are mandatory.

The Hill of The Apparitions

The Village of Bijakovici is where most of the visionaries live. Many pilgrims walk from the church to the village, a distance of about 2 or 3 kilometers, most of which is on flat, unpaved road. It's a pleasant walk early in the morning, when the air is cool and moist. The entrance to the hill of the apparitions, Mount Podbrdo, is at the side of a house. The path has been carved out of the rose colored dirt and rock by the years of pilgrims climbing, praying, suffering. We say suffering because the climb up the hill is penance. One of our catch phrases became *SOFFRENZA— PENITENZA*—Suffering and Penance. It becomes a humorous phrase of encouragement when the pilgrims are subjected to hardships and inconveniences they're just not accustomed to. Once accepted, it becomes an anticipation, a gift to be able to share in the physical suffering of Jesus, and the emotional and spiritual passion of His Mother, My Lady, Mary.

The climb begins. It's a steep hill, made up of rock, deep crevices, and sharp crags. It's difficult on the feet, but impossible on the ankles. It begins at a sharp incline, and never gets any better. So in addition to the unevenness of the terrain, the rocks and sharp boulders, it's uphill all the way. Conversion takes place on the hill. We've seen people who never walk in the United States, struggling with the hill, holding on to each other not to fall, praying the rosary all the way. We had seen an American woman at Mass. Her hair was the tight curl perm. Her fingernails and toenails were painted in coordinated colors, and manicured. She wore designer jeans. I recall having made the mental judgment, "What's she doing here?" As we were climbing up the hill of the apparitions, she was coming down the hill *Barefoot*. Her feet were full of the reddish clay. Her toenails had cracked. She was praying and crying. She embraced the hill. She came to love it, and the pain it provided her.

We were caught in a fierce thunderstorm at the top. The rain hammered at us like a spray of bullets. As we struggled to get down the hill, soaked to the skin, we passed the same woman, also soaked to the skin. She huddled under a bush, searching for any form of protection from the vicious rain. Now, in addition to cracked toenails, her hair was stringy from the rain, her eye make up streamed down her face; her designer jeans were covered with red mud, but she was still praying the rosary, and she was radiant.

Demands are made on the Hill. Mary requires drastic change through the entire Medjugorje experience, but nowhere is it so obvious as on the Hill of the Apparitions, and excruciatingly clear on the Mountain of the Way of the Cross. She's training us for hard times. She needs strength in her people. We said that Medjugorje is a training field in penance, suffering and hardship.

We continue up the Hill of the Apparitions, towards the top. Along the way, we pass rocks with crosses painted on them, markers which identify places where Our Lady appeared to the children. Marinko Ivankovic, one of the earliest supporters of the visionaries, placed these crosses at the various locations during the first seven days of the apparitions on the hill, so that they would not be forgotten. At last we have climbed as high as we must. Our path now takes us east on a rocky, but rather level ground, to an opening, an area without trees or shrubbery of any kind, just rock and boulder. This is where pilgrims, oftentimes barefoot, carry large wooden crosses up the Hill in procession. Names of Parish Pilgrim groups are inscribed on the crosses. Pictures of Jesus, rosaries, prayer cards and pictures are placed on the crosses.

The familiar chant of the rosary can always be heard, recognizable no matter what language it's prayed in. It provides the perfect accompaniment, a bead for each beat of the heart, for the struggle up the hill. Sometimes a priest will be giving a sermon to his particular group of pilgrims, but by and large, the chant is the meditative Life of Christ as it unfolds before us in the Mysteries of the *Holy Rosary*.

From this vantage point, high on the Hill of the Apparitions, we can see the church off in the distance, very tiny, nestled in the farmland. But here, way up on this hill, away from the whole world, with the soft chanting of the rosary as background, the church on one side, the Mountain of the Cross on the other, providing inspiration, we are "tenderized". We are so ready now, as

open as we will ever be, to listen to Our Lady as she *speaks* to us.
With suffering, our senses become extremely keen, acute. We are
raw. The slightest motion, physical or emotional, is felt. Take
time here. Listen to her. Act on what she tells you.

From the interviews with the children, none of them experienced the slightest difficulty with exertion, breathlessness, pain,
cuts from the heavy brush on the hill, or any of the difficulties that
just about *killed* me when I made the climb. In Sacred Scripture,
Our Lord Jesus says that when the baby is born, the labor is forgotten. This must be the case with the Hill of the Apparition and
the Way of the Cross. I don't recall ever having heard anyone
complain about the struggle to reach the top. I have only heard
about the joy of having made the sacrifice in the name of Mary.
People of all ages come from far and wide for the privilege of
ascending these sacred mountains. It's a badge of *honor*.

The Mountain of The Way of The Cross

It takes sturdy stock to climb the Mountain of the Way of the
Cross. The Franciscans don't really tell you what kind of physical
stamina is required to make this climb, and with good reason. We
go back to *Soffrenza—Penitenza*. Medjugorje is a place of *pain*
and *penance*. We have but to read Our Lady's messages since
1981, to know that she is asking for an extra special effort to do
sacrifice. Originally, she asked us, through the children, to fast on
Fridays of every week. Then, she asked us to fast on Wednesday,
in addition to Friday. The Mountain of the Way of the Cross is
just another way for us to lift up our suffering and hardship to Our
Lady, for the sins of the world. We don't carry crosses of *wood*
up this mountain. We carry the crosses of the *world*, the crosses
of our *family*, of our *loved ones*. We carry our *life* with us. And
if we are so blessed that our crosses are light, Our Lady asks us
to allow our brothers and sisters with heavier crosses to lean on
us for support.

We took our time, praying as we went. The mountain is
treacherous. To many of our people, the Medjugorje experience

would not have been complete without the Way of the Cross. We started at 8:30 in the morning, while it was still cool. It took an hour and a half each way. When we arrived at the top, we were amazed to see that the cross which appeared so small from the Church, rose majestic, 30 feet into the air. It was a sight to behold.

On our way up and back, we saw many people, mostly women, making the climb up the Way of the Cross. Their ages differed greatly, from the very young to the very old. The gifts they offered to Our Lord Jesus and Mary were based on their ages. They gave what they had to give, from their years and experience, and then some. Most prayed in petition, for special favors, or the grace to carry the heavy burdens of their lives. Others prayed in thanksgiving for favors received. This is what Our Lady asks for, the most that we can give, and then some more. It's needed. There are *tribulations* that Mary talks about which are unavoidable. But because of the enormous amount of prayer and sacrifice that has already been offered to the Son through the Mother, the degree has been *lessened*. We can do that. We have the power. It has been given to us. We just have to be willing to use it.

There is *power* in Medjugorje. There is *commitment* there. Our Lady makes demands there that she has never made before. She speaks very straight. We are in troubled times. We know it. It's been staring us in the face over the last twenty years. The permissiveness, pornography, abortion is running rampant. But there is backlash. The Lord is angry. The first case of **AIDS** was discovered in the United States in Atlanta, Georgia, in June, 1981. (Reference: Time Magazine, Aids issue) When did our Lady appear for the first time in Medjugorje? You guessed it, June 24, 1981.

Attitudes towards Mary's presence in Medjugorje are either very much in favor of, or violently against. We have never spoken to anyone who has been *lukewarm*. I can't explain why people are against it. There seems to be such anger against the possibility of her appearing there, that I have to remove myself from this anger immediately. Most of the people we share with are those who have been completely captivated by Our Lady at Medjugorje. Lives have been *changed* by Mary's demands at this very special place. I find myself completely recommitted every time I go there. I come back with renewed energy and desire to spread the word.

The place is desolate. You would think that nothing of any importance could ever come from there. Yet the *conversions,* the changes we've experienced not only in the United States, but in Europe as well, are beyond comprehension. You can't mention the name of Medjugorje in Europe without seeing people's eyes fill with tears. Looks of longing appear on the faces of those who have been there. We can be pushing and shoving with people to get into an audience with the Pope, and the moment we mention Medjugorje, these same brothers and sisters that we've been doing battle with, become saints.

Medjugorje exists for me. Mary is there, very strong, very demanding, very loving in Medjugorje. She has pulled out all the stops there. Miracles are reported almost as a normal course of events. The greatest miracles, those of conversion and reconciliation, abound in Medjugorje. Our priest commented on the hundreds of people sprawled all over the lawn, receiving the sacrament of Reconciliation. He couldn't help but compare it with Saturday night at many of the churches around the world, where our priests sit in the confessionals, waiting for the few to come. And in this place, there are not enough priests to hear the confessions of all who come.

A noteworthy thing happened to the priest who went with us. Our Pilgrimage of 28 days ended with a flight from Amsterdam to Los Angeles, which arrived on Saturday at 2 P.M. Most of us went home and collapsed from jet lag. Remember, we had been up for close to 24 hours. Our priest went to his Church, celebrated the 5:30 Mass, and then proceeded to hear confessions until 9 o'clock that evening. The next day, at the two Masses he celebrated, he shared about his Pilgrimage, and at the 5 P.M. Mass, he had Jennifer Hoefflin, the 13 year old girl who had been in the room of the apparitions with us, get up and share on her experience at Medjugorje.

Many people have mixed emotions about Medjugorje. The pattern of this series of apparitions is far different from any other we've heard of. The demands are greater. She makes us *uncomfortable*. She's talking about the end times. Jesus once said *"If you can't believe in me, believe in my works"*. I say the same thing about Medjugorje. If you have a difficulty with the apparition, forget it. Just do what the Lady *tells you*. Fasting, Abstinence, Reconciliation, not with Russia but with your next door neighbor, your brothers and sisters, this is the message of Mejugorje. It's completely in agreement with Church teachings, only in much stronger language. *Accept that.*

I personally wish that everyone would accept and embrace the Medjugorje experience, as given to us by my loving Mary. I would wish that you all go there at least once in your lifetime. You deserve it; you need it, and she needs you. However, don't expect any new revelations from her. She's repeating the same thing she has been saying in all her apparitions, her message at the Wedding Feast of Cana, her last recorded words in the Bible, **"DO WHATEVER HE TELLS YOU"**.

Epilog: The End . . . . or The Beginning?

We've come to the end of the story, or is it the beginning? This is not a book about apparitions. It is a book about love, Mary's love for us, and for her Son, Jesus. It is also a book about our love for Them. Our goal here has been to introduce you to Jesus' Mother, as we have come to know her,

AND BY KNOWING THE MOTHER, TO KNOW HER SON.

We find it so difficult to understand how our brothers and sisters in Christ think they can know *Jesus* without knowing His Family, His *Mother*. If your daughter were to bring home a young man she wanted to marry, you would want to know all about him, wouldn't you? You would want to know his background, what goes into making him who he is. Does he come from a good family? What is their philosophy? What does she know about his mother and father? Is she aware ho much influence his family will exert on their marriage? Would you not think it extremely important that she meet his family? There are so many questions you and she have about this person who will become a major part of your life, and that of your family.

We have to understand how important a part of *Jesus'* life His *Mother* has been. If God had wanted, Jesus did not have to be born at all. Why did He allow Himself to be born of a *woman* in the first place? Why was the first miracle of His life, God becoming Man, accomplished through this *woman*? Why did He choose her, above all His apostles, to stand at the foot of the Cross? If we truly believe in the power of Jesus, we have to know that He could have given the Apostles the *strength* to be there. But He chose His *Mother*. It was a special time between Mother and Son.

In Mark 3:33, Jesus made the statement: **WHO ARE MY MOTHER AND MY BROTHERS?** He continued with **WHOEVER DOES THE WILL OF GOD IS BROTHER AND SISTER AND MOTHER TO ME.** There are those who have taken this scripture Passage as being degrading to Mary, as if she were not that *important*. Actually, if we study this passage, Jesus is commending those *who have raised themselves from the human level*, to those **WHO DO THE WILL OF GOD**, as *Mary* has done. He has not brought Mary down to the level of the common man. On the contrary, He gives us the opportunity of **BEING LIFTED TO THE LEVEL OF MARY.** In addition, by reading John 19:26/27, **"WOMAN, THERE IS YOUR SON; THERE IS YOUR MOTHER"**, we have to realize that Jesus thought so highly of His Mother Mary, that He entrusted us, the people of God, His Church, to her.

Recently, Penny spoke to the owner of a book store who has carried and successfully sold our book **THIS IS MY BODY, THIS IS MY BLOOD, Miracles of the Eucharist.** She shared that when she was young, and her children were growing up, she prayed all the time to Mary. Mary was her best friend, her confidante, someone she could turn to, who knew how she felt, Mother to Mother. But since the children had grown up, and she had been Reborn in the Spirit, she had *outgrown* Mary. She was able to pray directly to Jesus now. My Penny, who has the wisdom of the saints, did not question her on this point. Instead, she said, *"How are other young mothers going to know that they can turn to Mary the way* *you did when you were young if you don't have anything in your store for them to read about Mary? Who will tell them about Mary, the Mother, the friend of Mothers? And how can we get the Protestants to understand Mary if there's nothing for us to use to tell them about Mary."* (A little aside—the woman bought a case of this book, sight unseen)

We recall a story Penny's mother used to share with us, about a Mother and her son. Oh, how much they loved one another. The son grew up and away from his mother; but they never stopped loving each other. The son met and fell in love with a girl, whom he really *didn't* know.

After they married, the girl showed her true colors. She told the son he could never see his mother again. The son agreed. It broke the mother's heart, but she was willing to accept it, if her son was *happy*. This infuriated the girl. She told the son he had to go to his mother's house, kill her, and bring the mother's *heart* back to her as proof. The son was so blinded by passion for the girl, he agreed to this *outrageous* demand. He went to his mother's house. She prepared a sumptuous dinner for him. After the son had eaten, he took a kitchen knife, and killed his mother. He opened her chest, and removed her heart. He put it in a box, and ran towards his home to show his wife how he had *obeyed* her. On the way, he tripped and fell. The heart fell out of the box. From the heart, he heard his mother say to him, **"MY SON, DID YOU HURT YOURSELF?"** Mary is that *perfect* Mother who never stops loving us, no matter what we do to her.

Mary is **TOUCHABLE**. We talked about this at the beginning of the book. Mary is **LOVE**. That's a part of our title. These are the two things we've tried to bring you throughout these pages. We used the apparitions as a frame of reference, because through her visits to us, we've been able to learn a great deal about her. We've tried so hard to let you know who she is, and how much she *loves* you. She has come to answer the prayers of the little people, as well as aiding big countries. In her most recent apparitions, she is attempting to save the world. In Fatima and

Medjugorje, she's given us a **WARNING AND A PROMISE.** The warning is, we've brought ourselves to the point of total annihilation. We're in the end times. This is Apocalypse. The promise is

IN THE END, MY IMMACULATE HEART
WILL TRIUMPH

We know the end of the story, but what we don't know is what will happen between the *warning* and the *promise*. She has told us that there will be tribulation. She has also told us that we can lessen the chastisement through prayer, fasting and reconciliation. In the final analysis, the decision will have to be ours to make. But she does not leave us on our own. She keeps trying to help us save ourselves. The road to the kingdom can be smooth or rocky. That determination is up to us.

We posed a few questions at the beginning of the book.

Why Is She Under So Much Attack?

We have to go back to before the beginning of time for the answer to this question, when Lucifer and Mary clashed for the first time, after he learned that she was to be higher in the kingdom than he. Or we can look in the book of Genesis, 3:15, *"I will put emnity between you and the woman, and between your offspring and hers."*

This prophecy, first made in Genesis, has been fulfilled over and over throughout the history of the Church. There has been a major war going on between Jesus and Mary on the one side, and satan on the other, from the beginning, and it will continue until the end of time. Satan has been able to use *good people* to say *bad things* about Mary from the earliest days of the Church. His attacks are always twofold. He attacks first the Eucharist, and then Mary. She has never hurt anyone, and yet she has always been the object of abuse and criticism.

The next natural question is

WHY DOES SHE KEEP COMING BACK WHEN PEOPLE ARE SO CRUEL TO HER?

The only answer we can give to that is **MARY IS LOVE!** We were given to her by Our Lord Jesus on the Cross. She has taken seriously the role of our Protectress, and Mother. When we are children, we have no problem listening to, and taking, our mother's advice. But as we grow older, we tend to believe we've outgrown her. When we *finally grow up*, however, we can shuck the cloak of pride. When we're free of the world, when we can embrace her as our Mother, the clouds of our life will part. The sun will break through. She's there waiting for us. She has been since the day we were conceived in our natural mother's womb. Every time we fell and bruised ourselves, whether it was physically or spiritually Our Lady cried out; her heart jumped. She tried to walk in front of us, to protect us from the rocks that would make us trip and fall. But ultimately, she had to wait until we were ready to come home to her.

Life can be beautiful, basking in the warmth of Mary. It can be **HEAVEN, HEAVEN, HEAVEN, all the way to Heaven.** Why do we fight it so much? All she wants is for us to be happy. She does one thing so perfectly. She loves. Why won't we allow her to love us? There's still time, we pray. But if I were you, I'd open the window of my heart to her right now, and let her love shine in.

Fr. Svetozar Kraljevic with Penny Lord and group from
Journeys of Faith Pilgrimage

Pilgrims climb the Mountain of the Way of the Cross at Medjugorje

Celebration of the Mass in the Room of the Apparitions at Medjugorje

Priests outside the Church hearing Confessions of crowds of Pilgrims at
Medjugorje

Bibliography

Beevers, John—Virgin of The Poor—Abbey Press, St. Meinrad, Indiana 1972

Broderick, Robert—The Catholic Enyclopedia, Thomas A. Nelson, New York 1976

De Marchi, John—Fatima, from The Beginning—Edicoes: Missoes Consolata, Fatima 1950

Dirvin, Joseph Fr—Saint Catherine Laboure—Farrar, Strauss & Cudahy, New York 1958

Kennedy, John—Light On the Mountain—Mc Mullen Books, New York 1953

Kraljevic, Svetozar Fr—The Apparitions of Our Lady At Medjugorje—Franciscan Herald Press, Chicago 1984

Laurentin, Rene Fr—A Hundred Years Ago Bernadette—Fetes E Saisions—Editions Du Cerf, Paris 1979

Laurentin, Rene Fr—Bernadette of Lourdes—Desclee Du Brower, Paris 1978

Laurentin/Durand—Pontmain Histoire Authentique—Apostalat Des Editions & Lethielleux, Paris 1970

Laurentin/Rupic—Is the Virgin Mary Appearing At Medjugorje?—The Word Among Us Press, Washington D.c. 1984

Neary, Tom Fr.—I Comforted Them in Sorrow—Custodians of Knock Shrine, Knock Ireland 1979

Neary, Tom Fr.—Shrine of Our Lady of Knock Guide Book—Custodian of Knock Shrine, Knock, Ireland 1979

New American Bible—Thomas A. Nelson, New York 1970

Pelletier, Joseph Fr.—The Queen of Peace Visits Medjugorje—Assumption Publication, Worcester Mass 1985

Ravier, Andre Fr.—Lourdes, A Land of The Gospel—L'ouevre De La Grotte, Lourdes 1983

Ricaud, L—Sanctuary of Our Lady of Lourdes—Institution of The Grotto, 1949

Sharkey/Debergh—Our Lady of Beauraing—Hanover House, New York 1958

Sharkey, Don—The Woman Shall Conquer—Franciscan Marytown Press, Kenosha, Wisconsin 1954

Smith, Jody Brant—The Image of Guadalupe, Myth or Miracle?—Doubleday Image Books, New York 1979

Strode, Hudson—Timeless Mexico—Harcourt, Brace and Co., New York 1940

The Saint of Silence—Shrine of Miraculous Medal, Paris 1968

The Wonder of Pontmain—R. Madiot, Laval, France 1978

Wahlig, Charles Dr.—Handbook On Guadalupe—Franciscan Marytown Press, Kenosha Wisconsin 1974

Walsh, William Thomas—Our Lady of Fatima—Macmillan Company, New York 1947

Werfel, Franz—The Song of Bernadette—Pocket Books, New York, 1940

Bob and Penny Lord

We Came Back to Jesus is the third book in Bob and Penny Lord's Trilogy, based on the Prophecy of St. John Bosco, which is about **the Body of Christ, the Mother of Christ, and the Church of Christ.**

Their first, *This Is My Body, This Is My Blood, Miracles of the Eucharist,* is about **the Real Presence of Jesus in the Eucharist.**

Their second, *The Many Faces of Mary, a Love Story,* is about **the Mother of Christ.**

The third, *We Came Back to Jesus,* brings it all together. The focus is on **Church,** how Bob and Penny left the Church after the death of their 19 year old son to an overdose of drugs, the long road back, and how Mother Church embraced them, showering them with all the gifts the Church has to offer.

Readers say this is the reason the first two were written.

"I got to page 30, and had to stop because the tears kept coming out like a deluge......it was a personal relationship"
Msgr. Vito Mistretta - Citrus Heights, CA

"The book is lovely.....I do hope it reaches many and touches their hearts." **Fr. Richard Rohr - Albuquerque, NM**

"I got goose bumps as I read through it. There were so many memories....and so much love....and so much hope."
Fr. Chuck Gallagher - Elizabeth, NJ

"All your books are Super, but this one adds a luster....because this is giving the other two Roots....You bared all of your own personal selves....you actually showed us How God works in our lives..."
Anna Buonicore - Saddlebrook, NJ

This may well be their most important work thus far. It is a book you will not only want to read over and over again, but will want to give to your loved ones and friends.

207 pages - Hard Cover - $12.95 ea   Paperback - $7.95 ea.

California Residents add 6% Tax - Make Checks Payable to Journeys of Faith
Please include $2.00 for postage & handling

Journeys of Faith

31220 La Baya Drive, Suite 110 - Westlake Village, CA 91362